LESSONS FROM THE BACK ROADS

Because Life Is Too Short To Use Interstates

by

John Hodel

First published by Dog Ear Publishing
4010 W. 86th Street, Ste H
Indianapolis, IN 46268
www.dogearpublishing.net

ISBN: 978-1-4575-0563-8

This book is printed on acid-free paper.

Printed in the United States of America

PREFACE

June 12, 1995: As I gaze up toward the heavens this night, my soul is over-flowing with joy and expectancy. I know my thirst for adventure, for lessons yet to be learned, is soon to be quenched. I take inventory of the scene around me: tent, roaring campfire, pine-filled forest, my motorcycle...and me—alone. I laugh to myself, realizing how similar this setting is to the many times my imagination has taken me to such a place. But now, when I open my eyes, it does not disappear within my current reality...it is my reality.

The tall pine trees, swaying gently back and forth in the breeze, seem to wave their approval at my attempt to define the unknown, both in this world and within myself. I am unsure of what lies ahead, but I will not dwell on the unknown just now. I simply sit back and enjoy this sense of peace—a peace that surpasses all understanding.

This is the first night of a motorcycle journey to places yet unknown. A journey that will take place on the back roads of North America as well as a journey found deep within myself...the latter journey being the more fright-ening of the two. Although I feel secure that I can handle most physical situ-ations that will challenge me over the next several months, the uncharted regions from within open up much riskier roads—these roads that are destined to transport me to places where long-kept emotions lie in wait to be discov-ered, whether I want to discover them or not.

I had grown tired of my sluggish attitude toward life and my willingness to let complacency be my steady companion. My passions for new experiences had all but deserted me, and I felt that I was no longer willing to trade my life for what was behind door number three. I had only wanted to settle for the sure thing, the choices void of risk. I had not been living the life I was preach-ing to others, and I knew I needed to reverse this hypocritical path I was on. This trip would represent my attempt to begin the reversal process.

This is my story of stepping outside life's comfortable boundaries, discov-ering the hidden wonders of this land and its people, and learning a lifetime of lessons in three and a half months. A story of where interstates are con-spicuous by their absence, replaced by the back roads of this great land, these black ribbons of learning that slowly wind through each small town, provid-ing me the gift of life's small details, where I can behold peoples' faces, hear their words, smell the wind, and experience life.

Traveling throughout North America, I discovered that it is not necessary to sit in a classroom to be taught powerful lessons. Every day of our lives, we are surrounded by teachers—ordinary people who have persevered through experiences and trials in their own lives and who have triumphed in their own personal battles. People who have chosen to take responsibility for themselves and face life's problems instead of curling up in an emotional fetal position, blaming others. I learned from their victories as well as from their mistakes.

Perhaps the greatest teacher of all is found within us as we take the time to reflect and think upon our own lives. We can draw strength from these worthy instructors, or we can ignore the valuable lessons they provide us. It is our choice.

I met many such learned scholars on my journey, and I was taught much. Perhaps the education I received will motivate others into looking at new roads within their own lives. New roads that may lead to welcomed lands.

It's a great lesson plan.

CHAPTER 1

The Journey Begins

I bolted upright to a sitting position in my warm and comfortable bed as classic rock music filled my bedroom, signaling the beginning of a new day. Half asleep, I fumbled for the button that would turn the volume down to an acceptable level. A morning person I am not, and normally, I would have made an instinctive grab for the snooze button, gladly accepting the priceless gift of ten more minutes of slumber. This morning, however, my anticipation thoroughly overcame my desire to roll over. This was not just any morning, it was a morning I had been waiting for my entire life.

As the Eagles' song "Desperado" was nearing its finale, I looked at the digital display of the radio with half-opened eyes and saw that it was 6:30. Swinging my legs out of bed and onto the floor, I walked toward the shower, in a stride more like Quasimodo's than my own, working the blood back into my legs, and as the comfortably warm water hit my face, the only thing I couldn't wash away was the stupid smile on my face.

As I swallowed my last bite of soggy cold cereal, I pulled the kitchen curtains aside and peered out the window. My eyes instinctively shut as the bright sunlight invaded my still-dilated pupils. I was relieved to find that the weather was fully cooperating with my plans, providing cloudless skies on this Southern California morning. All systems were go! It was nearing the time for takeoff.

With my heart beating just a little faster than normal, I lumbered down the stairway and into the garage, where my fully-packed motorcycle anxiously awaited me. As my eyes met my motorized riding companion, I found myself suddenly void of movement, staring at her in a trance-like gaze. She is a maroon 1990 Harley–Davidson FXR Superglide, and she was no rookie, boasting over 30,000 miles of past experience. She did not sport the large fiberglass faring that adorned the front of many touring bikes, nor did she provide a giant windshield used by many riders for long-distance trips. She wasn't all that pretty or special…but she was mine. There would be no radios, headphones, or heated hand grips…just myself, my bike, the road, and the wind. The way it should be.

1

I could not remember ever feeling so free in all my life. I lifted my leg up and over the seat and slowly began to back her out of the garage and into the driveway. I felt like I was in a dream and that I would be awakened any minute by my alarm clock reminding me I had a business meeting on the agenda that day, but as I started her up and the distinctively loud Harley noise filled the air, my heart skipped a beat and I didn't wake up. This was it. I wasn't dreaming…I was living. No, I was living a dream.

I shifted into first gear, slowly let the clutch out and traveled the first inch of what would be an 18,000-mile ride. I accelerated onto the busy six-lane surface street near my home in Lake Forest, and as I slowed for the first red light of many to come, I noticed the multitude of stares I was receiving from the vehicles around me. Looking at my setup, it was easy to see why. I looked as if I were running away from home and taking most of my home with me.

Most of my clothes were packed in a black canvas bag that had a pocket sewn into the back, which tightly slipped over the seat's backrest. The bag sat about three feet high, and when its contents were packed correctly, it protruded far enough forward as to provide an excellent backrest with ample lumbar support. My rolled-up black sleeping bag crowned this vertical luggage mountain held by a thick black meshing with quick-release connectors. So high was this arrangement that, basically, I could not be seen from behind.

A small chrome luggage rack located directly behind the backrest served as the foundation for a pyramid of additional supplies consisting of a black duffel bag full of reading material, cooking gear, my repair manual, and many little things I thought might come in handy. It was still not enough "stuff," though, so I had also stacked a black nylon bag containing all of my camping gear and crowned by a bright red cargo net which held my full face helmet and anything else I wanted to shove under it for quick retrieval. All was held in place with black bungee cords. Basically, I had no idea what I was doing or what I would need, so I was taking a lot.

The weight and height of all these possessions made the bike's handling a little shaky and unfamiliar, and the first goal of this trip was a simple one—don't fall over at the first light. Fortunately, my first goal was soon achieved, and ten minutes later, I was accelerating down the same Lake Forest Avenue to the I-5 freeway on-ramp I had used many times before, but never with more anticipation.

As usual, the Southern California morning commute was thick, and I began to weave my way around the slow-moving vehicles, being careful not to catch a piece of luggage on a side mirror. After thirty minutes, I broke free of the congested traffic and turned my handlebars east on Highway 91 and then north on I-15 toward the Mojave Desert.

Within an hour, the temperature in the desert easily capped the 100-degree mark, and my black leather vest and boots were doing their best at absorbing every degree of it. My fingers were left bare, because the black gloves I was wearing covered my hands only to the knuckles, and I felt a constant burn as the hot wind passed over them. My posture was relaxed as I leaned back against my T-bag, my legs fully extended forward while resting my feet upon the highway pegs mounted toward the front of the bike. No matter how hard I tried, I couldn't stop smiling.

My love for the desert is a deep and reverent one due to my dirt-biking passion, and I reveled in my surroundings as I gazed out over thousands of acres of the flat brown landscape dotted with sparse vegetation and the occasional Joshua tree. Every so often, the flat land would be broken up by an occasional rock-strewn mountain seemingly void of anything that resembled life. The distinctive aroma of creosote bushes hung heavy in the air, and I breathed it in deeply until my lungs were full. The little gifts the back roads provide over freeways. It would be my theme to focus on the journey rather than the destination.

Interestingly enough, this philosophy of travel was the antithesis of the way I had been living my life. In many ways, I felt I had been living my life as a freeway driver, with life passing me by at a 70 mph blur, my eyes determinedly focused ahead of me, as if quickly arriving at my final destination was my only objective. In the end, the final arrival is death. Why was I rushing? Why was I ignoring the experiences around me? I realized that if I continued living my life in this fashion, I would, indeed, quickly reach the end of my life and look back upon it not with feelings of accomplishment but with feelings of regret. I knew I had only one shot at this earthly existence, and when it was over, I wanted memories that were etched deep in my soul—smells that would forever linger in my nostrils. Adventures I could revisit in my mind over and over again. Taking the back roads was a step in the right direction.

After the first few hours in the desert, I pulled into a gas station at Kramer Junction, located in the heart of the Mojave, where Highways 395 and 58 intersect. The sudden absence of wind made me realize just how hot it really was, and I quickly reapplied another coat of sunblock over my arms and face. I looked into my mirror. My nose was already sporting the Rudolph look. As I dismounted, I glanced over to my right and noticed another bike gassing up, also loaded with supplies, and with an Alaskan license plate. Time to bond. After I had spoken to the rider for a few moments, he told me of his goal of riding his motorcycle from Alaska to New Mexico but had found the heat to be too much of an obstacle. He was turning around to go back north.

Although he was sporting a sleeping bag as part of his supplies, he admitted it was more cosmetic than anything practical. He had mostly been staying at motels. His remarks made me reflect on my own abilities and weaknesses. I found myself wondering if I could really handle not watching cable TV or relaxing in a warm bed throughout this trip. Could I handle the cold and the rain? Would I let the weather drastically affect my intended plans? I had committed myself to no U-turns on my dream's adventure, yet here was a man letting outside elements affect where he really wanted to go. Only time would tell if I would do the same.

I continued north on Highway 395, and after an hour or so, I could finally see the smaller mountains that mark the beginning of the majestic Sierra Nevada mountain range. This range of high mountain peaks parallels the California–Nevada border and extends nearly 300 miles north from the Mojave Desert. These mountains are where fighter pilot Chuck Yeager settled down, saying it was the most beautiful place of all the areas he had visited throughout the world. The range is home to Yosemite National Park, Lake Tahoe, and the highest mountain peak in the continental United States, Mt. Whitney.

As the highway swept right of the range, the mountains seemed to explode from ground zero straight up toward the heavens with hardly a slope initiating the climb. Almost before I realized it, the steady hum of my Harley's engine had transported me up Owens Valley, where I gazed over my left shoulder at a series of desolate and rugged peaks above the town of Lone Pine, one of which was Mt. Whitney. To my right was the road that could take me to Death Valley. How diverse—within a few hundred miles were both the highest and lowest points in the continental United States.

Because of California's extremely wet winter that year, an abundance of snow still blanketed much of the range, making this panoramic masterpiece even more beautiful than usual. I took it in minute by minute as time seemed to slow down just for me, allowing me to savor these first day's moments as the clean, crisp air filled my senses. Throughout all my travels, the Sierra Nevada range still remains one of the most breathtaking regions in all of North America.

I soon passed a familiar sign telling me that I was entering the small and historic town of Independence. I had always loved this little community and had actually written a high school term paper on portions of its historical mining operations of the late 1800s. During past trips through this town, I had always noticed the museum sign pointing toward a place a few blocks off the main street but have never once taken the time to stop. I had always wanted to, but my internal program of interstate living had always been in full swing, and getting to where I was going, usually in record time, had always seemed to take priority. I decided that this time, I would practice my back-roads philosophy and force myself to take a little time to investigate the knowledge contained within the museum's walls.

The museum was a tiny stone building surrounded by small residential homes with the 14,000-foot snow-covered Sierra peaks as their backdrop. A smattering of old, rusty tractors and mining tools were strategically scattered around the building, which seemed quite fitting for a museum such as this. I pulled my bike into the gravel parking lot, and as I was removing my helmet, a couple in their fifties who had just left the museum glanced my way. Instead of entering the car through the door the man had just unlocked, the couple moved in my direction and began asking me a myriad of questions. As it turned out, they had lived in Independence most of their lives, and we shared information that we all found interesting—theirs about life in Independence and mine about why I was doing what I was doing. After we said good-bye, I secretly envied the fact that I was actually the character in the story I was telling.

I entered through an old wooden door located on the north side of the building, and a little grey-haired elderly lady, who seemed to be in charge, quickly gave me a huge smile followed by a friendly hello despite my "biker" look of unshaven face and black leather. I quickly returned the smile along with a friendly squint. I spent the next few hours poring over hundreds of old photos and relics detailing stories of the mountaineering adventures and mining history of the area. I read about Manzanar, the Japanese relocation camp that had been located just outside of town in the early 1940s. It was nearly impossible to believe that such a beautiful place could be used for such a travesty of justice. As I walked out the door and sauntered back to my bike, I realized how much I had missed by not stopping before. The Independence museum was an important victory that first day, as it would help set the stage for the rest of the trip.

I continued to ride north along the base of the regal Sierras. The scenery's intensity did not diminish the rest of the day. As I saw the sign telling me that Yosemite's turnoff was ten miles ahead, I knew I was close to my final destination for the night. My first campsite of the trip would be an isolated place near Mono Lake, an area that has always held a special place in my heart. My brother Eric and I had camped and ridden dirt bikes in this area several times, and the brotherly talks we have had, combined with the beauty of this place, set it apart from many other places others I have visited and loved. Because I am an avid Clint Eastwood fan, the fact that the movie *High Plains Drifter* was filmed here only makes it better. Ah yes, the perfect place to stay.

I had traveled nearly 400 miles since being awakened to "Desperado" that morning, and I realized I was pretty tired. Five miles past the Yosemite sign, I turned right onto Highway 120 and rode the winding two-lane road eight miles before finding a dirt trail that would transport me into the pine-ridden forest. I carefully made the transition from pavement to deep sandy soil and bullied my heavily laden Hog forward, struggling to keep her upright in the process, fighting the desire of my tires to follow whatever rut was available. After off-roading for 200 yards, I found a perfect location in an open area of the woods and made camp.

Turning off the engine plunged me from the low roar of the Harley motor to absolute silence with the exception of the wind rustling through pine needles. The sun was beginning to set behind the 13,000-foot snow-covered peaks to the west, and the clear, crisp air began to turn slightly cooler. Good timing. I excitedly unpacked my supplies for the first time, set up my tent, blew up my air mattress, unrolled my sleeping bag, and sat down on an old fallen pine log, staring in awe at my first campsite.

All that was missing was a crackling fire. Surveying my surroundings, I noticed a bountiful supply of dry timber lying amongst the discarded pinecones that covered the forest floor. Even this Boy Scout reject could start a fire with all this easily combustible fuel. I walked through the woods and collected pieces of dead wood as dry pine needles snapped loudly under the weight of my feet. My feelings of freedom had reached new heights, and I couldn't tell if my deep breathing was due to the 7,000 feet of elevation or my heart having trouble keeping pace with my heightened emotional state. I couldn't have wiped the silly grin off my face even if I had wanted to. As I continued the chore of collecting wood, my mind began to wander back to the events that had led me to this place in my life…that which had awakened the spirit within me.

Only three months earlier, I had been a typical 34-year-old single male employed in the "exciting" world of computer software sales. This was quite ironic because I remember telling my mother at the age of 23, when sharing my future's uncertainties, that there were two areas of work I absolutely would not do—computers or sales. I have learned to never say "never" anymore.

This vocation, however, had turned out to be mildly lucrative for me, both financially and educationally, and had provided me an opportunity to travel all over the country courtesy of the ever-giving expense account. Life was good. I had the luxury of working out of my home, I owned my own condo in Southern California, I had all the toys I wanted, and, according to most people, I had it made. There was just one little problem with this perfect picture: I was not passionate about what I was doing with my life. Heck, I wasn't feeling passionate about much of anything of late. I was finding that my level of dissatisfaction with my current profession was directly proportional to the stress level I was beginning to experience. Deep down, I knew I needed a change, but the thought of giving up the security of a well-paying job and trying something different struck fear into my very soul.

In addition to these feelings, I had also been struggling with areas in my life where I felt I needed improvement but was doing little to resolve the problem. I wanted to take more risks in achieving certain dreams, I battled with my lack of discipline, I ignored weaknesses in my job skills, I gave very little of my time to others, and the list went on. Even though I was not happy with these areas in my life, the security of a paycheck every other week allowed me to conveniently ignore them. Complacency was suffocating my desires and my need to expand my experiences and myself. I had jumped from life's path straight into a rut.

Someone once told me a rut is nothing but a grave with the ends knocked out. Having raced dirt bikes, I knew that falling into a rut at speed was often disastrous....You either rode it out or crashed hard, but either way, the rut was in control. I was beginning to identify. The answer was clear—I needed to stop and pull myself out.

In September 1994, I read an article by Tom Peters, whose column appeared in the weekly business section of the *Orange County Register*. He discussed how we must renew our lives using little renewal and big renewal. (He called it little r and big R.) Little r consisted of changing everyday habits and doing something different such as going for a walk in the middle of the day, or taking off for a few hours to a place we may not normally visit. Big R dealt with life-changing experiences such as taking six months to a year off work, learning a new language, trying a new line of work that you're passionate about, getting a degree, or joining the Peace Corps.

This article had hit me right between the eyes. I had promptly cut it out and hung it on the corkboard in my office and read it often. Six months later, I was heading out the door to catch a plane to Oakland to attend several business meetings. As I climbed into my Toyota 4Runner, I suddenly remembered to grab the newspaper. That small decision would change my life. As I situated myself in my Southwest Airlines aisle seat, I pulled the newspaper out, found Tom Peters' article, and began reading.

As my eyes absorbed his words, I soon found that it would be his last article for quite some time. Coincidentally, he referred to the same September 1994 article I had hung in my office, saying he had recently reread this article and discovered that its message applied to him as much as anybody. He would indeed take his own advice and would take some time off and change his life.

Then and there, I decided I would do the same. I had been staring at the fork in the road for too long, and with that decision, I had finally taken the first step on the path I would take. I had lunch with my boss that very day and told him of my plans to take six months off work starting in June. He told me he would do his best to work with me on this but there would be no guarantee that a job would be waiting for me. I understood. At that time, I also had tens of thousands of dollars in future commissions based on sold deals but unsigned contracts. This money would be forfeited should I leave. The temptation to stay was great. *Just wait until I receive my commissions, then I will leave*, I thought. But then I realized there would always be outstanding commissions and there would always be a reason not to go. I decided to do this no matter what the cost.

I was euphoric all day over my bold decision to change my life and excitedly told many of my coworkers of my daring plan. "I am Sabbatical Man!" I was no longer a talker, I was a doer! To be honest, I was feeling a little on the cocky side as people congratulated me on my courage and raw guts. I could sense their envy as I smiled while nodding my head, soaking up the attention and acting like the decision had been no big deal. I felt like I could conquer the world.

Once I returned home that night, my euphoria and daring exterior transformed into two other emotions, panic and horror. Fear hit me like a Mohammad Ali uppercut. "Am I nuts? What am I doing? How am I going to live? What if I can't find another job?" I don't remember if I slept in a fetal position all night or not, but I'm fairly certain my sleep began that way. The cocky tough guy had left the building.

I came to discover that the feelings I felt that night were very natural emotions when confronting major change in one's life. When these feelings are present, it usually means we are on the right track in our search for transformation. The road of change is not easily traveled. Unfortunately, this same road provides its travelers many opportunities for U-turns and people too often take advantage of this easy way back to the place where they began. I was determined to make this a back road with no exits.

I didn't have a large stockpile of money saved up, but I had enough to get me through the next seven months, and I had managed to pay off all my debts with the exception of my mortgage. I planned to begin my ride on June 12, 1995, and return sometime in early October. Although I had a vague idea of where I wanted to travel, I didn't plan a specific route. I made the decision to take things more on a day-by-day basis and not risk choking my spontaneity with stringent planning. My basic plan would be to ride the perimeter of the United States and parts of Canada using back roads all the way.

I also decided to make this ride alone, feeling that the overall experience would be enhanced by my ability to reflect and be by myself. It would give me an opportunity to meet more people, as they would be more likely to talk with a rider by himself versus two or more men together. Being 34 and single, I must admit that I am a bit strong-willed about what I want to do and when I want to do it. My goal on this ride was to be as free as possible, both in action and in spirit. Another rider could easily jeopardize this objective. As it turned out, I made the right decision.

After my announcement at work, I spent the next two months preparing. There seemed to be an endless list of things to do: deciding what camping gear to take, buying rain gear, setting up bill payments, putting together the phone numbers and addresses of those I could stay with on the road, making a will, and on and on and on. I needed to be as detailed as possible when selecting my supplies because I had few plans to use motels or campgrounds on this ride. I would camp where I could find places to sleep, and that meant any- where and everywhere. Cell phones were large and bulky and service would be non-existent in the places I would be riding. For most of my trip, nobody would know where I was and help would not be conveniently accessible.

For this reason, I was a bit concerned with the safety factor, both in the two- and four-legged variety of animal I might encounter, especially at night. Although I would have my trusty knife with me, I could just imagine pulling that mean six-inch blade out against an angry grizzly as he charged me from the woods. The only way that knife would save my life would be if the griz- zly fell over from laughing...and I wasn't even sure if bears laughed. I realized that there was no way to be completely prepared, which made the trip that much more exciting.

As June approached, my fears about life, my job, and my security began to melt away like the Sierra snowpack in summer. Not one of these fears could overcome my desire to leave. It was full speed ahead into the unknown. I was so glad I had made my decision.

My arms were beginning to ache as I carried the last load of dry timber and threw it upon the now healthy pile of wood strategically located next to the fire ring. There would be a fine fire tonight! The culmination of the past three months had brought me to this place, and I was experiencing tremendous peace as I leaned over the fire ring containing pyramid-stacked wood and struck a match into the dry pine needles I was using for kindling. Within five minutes, the fire was perfect.

Around 10 p.m., sitting in my small portable chair, I drew heavily upon a cheap cigar, and the combination of smoke and cold misty breath left a long plume of white vapor high above my head. The brilliance of a full moon that night slowly rose behind me and illuminated the dormant volcanic craters off to my left, draped in pure white snow. The moon's light began to silhouette the majestic mountain peaks in front of me, and the magnificence of this place enveloped me in its arms. Tears came to my eyes as I felt closer to God, to myself, and to my surroundings than I have in a very long time. That same feeling of serenity floods my soul each time I close my eyes and remember that first night.

After several hours, my eyes became heavy, and I slowly and somewhat reluctantly unzipped the door to my tent and crawled inside the domed structure. I felt like a little boy camping in my parents' backyard again. As I lay on my back upon the comfortable air mattress, I glanced around my miniature domicile, my home for the next several months. My sleeping bag was positioned in the center, with my supplies stored along the sides. The three-man tent provided plentiful space. The outside air was still and silent, and the moon's bright glow reflected against the thin walls. I remained awake for only a few minutes, as my relaxed body soon drifted off to sleep. Classic rock would not wake me in the morning, and there would be no business meetings to attend. My first three items on tomorrow's agenda would be to arise, smell the aroma of the woods, and eat breakfast.

My dreams would be plentiful that night, but they would not end with the sunrise.

First day

First Campsite - Mono Lake (Mono Crater in background)

CHAPTER 2

New Roads in a Familiar Land

I awoke with a slight shiver, as the air's temperature had dropped into the low forties during the night. It had been a good night's sleep. The early-morning sunshine was doing its best to reach me as its rays wove around the tall pine trees, and I groggily glanced at my watch to confirm what I already knew—it was early. As the blurred digital display of 6:30 slowly came into focus, I thought it coincidental that I had awakened exactly 24 hours earlier in a much different place and in a much different way. My one-day anniversary was now complete.

After resurrecting the hot embers from the previous night's fire into a new morning blaze, I huddled near its generous warmth and felt the chill begin to leave my body as I sipped a cup of hot instant coffee. Once my body temperature reached an acceptable level, I packed up camp and went through the process of loading my supplies back onto the bike, blowing into my hands to keep them warm. I knew it would take me several attempts at this ritual before I really got it down to a science, but that was a task I would not mind rehearsing. Before leaving, I looked toward the west, where the rays of the rising sun were glistening off the high peaks of the Sierra, causing them to glow like a candle on a dark night. I felt the need to kneel before this majestic scene and thank the Lord for the incredible opportunity He had given me.

The nearby town of Lee Vining was a short fifteen-minute ride away. It is one of those quaint mountain towns whose primary survival is based on the thousands of tourists who pass through each year. It is a very small town consisting of perhaps thirty buildings bordering each side of Highway 395, nicely centered between the western shore of Mono Lake and the Sierra Nevada mountain range. The small restaurant was very busy that morning, mostly with people "just passing through," and I received more than one long stare as I pulled my two-wheeled motor home in front of the large restaurant window.

As I walked toward the counter to lay claim to a vacant stool, I noticed a young European-looking couple sitting in one of the booths across the dining room. Now if someone were to ask me what "European-looking" actually looks like, I probably could not describe it. I just knew. Their attire consisted of black leather jackets, red scarves tied around their necks, and large black leather boots. The woman had somewhat stringy and thin blonde hair that fell upon her shoulders, and her face was absent of any makeup, making her very plain-looking. The man's features were similar to hers, except for the shorter hair, and I wasn't sure if he was a boyfriend or a brother.

I had noticed two BMW motorcycles sitting outside the restaurant, fully packed, with what looked to be about fifty pounds of dirt and grime sporadically deposited everywhere but the seats. Being the intuitive and intellectual giant that I am, I quickly deduced that this couple must be the owners of these bikes. Normally in this type of setting, I would not have made a move to initiate a conversation with total strangers, but I was determined to turn over a new leaf and attempt those things I would not normally do. I needed a good opening line, something that would really grab their attention. I ambled over to their table, and as their eyes met mine, I said, "Hi. Those your bikes?" I've always had a way with words.

They responded in the affirmative with unmistakable German accents (I told you they were European) and motioned for me to sit down. They shared with me their experiences of riding throughout the United States over the past three months and then spent a few extra minutes describing their ride through Oklahoma amidst the terrible flooding that had taken place only a month earlier. Their trip was nearing an end, and their faces displayed a mixture of enthusiasm and weariness. I found myself envious of their adventure stories but quickly realized that someday soon, I would be sharing the same kind of tales with others. I didn't visit very long but was proud of myself for taking the time to chat. It was another small victory in the battle of change.

As I was devouring my hotcakes and sausage at the counter, a gentleman in his late fifties sat down on the stool next to mine and began engaging in active discussion with another man eating a few feet away. Based on their subject matter, it was obvious they were both local Lee Vining men and that the man next to me seemed content to do most of the talking. His conversation contained more than one reference to the rat race and how he would be better off moving out of the country to some land he owned in Baja California, Mexico. He seemed to be going through some trying times. "There's got to be more to life than this," I heard him say. My ears immediately perked up after hearing this comment. I saw this as a good opportunity to interject and began to talk with him.

As I shared my brief story, he listened with intense interest. He would be the first of many who would respond to my account with the regretful phrase, "I wish I would have done what you are doing when I was your age." He looked at me with eyes of conviction and said, "Man, you are doing this the right way. What I wouldn't have given to take a trip like this. You know, when you put these kinds of dreams off till you're older, you find that they often won't happen. The body tends to give up on ya."

There was a sadness as he spoke, and I knew the regrets he spoke of were from personal experience. He was confirming, through life, what I was beginning to learn…that we must seize the day. I tried to encourage him, assuring him it was never too late to start living those dreams that are still attainable, but my words seemed to fall on deaf ears. He had obviously given up long ago and had resolved himself to settle with life instead of changing it. Looking back, I wish I had pursued learning his reasons why. Perhaps I could have made a difference.

I thought back to a poster I had seen once in a motorcycle shop. The poster displayed a man who looked to be roughly 101 years old and 95 pounds, wearing an old-fashioned wool suit and fedora hat, sitting on the seat of a dirt bike. He looked confused, helpless, and sad. The caption read, "Be sure and work long and hard all of your life so that when you get old, you can afford to buy the things that you can no longer use." I smiled to myself as the lesson hit home.

After thirty minutes of motoring north from Lee Vining, I stopped in the town of Bridgeport for refueling. Bridgeport was another small town located in an expansive valley of deep green rich grass and quick-flowing streams, where hundreds of cattle could be seen grazing at the base of the range. While pumping the high-octane fuel into my four-gallon tank, I marveled at how well things had gone so far. Hard as I tried, I could not recall one single problem. *This isn't so hard*, I mistakenly thought to myself. I was soon to find that one should never say or think this. Luck turns faster than a night in Vegas, and I was just asking for it when I began to display any cockiness whatsoever.

As I pulled out of the station's driveway, my back tire fell into an unseen yet deep hole in the roadway and jarred the bike and me pretty hard. "Nice going, Ace," I sarcastically said to myself, but I didn't give it much thought at the time. About ten miles down the highway, I glanced back for a casual inspection of my cargo and noticed that my bright maroon full-face helmet was riding about six inches off the road's asphalt! This was not good. Both bags had fallen completely off the rack, probably when I had hit the hole, and the black bungees were straining for all they were worth to hold things from scattering all over the highway.

I immediately pulled over, unpacked all of the bags, and tried to arrange my contents in a different manner and weight ratio so as to remedy any similar occurrences in the future. After spending a half hour on this task, I was back on the road. Twelve miles later, as I was passing a car on the left , something caught my attention out of the corner of my right eye. At that moment, my sleeping bag completely unfolded, flew out of its netting, and bounced off the car's windshield. Unfortunately, I had just stuffed a number of items into the sleeping bag so I could easily access them...items that were now nicely scattered everywhere. The old man driving the car quickly passed me back and shot a disgusted-looking scowl my way as if I had planned the entire event just to tick him off.

My macho ego was definitely a bit deflated at this point. There I was, rolling up my sleeping bag on the side of the road and picking up my maps, money, and other such items from out of the ditch and off the highway covering about a quarter-mile area. As I began to put everything back in its place, I gave a hard pull on the strap that held my sleeping bag in position so this would not happen again, and in doing so, I broke the plastic buckle in two, slamming myself in the nose with my fist. Relieved to find I had not given myself a bloody nose, I shook my head at how stupid this must have looked, expecting Moe, Larry, and Curly to show up any minute to advise me on how to perfect my act.

Shaking my head and muttering to myself, I mounted my bike and, once again, headed down the highway. Ten miles later, I realized I had left my brand-new leather gloves on top of the sleeping bag and they were now lying somewhere on the highway behind me. I was not going back! The cockiness curse had struck swiftly and fiercely. Lesson learned.

I needed to turn my direction westward, toward the interior of California, which would require crossing the Sierra Nevada range. My initial plan had been to use Tioga Pass, which would have taken me through Yosemite National Park, but the heavy snows during the winter and spring had kept this mountain road closed much longer than usual. For this reason, I chose Highway 108, the Sonora Pass, as my alternative. Thirty minutes after my self-beating, I stopped at the Sonora Pass turnoff and fitted myself with warmer clothing in preparation for the higher elevations I would soon be experiencing. Luckily, I had brought a second pair of gloves.

As I was standing next to my bike, a car pulled in behind me and out stepped, yes, a European-looking gentleman. His accent was extremely heavy, and I would guess he was from Germany, much like my restaurant friends. He was holding an unfolded California map and just stared at me with a sort of pouty, "I need help" look. I raised my eyebrows a bit and said, "Yes?"

He said, "Yoss Emight?" and pointed toward the mountains. I had no idea what he was trying to convey to me. Noticing my confused look, he repeated, "Yoss Emight!" but louder this time, as if the change in volume would help me understand.

I decided to respond with the intellectual reply "Huh?" and also by speaking loudly. This interesting verbal interaction continued for several frustrating minutes, until I finally realized he was trying to say Yosemite. It took me another ten minutes to explain that the pass to Yosemite was closed and he needed to take the Sonora Pass route and enter the famous park from the other side.

He smiled and said, "Thank you," but I'm not sure if he had really understood what I was trying to tell him. I had taken German in high school, but for some reason, the only combination of German words I could recall was "Du bist ein Esel," or "You are a donkey." Because this is a German insult, I decided it would be best to stay with my native language.

Sonora Pass was breathtaking, as it cut through deep forest, high mountain passes, grand waterfalls, and wide, open valleys. Because of the heavy snows, I found myself riding next to fifteen-foot snowbanks at the 9,624-foot summit, and it made me feel very small. I was often forced to ride much slower than normal because there were many places where melting snow had produced slippery conditions of water and gravel. I cringed at the thought of my clean, bright chrome being dulled by the road grime now being flung upon it. *Oh well, better get used to it*, I thought. There would be plenty of places where my chrome would lose its luster.

After crossing the Sierras, I continued down through the foothills of California, an area rich in history for its mining and gold discoveries of the 1800s. The air temperature began to quickly climb, and I soon found myself once again riding in temperatures that exceeded 100 degrees. After indulging in a thrifty lunch consisting of a ninety-nine–cent Whopper and glass of water, I began to near the area where I had been born and raised—Lodi, California. Yes, as in Creedence Clearwater Revival's "Stuck in Lodi Again."

Lodi is a mid-sized town whose population consists of 50,000 people. It is located thirty-five miles south of Sacramento in the Central Valley. I was not actually raised in the Town of Lodi but seven miles from the town's limit, amidst acres and acres of grape vineyards for which Lodi is famous worldwide. It felt good to be nearing deeply familiar lands, a place of security where my roots ran deep.

I was the youngest of three boys and had been born into a ready-made nuclear family that had been around for quite some time before my surprise entrance. My oldest brother, Eric, was almost 18 years old when I made my way into this world, and I was fourteen years behind the next in line, Mark. Dad was 44 years old and Mom was 42. Can you say whoops?

To say that Dad was not enthralled with the idea of a newborn at the age of 44 would definitely be a gross understatement. Being older, I have come to understand my father's sentiments a bit more clearly now. I compare it to running the famed Ironman triathlon in Hawaii, finishing the race in the best time of your life and then, as you crawl across the finish line, hearing, "Okay, once more around the island!"

I seem to be one of those rare people who actually was raised in a fairly functional home, which I am sure has cost me thousands of dollars on the talk-show circuit, but am thankful, nonetheless. A primary reason for this stability was the grounding we had had in our Christian faith and our relationship with our God and Jesus Christ. This had always been an overwhelming priority, especially through my mother's actions. Values were not only preached but were demonstrated to me in many ways as I grew up. I consider myself fortunate to have been raised in such a good home.

As I cruised through the back roads of my youth, fifteen miles from Lodi, more and more landmarks sparked small memories of years gone by. Many a smile came to my face as I simply remembered. It was mid afternoon, and my skin glistened with sweat as the 105-degree temperature mercilessly beat down upon me. I was relieved to see the road sign that told me Lodi was only seven miles away. I turned right onto Highway 12, the highway I had traveled thousands of times during my lifetime, and my heart began to pick up speed as I neared the home where I had spent so much time growing up, a place I had left eleven years before.

I slowed my bike to almost a crawl and putted past the house of the neighbor whose lawn I had cut as a 12-year-old, my first job ever. I really despised mowing lawns, and when you live in the country, everyone seems to have a huge one. I cut so many lawns as a child that the smell of cut grass was not actually a pleasant aroma again until I was in my late twenties. I thought it interesting how time can change a detestable experience into a cherished memory.

A few moments later, I found myself in front of my "real home," the place where I had grown up. I pulled my bike onto the wide shoulder of the highway, turned off the motor, and stared at the familiar structure for a good while, letting feelings wash over me like a cool shower on a hot summer's day. So many memories.

Although the scene was now somewhat physically different, my mind could picture exactly how it had looked years ago. It was a pink stucco house (the kids on the bus loved this one) that was connected to the highway by a U-shaped gravel driveway, the interior of the "U" filled in with grass and a walnut tree in the middle. It was a one-story ranch house, with three bedrooms, a huge backyard, a large red barn, and five acres of flat, barren land, hemmed in by a border of barbwire fencing.

This was the place where I had bicycled to and from elementary school every day, four miles round trip. Here was where I had learned to drive a motorcycle, a car, and a tractor. Here was the barn where I could still smell the aroma of musty hay and where I had raised rabbits as a 13-year-old boy. Here was where I had dealt with death and loss. The place where I had become a man.

I don't believe I had ever realized just how special this country home was to me until that very moment. Memories began to flood my mind so fast, I could barely take them all in, and I could feel my emotions churning like the waters beneath a waterfall. A surprising event was taking place: This journey was not only setting me free to follow my dreams but also putting me in closer touch with where I had come from. I found myself focusing on feelings I had not taken the time to remember for quite some time, reminiscing on events that had made me the person I was today, like the night I had come home after a church meeting during summer vacation only two weeks before the start of my senior year in high school. I had been going through a period of intense teenage rebellion throughout the past year. My "I'll try anything once" philosophy had gotten me in trouble with drugs and drinking and I wasn't about to let any adult tell me what to do, especially because I knew it all already. The relationship between my parents and me had definitely become a strained one. Recently, I had finally begun to return from these ways, and I was slowly coming back to the family foundation on which I had been raised. It felt good that my parents and I had had a great dinner together that night. For the first time in a long time, we had been talking and laughing instead of arguing and yelling. We had left the table as friends for a change, with hope that things were finally getting better.

I had been in a great mood that night as I drove the last half mile of Highway 12 before reaching my home, but it hadn't taken long for the good times to change. As I had neared my home, I had known something was terribly wrong. My headlights began to outline a number of cars parked along the shoulder of the highway, and as I drew nearer, I saw even more cars parked in our driveway. Every light in the house seemed to be shining brightly as if there was a huge party going on, but I knew there was no party that night. Feelings of dread twisted my stomach in knots as I slowly passed my house, unwilling to face the inevitable truth that waited for me inside.

Instead of turning into the familiar driveway, I had continued on, pulling over to the side of the road a few houses down, feeling scared and alone. My parents had planned to go for a drive that evening, and I was assuming the worst. Shock gripped my body as I stared aimlessly out of the window, wondering what I would do with both my parents gone, trying to prepare myself for what was soon to come, knowing everything was about to change. With my heart in my throat, I slowly turned the car around, parked in the driveway, and waited. Almost immediately, my brother Eric came out to meet me. His face seemed stoic behind his black beard, but I could tell he was fighting emotion. As I was standing next to my car, he looked me in the eyes and cut to the point. "Dad was killed tonight on his motorcycle." For a brief moment, I was almost relieved in hearing that one parent had been spared, but it did not take long for the grief to hit me. We hugged each other, and cried, saying little. Dad had been killed only two months before retiring from a job he had disliked for most of his life, working as a machine mechanic in a factory. All he had been looking forward to was retirement. It didn't seem fair. I couldn't believe he would not be around during the time of my life when I was becoming a man and would need his guidance more than ever.

I still miss him.

This same house is where I had walked through the front door as a 7-year-old boy returning from a hard day of second grade, ready to get on with the business of playing outside. As I had walked through the kitchen, I had glanced down the hallway and seen my mother standing toward the end of it, near the bedroom from where she had just come. She had motioned for me to come to her. "I have something very important to tell you," she had said, her tone low and serious. Her face seemed red and a little puffy, and even at my young age, I could tell that something was not right. She kneeled, and as tears began to well up in her eyes, she told me in a trembling voice that my middle brother would not be coming home, he had been killed in Vietnam.

I had burst out sobbing. Mom and I had cried together for five minutes as the comforting security of my mother's arms held me close. Then, as quickly as I had started crying, I stopped. Mom looked at me a bit strangely and asked why I had stopped so quickly. "I'm not going to cry anymore," I said. "I know Mark is with Jesus and he's really happy now," and I had walked out of the room, confident in my reasoning. Mom later told me that this one short statement had dramatically helped her during that mournful time of loss. Yes, we had gone through some tough times in this house, but tragedy could not destroy a family's love. It only made the love stronger.

I remembered the plans I had made for myself as a naive and simple young boy. I had assumed I would stay in this area my entire life, graduate from college, marry in my mid-twenties and have two or three kids by the time I reached my thirties. After all, that's what everyone else seemed to do. Marriage would also come easily, I figured. You meet the right girl, fall madly in love, and get married—no big deal. I had just known my life would be perfectly executed according to the fine plan I had designed. Now, sitting in front of my old house, I smiled and shook my head as I thought just how opposite my life had turned out compared to that "fine plan."

Although I had accumulated more than 100 credits, I had never received a four-year degree from college, nor had I remained in Lodi very long. I had moved away from home and gone to Colorado when I was 20, attending Rockmont College, a small Christian college in Lakewood, probably more for its skiing than its academics. Wanting to get on with my life and never deal with homework again, I had then quit college early and worked in my brother's computer software company. After ten months, I had been offered an opportunity to work in New Bedford, Massachusetts, for a short time, at the age of 23. This job transfer was to last only two months, but as it would turn out, it would end up being a permanent move from my hometown. So much for a college education and staying in the area.

My marriage plans did not exactly go according to schedule, either. Many of the relationships during my twenties turned out to be unfulfilling long-distance affairs, primarily because of the extensive travel I endured on my job and because of my growing reluctance to commit to one person. As time passed, I knew that my plan of being married before I was thirty wasn't going to happen.

A few years after being transferred to Southern California, I met a girl I'll call Leslie. She was 23 years old, four years my junior, and a very personable and attractive young lady who also had a great sense of humor. We hit it off quickly, and for the first time in years, I was regularly dating someone who actually lived within driving distance. After only a few months, we were discussing the subject of marriage and I felt that I may have finally found the one I was looking for.

As the relationship progressed, however, the likelihood of marriage did not. I thought it might be the lack of passion I was feeling toward her. I had never really felt that passion, but I had written that off as unimportant and shallow. It isn't. I was also concerned with her drinking habits but was very naive about the tell-tale signs of alcoholism because I had never really been exposed to it before. Whatever the reasons, our relationship made little progress over the next five years, and although I often felt I should end it and move on, I was too weak to let go of the security and good times we had together. That weakness would dramatically change my entire life.

Despite our troubled relationship, Leslie and I were married in August, six years after we met, at a small church in Mission Viejo, California. My nicely decorated Harley would serve as our transportation to the reception. This brief twenty-minute ride, made in full wedding garb, was and is, to this day, a very good memory. Unbeknownst to me, during the reception, two of my very good friends had been told some distressing news by one of Leslie's friends about Leslie's unfaithfulness of the past. Why she waited until the day of the wedding, I will never know. My friends, Jim and Chris, at the risk of ruining a valuable friendship, made the decision to pursue and investigate the allegations and collect as many facts as possible before speaking with me. What they discovered while I was on my honeymoon would be devastating.

Ten days after the wedding, Jim and Chris told me the news. Much of the innocent past Leslie had portrayed to me had been a lie. She had also been consistently unfaithful during our relationship. One infidelity had taken place only two months before our wedding. To make matters worse, I was told that her drinking problem was much worse than I had thought, especially during times when I was not present. The reality of the situation hit me like a locomotive—I had married a person I did not know at all! This pain was increased tenfold when I found that one of my best friends had been with her as well. I had never experienced betrayal of that magnitude before in my life. One by one, my innocent views of the way life should be were being destroyed by the reality of this unfair world.

The marriage was over that night and was annulled six months later. I began to live my life alone again, letting time slowly heal me as I continued on with my daily rituals. I consider myself lucky that I had been told the truth when I had. Through this difficult period of my life, I had grown like never before.

Now, sitting along the highway, looking at my house, it was hard to believe I had ever been that naive young boy raised in this country home. Life had been much harder than I had thought it would be. It still is. I began to realize that my *real* journey had not yet actually begun. This ride had been intended to take me away from my comfort zone and transport me outside its walls, to the world of the unknown, but so far, I had simply ridden toward my comfort zone and to the well known. Until I left the comfortable surroundings of this place, my "true" home, my journey would not truly start. I had learned a little more about myself sitting there on Highway 12 that afternoon. I discovered a few new roads in a familiar land.

I stayed in Lodi for two days, enjoying time with my family and appreciating them even more than usual this time. Of course the family had grown a bit since my years in the country, no thanks to me. Eric and his wife, Gloria, had three daughters, all two years apart, and all of whom were now married. You know you are getting old when all of your nieces are married before you.

While visiting Eric at his Lodi home, I meandered outside to his fenced-in backyard, margarita in hand, and took a seat on one of his patio chairs. As I was relaxing, letting my mind wander toward the memories yet to be experienced, Eric strolled over to where I was and, with somewhat of a smirk on his face, said, "Did you see the weather report?"

I knew he would not be taking such pleasure in this comment unless it leaned toward bad news. "Nooo," I replied hesitantly. "Why do you ask?"

"Rain up and down the coast," he nonchalantly said as he strolled back into the kitchen. I couldn't believe my ears. This was California…it hardly rains in the winter, let alone the summer! I rushed into the house, turned on the weather channel, and witnessed the long line of clouds that seemed to be covering the entire western coast from Northern California to Canada, exactly where I had planned to ride.

I had known that riding in the rain was inevitable but had not planned to do so on only my third day on the road. My family and friends had a heyday with this news as they listened to my ever-increasing whining. I believe the phrases "fair-weather rider" and "wimp," along with various choice words I have conveniently deleted from my subconscious, were viciously hurled in my direction with great enjoyment. I simply chalked up their ridicule to extreme envy of my six-month vacation from work and left it at that.

My nights in Lodi were spent at my favorite bed-and-breakfast…Mom's. I don't care what anybody says, the world just seems a little better when you are with your mother. The night before I would be leaving, we sat around the dining room table and talked a little about everything, something we didn't do often enough. We shared a lot of feelings about our family, each other, Mark, and Dad. She told me stories of their lives I had never heard before, and we shared laughter as well as tears. It was a fitting time together in light of all I had remembered just two days earlier. It set the stage for how I wanted to leave.

The alarm's obnoxious beeping catapulted me from my deep sleep, and the morning of departure was once again upon me. My sleep had been deep, and it took me a good thirty seconds of looking around the room to finally realize where I was. Once my mind shifted into gear, I was more than ready to begin the first day of my "real" journey.

I had said my good-byes to the rest of the family the night before, and now it was just Mom and me. As I watched her make my favorite breakfast in the world, thin pancakes, I realized how fortunate I was to have her as my mother. Everyone loves Mabel. She looked much younger than her 76 years and is probably healthier than I am. In fact, Eric and I have a running joke that the making of her will was a waste of time because she will most certainly outlive us anyway.

Mom always seemed to be the glue that held the family together, and never have I seen her Christian principles compromised in any way. She is the one who is always willing to visit someone in the hospital, to help someone in need, or to just be a listening ear on the phone. She is the epitome of the phrase "actions speak louder than words," and I will always credit her examples throughout my life as the cornerstone for my character, my values, and my beliefs.

After breakfast, Mom joined me in the garage as I was loading my supplies on the bike, and she seemed genuinely interested in helping me get ready for the trip. Although she put on a good front, I could tell it was extremely hard for her. She had said good-bye to another son in 1967 as he boarded a plane to Vietnam during the Christmas holidays. He, like me, had been leaving, unsure as to what the future held for him, and she had constantly reassured him they would be together again the following Christmas and that this dark chapter in his life would soon be over. That was the last time she saw him.

It wasn't an airport, only a garage, but I wondered if this good-bye scene was replaying in her mind once again. I admire her for not placing guilt upon me, as some mothers might, or failing to support me in my quest. She has always placed me in God's hands and allowed me to do those things I felt I needed to do. It takes great faith to let go and put others first, and this was demonstrated in a mighty way by her actions that day.

I felt somewhat ambivalent about my feelings as I backed out of Mom's garage and started the engine. I was excited for what lay ahead, yet sad for what I must be putting her through and the outside chance I may never see her again. I gave her a hug and told her I loved her, and with a twist of the throttle, my official journey finally began. Just before I turned the corner, I looked back over my right shoulder and saw her standing in the driveway, wearing her bathrobe, waving. What a great image to leave with. I knew her prayers were with me.

Although the sky was overcast and threatening, I was still hoping for the best. While suiting up in the garage, I had adopted a positive "aw, it won't rain on me" attitude and decided to forego my bulky rain gear of rain pants, jacket, booties, gators, and full face helmet. I just had no desire to put all this mess on. I was confident that if I thought positively enough, the rain would flee my positive aura to some other less menacing region of the world. *Wrong!* Not twenty miles west of Lodi, I felt the first raindrops begin to sting my face. By the looks of the clouds ahead, this was not going to be just a light shower.

I reluctantly pulled over to the side of the road, unbuckled my left saddlebag, which held my water-repellent garb, and went through the rigorous process of suiting up like a knight getting ready for battle. After unfolding the bulky blue plastic pants, I pulled them over my jeans and black leather chaps, somewhat thankful that the baggy look was currently the trend. The oversized waterproof jacket completely covered my torso, including my tee shirt, black vest, and black leather jacket, and I buttoned it clear up to the bottom of my chin. I reached down and placed my black riding boots through the elastic strap of the waterproof gators that would cover my legs from the middle of my boots to just below the knee. To finish off this fine ensemble, I covered the rest of my boots with plastic booties to make certain my feet would stay as dry as possible. I retrieved my full face helmet from beneath the red cargo netting and replaced it with my open half-helmet and placed the claustrophobic hat over my head.

When I was finally through, I felt like the Michelin man. Those who really know me are fully aware of my disdain for excess clothing, and this gear was nothing but excess clothing. I don't even like wearing long-sleeved shirts. I was convinced that if I ever fell while wearing this suit, I would be at the mercy of strangers to place me back on my feet, like a tortoise on his back with his belly facing the sun. That was not the way I wanted to die. I started my machine and continued on through a ten-minute deluge of rain…and then the sun came out. Well, that was worth it!

As I continued toward the Pacific coast, just north of San Francisco, I entered the beautiful Napa Valley and found myself surrounded by exquisite rolling hills professionally carpeted with thousands of acres of grapevines sporting the fruit that would eventually fill many wine glasses all over the world. The recent rains had produced crisp, clean air heavily laden with smells of open land, grass, and grapes, and I was transported not just by my motorcycle but also by my senses.

Before I realized it, I suddenly and unexpectedly was met by the Pacific Ocean, stretching before me in what seemed to be an infinite blue carpet, marking my furthest point west. My heart did a little high five as my direction soon turned north on scenic Highway 1, where the waves of the cold Pacific crashed loudly upon the shore to my left and beautiful green hills towered high to my right. I was now, outwardly this time, experiencing new roads in a familiar land. For the very first time, I felt I was beginning to break away.

Mother Nature had chosen not to dampen my spirits since the ten-minute deluge earlier, and I decided to strip off the bulky rain apparel and return to my black leather garb. Ah, so much better. The next five hours would be spent hugging the ocean's coast over the slow, tight, and twisty road that makes Highway 1 a heavenly experience for bikers around the world.

In late afternoon, I continued to follow Highway 1 as it began to cut inland over the coastal mountainous terrain now covered with its world-renowned mighty redwood trees. Twelve miles later, it terminated into Highway 101, a somewhat larger highway that would eventually meet the coast again at the small town of Eureka, California. The winding mountain road soon began to climb, and the weather started to turn drizzly and very cold. I had been on the bike for eight hours now, and it was time to find a place to spend the night. It was the first time that my lodging plans had not been planned in advance.

Let's see, where would I lay my head for the night? How would I initiate this first evening of the true journey? Perhaps a clearing amongst the trees of the forest, an abandoned cave, some thick brush, or beneath a rocky overhang...hmm...how about...a motel? Yes, a motel would be good. My defenses immediately kicked in, and I rationalized my weenie decision through the logical determination that roughing it too soon would be a bad thing. I still have not come up with a reason why it would be a bad thing, but the hypothesis held up that night.

As I approached the 101 turnoff, I found a cheap motel in the town of Leggett, near Smithe Redwoods State Reserve, the famous park where, among other things, a car can be driven through a live redwood tree. From what I could see, the metropolis of Leggett consisted of two motels, a diner, and a post office. I thought, *Not much nightlife tonight.* Redwood trees were sprinkled among their pine and fir cousins, nicely located outside and within the small town. The gray and chilly weather did little to alter the smile on my face. I was already forgetting what stress felt like.

I staked out one of the motels and slowly putted my bike to the sign that said "Office" and, with the turn of the key, returned my surroundings to silence. The fragrant smell of burning pine wafting in the air turned my eyes skyward to witness all the cabins' fireplaces seeding the air with this delectable aroma. I walked into the motel office and was greeted by two cats eyeing me from atop the check-in counter, with an old, gray-haired "earthy" woman barely visible in the back room, watching TV. As I walked over to the felines, I said something like "nice cats," whereby she proceeded to share with me their entire life histories. I'm pretty sure I could pick either one out in a lineup. I had picked this place because the rooms were actually tiny cabins. I asked her how many TV channels were available. "Hard to say," she replied, "depends on the weather." Okay. Total motel bill—about thirty bucks. Not too bad.

It was a cozy little room, with emphasis on the word little. It consisted of a bedroom, which was a fitting name in this case because the bed took up the entire room. Oh, there was a bathroom, fully equipped with a tiny bath and shower. It was still better than a rocky overhang. Normally, I'm not a bath man. I don't mean to be stereotypical, but I have a difficult time visualizing a macho guy soaking in a tub of suds (not that I make it a habit of visualizing macho men in tubs). I couldn't remember the last time I had actually taken a bath, but I had to admit, I had been fantasizing about a nice hot bath for the last two hours of my ride, during which time my body temperature had dropped to that of a lizard. I decided to just go for it. I plugged up the tub with its little chained rubber stopper and reached for the water knob with high expectations of settling down in the soothing hot water and reading a good book.

I turned the hot water handle to the left, and after a few ominous plumbing noises, water began chugging from the old faucet. Well, it had the chemical principles of water, although rust colored and a bit thicker than I was used to. After filling the bath to the top, I was a bit chagrined to find I could not actually see the bottom of the off-white porcelain tub. I shrugged it off and took the bath anyway, rationalizing that the iron content, or whatever it was, was probably therapeutic and my skin would be much smoother and softer after exposing it to these ingredients.

After my mineral bath had returned my body temperature to that of a human, I ventured to the greasy spoon next door and ordered up a jalapeno burger and a cup of coffee. I then learned another valuable lesson from the back roads—do not drink coffee while consuming jalapeno peppers. I returned to my room with my swollen tongue and watched a made-for-TV movie through more snow than a Rocky Mountain blizzard. The room might not have been fancy, but it gave me warmth and it would allow me to get a fresh start on a new day.

The morning's air inside my miniature cabin was probably in the thirties, as I had failed in getting the heater to cooperate the night before. I leaned out from the foot of the bed and, while shivering from the cold, peeked out the window with high hopes of seeing nothing but blue sky. The tall redwoods around me blocked much of my view, but I could still tell that the sky was mostly filled with clouds and that only hints of blue patches could be seen. I would find that this would be a morning ritual...awakening with weather expectations, as this would always set the tone for the day's ride.

Walking toward the bathroom, I was relieved to find that my skin had not developed any cancerous lesions or any other skin disorder because of my bath the previous night. Starting with the brushing of my pearly whites, I began the morning ritual of getting ready for a long day's ride.

Although the weather was chilly, my black leather chaps and jacket seemed to suffice in keeping me warm enough. Highway 101 alternated between being a four-lane and two-lane highway, and although it was fairly busy with summer vacationers, the beauty of the forests around me seemed to make the traffic disappear.

There were numerous places where scenic loops were provided to take travelers off the main highway and allow them to drive through the mighty redwood forests, viewing them up close and personal and then eventually looping back to the highway. More than once, I found myself riding in places where the tops of the trees on one side of the road would reach out and touch the treetops on the opposite side, forming a natural tunnel that would stretch out over a mile or so. These scenes were not available for viewing to the traveler of the interstates. These scenic detours were breathtaking, especially on a motorcycle, and I took every one that was made available to me. Hey, this "enjoy the journey" philosophy was starting to become second nature! I had never realized how freeing it could be to bury my watch deep in my pocket and not let time dictate my life. There is so much to see.

The moment I left the shelter of the mountains and returned to the ocean's edge, I began to encounter a very cold and intense westerly side wind that seemed to snatch the dampness from the surface of the frigid ocean water and transfer it to shore. It was absolutely brutal. The half helmet I wore had no protection for my ears, and it felt as if every square inch of the ocean's air was aimed directly into my left acoustic organ. I was tempted to exchange my helmet for the full-face version beneath the netting but felt the muffled and claustrophobic feeling I received from it was the worse evil of the two.

The wind became so bad at times, I would find myself suddenly moved over six feet by an unexpected harsh gust, a nerve-racking experience when riding on what had turned into a narrow two-lane highway. To neutralize this unpredictable change in direction, I forced myself close to the center line, which in turn, didn't provide oncoming traffic much room for error as they passed me going the opposite direction. I had also noticed that the exposed skin on the fingers of my right hand seemed to be drying up, cracking, and bleeding, causing me a good deal of discomfort. I could only figure they were not used to the cold weather and the constant bending and gripping they were suddenly being subjected to. Hopefully, they would eventually toughen up as the trip progressed.

The Northern California coast was a ruggedly beautiful place and was nothing like the coastline I was used to in Southern California. The place where land met sea was not a gradual and friendly slope that I was familiar with, where one could walk down to the ocean and enjoy its benefits, but was a mixture of jagged rocky ledges and steep vertical drops. Sandy beaches were rare, and the white-capped waves crashed with a mighty force against the rocky walls, sending cold ocean spray high into the air. Tiny rocky islands protruded throughout the bays as if warning potential visitors to stay away. Because of the storms, the ocean swells rose high and often, as if the Pacific was struggling to catch its breath. The deep grayness of the sky seemed to only accentuate this foreboding place. What struck me most was the unfriendliness I felt, as if the shores did not want me there. As much as the Sierras had urged me into its waiting arms, it seemed as if this region was doing its best to push me away.

Early that afternoon, I passed the "Welcome to Oregon" sign, and a smile immediately came to my face. Now it really felt as if I was leaving home. I wondered how many more state signs I would see over the next several months. Time would tell. After a few more hours of riding, the wind had taken its toll and I was ready to stop for the night. This time, my rationalization for another motel was unsuccessful, and I settled for a campground instead…baby steps. I found a fairly cheap KOA campground in Bandon, Oregon, that was located a short distance off the highway, and I chose a campsite surrounded by trees. It wasn't Mono Lake, but at least I felt somewhat secluded from the other campers.

After setting up my tent and its indoor furnishings, I decided to fend for myself and cook my own dinner. No restaurant for me. It was time to rough it. Well, if you consider opening a can of chili and heating it up in the office's microwave oven roughing it. I know it wasn't exactly trapping my prey in the woods, but again, I needed to slowly work my way into the wilderness habits.

Although Mother Nature had been gracious and had not rained on me all day, she made up for it that night. I was awakened at three in the morning by the insistent tapping of rain drops pelting the top of my tent. My heart sank, and I felt bad that my bike was sitting alone outside in the elements while I was nicely protected from the weather's fury, but it didn't take long for the guilt to pass and for me to quickly return to my state of slumber.

After waking up around 7:30 that morning, I could still hear the steady pitter-patter of rain. A wet day was ahead. I slowly managed to sit up in my sleeping bag and started looking around the "room." Something toward the front entrance caught my eye. What was it? It seemed to be moving. Then, the sad realization began to take hold that it was water. My tent leaked! I knew I shouldn't have bought the cheap one! My eyes darted to the other side of the tent and focused to the spot where my clothes were piled. I slowly reached over and grabbed a shirt—squish. About a third of my clothes were now completely soaked. To make matters worse, my stomach was having its own internal battle with the chili I had eaten the night before. Although not real happy about my new laundering process, I packed up my wet clothes as best I could and prepared to get on the road. I would worry about drying them later.

The light rain continued throughout the morning, and because of my vain attempts at trying to keep my supplies as free from the mud and rain as possible, my packing and loading ritual became extended to about an hour and a half. The rain-gear issue was an obvious one, and the bulky suit only added to my increasingly foul mood that morning. At this point, the only thing that could turn my negative attitude around would be to get on the road and put some miles behind me.

I heaved my baggy blue leg over the seat and sat there like a big old lump, breathing heavily inside my enclosed helmet as my visor began to fog up. I pulled the carburetor choke out with my left hand and reached for the start button with my other. Ah yes, I would soon hear my loud pipes confirm successful ignition as my engine would roar to life. My morning hell would be over! I pressed the start button and heard...nothing. My eyes went into a cold, emotionless stare as the reality of what had just happened hit me. I laid my head against the handlebars and just sat there feeling very depressed...and very big.

I knew it was an electrical problem. Just to look at my battery required that the seat be removed, which required the removal of *all* of my gear from the bike. I was still sweating from putting it all *on* the bike. I tried the starter again—nothing. I checked the headlight and saw that it was on. This was somewhat encouraging; at least there was some electricity getting through. As I tried the starter a third time, the engine barely turned over once, twice, and surprisingly started on the third rotation. I would have kissed the tank, but I had my full face helmet on. Needless to say, I was ecstatic! Although my concern was very real about what the problem might be, I successfully put it out of my mind and headed out. I'd deal with it later.

It rained on and off that day, and the wind was actually blowing harder than it had the day before. When I could no longer take its cold, vicious pounding, I decided to turn inland around mid-Oregon. My destination for the day was the house of Bruce, whose name I had been given by a friend in Lodi. Although I didn't know Bruce personally, I did know that he used to race dirt bikes in the Lodi area and actually raced against my brother a time or two. I had spoken to him once over the phone, preparing him for a possible visit, and he had seemed very willing to put me up for a night if needed.

Riding that day was fairly uneventful as I took country roads through Oregon's interior, consisting of mostly flat country roads where small towns seemed to pop up every 15 minutes, along with its traffic signals, stop signs, and miniature traffic jams. The intermittent downpouring of rain kept my attention fairly focused ahead, and if there was scenery worth noticing around me, I didn't see it. I reached Portland around four in the afternoon and decided to stop in a mini mall parking lot to confirm directions to Bruce's place.

I found a phone booth and dialed Bruce's number. He answered the phone on the first ring and seemed genuinely glad to hear from me. He gave me a myriad of detailed directions, which included many small country roads required to get me there. It seemed a bit complicated because he lived so far back in the woods, just over the Washington state line, but I was fairly sure I could figure it out. In high anticipation of a warm dinner and comfortable lodging soon ahead, my finger pushed the starter button, and the sound of silence once again greeted my ears. In the eight hours of riding that day, I had forgotten about my little problem that morning. At least this time it was not raining and I was much more relaxed after a good day's ride.

I unpacked all my gear, spread it all around me in the parking space I had commandeered, and received many a look from the nearby locals looking for a place to park. I decided to check the battery first and, fortunately, found the simple problem. The bolt connecting the negative ground cable to the battery terminal had worked its way loose...nothing a few turns of the wrench couldn't cure. If that was the worst mechanical problem I would face on this trip, it would be smooth sailing, but I knew that wouldn't be the case. I packed everything back up and headed for Bruce's house.

I rode the dreaded freeway for only a short while and quickly found the exit I had been told to take. Many of the mountainous back roads apparently didn't require street signs, and after several wrong turns and one more phone call to Bruce, I finally found the one I was looking for. As I had been told, the pavement eventually turned to dirt, and soon, I was riding through an area covered with an expansive array of pine and eucalyptus trees mixed with open green pastures. Single-story ranch-style homes and separated garages were sporadically sprinkled about on their own large parcels of land and seemed to be a perfect Norman Rockwell print. I correctly identified the correct driveway and saw Bruce standing in front of his open garage door, motioning me to pull my bike inside.

Bruce looked to be about six feet tall and in his early fifties and seemed to be in good physical condition. His ruffled gray hair and neatly trimmed gray mustache gave him something of a rugged, Marlboro-Man look, and he readily smiled as I rode my bike into the garage. He was quite friendly, but I also sensed a hint of caution. After all, why shouldn't he be cautious? He didn't know the first thing about me, and I could tell that he was going to withhold judgment until he knew a little more. On the flip side, this was also my first experience of staying with a complete stranger, and I found myself dealing with the same issues of uncertainty.

After a few hours of good conversation, any barriers that had been present had long been broken down, at least from my end, and I began feeling very comfortable as Bruce's guest. Bruce's girlfriend, Linda, also joined us, and she turned out to be one of the nicest ladies I had ever met in my life. Between the three of us, we did not lack for good banter.

Bruce turned out to be the first of many people I would meet on this trip who greatly impressed me by taking on challenging tasks in his life using nothing more than his mind, his own two hands, and the discipline to make it happen. He was a man who accomplished things by jumping in head first and learning through the process. That has always been a trait I have admired in people...being a doer, not just a talker. Unfortunately, I tended to be more talker than doer.

Bruce was a man of high energy who had built his own house, cleared his own land, created an expansive motocross track through the trees, and dug his own pond. He was also a former dirt bike racer, and the barn loft was filled to capacity with trophies he had won over the years. As he was showing me around his place, I asked, "How did you start building a house when you had never done it before?"

He looked at me and said matter-of-factly, "You hammer pieces of wood together."

"You don't need to be so detailed," I replied with a chuckle. I caught the meaning. The real answer was, you just start doing it.

Among Bruce's many completed projects, the one that impressed me the most was a device he had made from a Leonardo da Vinci design called a water ram. It looked like a round metal cylinder, about two feet high and twelve inches in diameter, that sat in a stream of water. Attached to the cylinder was a long piece of white PVC pipe that worked its way up a slight slope under the road and ended in the end of his pond about 100 feet away. Water flowing into the cylinder from the stream is manipulated through a series of spring check valves within the canister, creating its own internal pressure. Once enough pressure is built up, water is pumped through the PVC pipe. It had taken him two years to figure it out, but there it was, clicking away and pumping water a football field away using no electricity…uphill.

When I heard the story behind the creation of this device, it really started me thinking. I had so often dismissed certain dreams or tasks in my own life because I had felt they were too hard or too time-consuming or that I wasn't smart enough to accomplish them. This was the first lesson of many that would teach me that true education is not always learned by reading how to do a task, but by doing it—getting my hands dirty and taking the chance that failure will follow. How many times had I given up before? Too many to count.

When I was asked upon my return of all the lessons I had learned, which stood out as number one, it was clearly this: "To attempt that which is fearful is guaranteed victory; to succeed is a bonus." I had a long history of overevaluating my goals and calculating my chances for success. If success seemed to be a long shot, then I would often choose to not even try. Those times I would try, I would place tremendous pressure on myself to succeed, and if I didn't, I would view the entire process as a waste of my time. I had robbed myself of the pleasure of trying. I was discovering on this journey that "failure" and "wasted time" were not the same things.

I am convinced that Bruce had many setbacks, frustrations, and headaches in achieving his results, which I was now witnessing. The painful memories always seem to fade once the project is over, however, and only the positive results live on.

Sunday morning brought rainy skies once again, and I decided to hold up one more day. Bruce, Linda, Bruce's daughter, Barbara, and I spent much of the day playing dominoes, talking, and laughing. I was having a great time, and, more importantly, it wasn't costing me a penny. I was trying to keep a tight rein on my expenses, and my goal was to average between $40 and $50 per day for absolutely everything. I knew this would be a challenge but also knew that with a little discipline and a lot of luck, I could do it.

Monday morning soon came to call, and as I wearily rolled off the couch, I walked over to the window and peeked out, hoping for clear skies. No such luck, but at least it wasn't raining. Bruce offered his place to me for one more day, but I was getting antsy to move on. I had a friend named Randy in Birch Bay, Washington, who was waiting for me that night and who had taken ten days of vacation from work primarily because of my visit. We planned to spend most of it together, and I didn't want to show up late. I headed out that morning thankful for the hospitality I had been shown and thankful for the lessons Bruce had unknowingly taught me.

Instead of riding straight to the Canadian border, I decided to make a detour and view the Mount St. Helens area to witness the volcano damage I had read so much about. The weather was drizzly and very cold, and its icy fingers seemed to penetrate my five layers of clothing with little effort. After an hour or so, I turned onto another side road, which began my ascent toward Mount St. Helens' summit. As I climbed the narrow, wet, and slippery roadway, the temperature began to plummet and I was surrounded by patches of snow and distant fog. The dreary weather was compounded by the lack of other vehicles, and I realized I had not seen another car for the last thirty minutes.

I continued riding on the narrow two-lane road through the dense green forest, wondering when I might see any hint of the destruction that had taken place so long ago, wondering if I would see any at all. My shivering body outwardly expressed the deep cold I felt, and I wondered if this detour was even worth it. Then, to my extreme disappointment, I found that the summit was completely hidden from view by the low clouds around me, and as I continued along, I chastised myself for taking the diversion.

Suddenly, as I exited a right-hand turn, the trees all but disappeared to my left and my eyes fell upon a sight I had not prepared myself for or will ever forget.

Where two seconds ago, I had not been able to see more than one hundred yards because of the forest's trees, I could now see for tens of miles, as there was no longer anything to block my view. I pulled my bike to the side of the road and slowly got off, slowly unbuckling my helmet, setting it on the seat while never pulling my eyes away from the scene before me. What had once been beautiful green forest was now a devastated landscape of brown fallen trees stripped of all life and lying all around like a discarded pile of Lincoln logs. It looked as if the eruption had taken place the previous week instead of fifteen years earlier. The piercing cold and gray weather seemed to mirror the cold and lifeless land as I could do nothing but stare at the devastation around me. My small presence on the planet seemed very insignificant at that moment when compared to the power of a single act of nature. I sat on the ground and stared at it for the next fifteen minutes.

I came upon a single-lane road, absent of a center line, which took me through the heart of the devastated area. I was now within a few feet of the large fallen trees I had witnessed from far above. I stopped again. There was nobody around, only me. My mind could not begin to imagine the forces that had leveled this place, and I tried to imagine what the process of devastation may have looked like had I been there the day of eruption. I left the area of destruction in subconscious silence, having not expected to be as humbled as I was. As I slowly traversed the descending snaky road, I was suddenly catapulted from barren and desolate land to lush forest and living things once again. I had crossed the line from death to life in a matter of moments.

In a way, I guess that's what this journey was doing for me.

Overlooking Mono Lake

Backing out of Mom's driveway (The real adventure begins)

Near Pt Reyes on Pacific Coast Hwy

Slight detour from PCH overlooking the Pacific (Enjoying the journey)

Northern California forest.

California Redwoods

Bruce & Linda (Oregon)

Entering Mt. St. Helens - Wet, freezing cold

Mt. St. Helens - Beginning of devastation (This was once lush forest)

Mt. St. Helens - Humbling

CHAPTER 3

Comfort Zones, Time Zones, and Tattoos

It had been a long day of riding, and the cold weather of Mount St. Helens had taken its toll. I decided to temporarily veer from my back-roads philosophy and take the I-5 freeway north because I would never make it to Randy's place before dark any other way. After two hours on the speedy but boring artery, I knew I was getting close when I caught a glimpse of the "Birch Bay" road sign…fifteen more miles. I had denied myself any rest breaks over the past two and a half hours, and I was feeling very stiff in the saddle. I glanced at my watch and calculated my arrival time at 7:30 that evening. I was definitely ready to stop.

Although the hour was late, the sun remained fairly high above the northwestern horizon, and its long, bright rays exploded through the nooks and crannies of the gray clouds above, reaching out to the ground as if the fingers of God Himself were touching this place. I love the long days of summer. Randy's house was located only a short fifteen-minute ride from our neighboring country to the north and I must say, I felt a slight swell of accomplishment at having successfully reached the Canadian border all the way from sunny Southern California. Although I really had not been forced to "rough it" yet (despite the chili experience), I didn't let that fact spoil my sense of achievement. I was confident there would be plenty of opportunities for roughing it ahead. No, I was going to savor the hospitality of warm, comfortable shelters offered to me by friends and acquaintances for as long as I could.

I was very much looking forward to seeing Randy again. He and I had worked for the same computer software company for several years, and although we never lived near each other, business trips had thrown us together several times. We had hit it off the first time we met, over three years previous. Randy is a very likable and easygoing man in his mid-thirties with a wicked sense of humor. His choppy laugh had a flavor of Beavis and Butthead but was much more acceptable. His salt-and-pepper hair (more salt than pepper) made him look a bit older than he really was, and we could almost pass for brothers because we were of similar height and weight and both sported mustaches.

Prior to his computer days, Randy had worked as a guard at one of the local Canadian correction facilities. He never fails to entertain me with interesting and sometimes shocking guard stories of the past. Randy also shares my thirst for adventure and had so long before I was traipsing around the country on my Harley or racing dirt bikes in Mexico. He had begun his own travels throughout various parts of the world when he was in his early twenties. Now this may not seem overly adventuresome at face value, but considering he traveled on foot for months at a time, completely alone, and usually with nothing more than a bedroll, the adventures definitely take on additional merit. His "Indiana Jones" stories of Guatemalan jungles, Himalayan villages, giant spiders, wild dogs, and remote villages had done much to inspire me to get out of my little world and begin experiencing my own escapades.

Randy's place was located only a few blocks from the shore of Birch Bay, a quiet little cove in the state of Washington that extends about three miles west before opening out into the Pacific Ocean. His little domicile looked more like your small everyday house than the mountain-type cabin I had expected. It was a small one-story, two-bedroom structure with a little grassy front yard, located among a row of similar type homes, most of which were separated by trees and shrubs...a quaint neighborhood. As I slowly guided my bike along the north side of the house, I could see people talking in the moderately large backyard as they were standing around a two-foot–wide fire pit, holding cans of beer and enjoying the warmth of the fire. All eyes quickly turned toward the loud thumping sound of my Hog, and I stopped the bike just short of Randy's unattached wooden garage. I looked over at the group, took off my sunglasses, and shouted, "What's for dinner?" Randy's infectious smile greeted me, and he couldn't seem to stop that choppy laugh as he took inventory of all the stuff I had managed to load on two wheels.

"Did you leave anything at home?" he asked with a crooked smile.

"Yeah, the stereo turned out to be way too bulky," I replied, "and the extension cord would have cost me a fortune." I didn't bother to unpack right away but instead chose to grab something to drink, sit around the fire, and share some of the stories of the past few days with Randy and his friends. It felt good to tell some tales of my own, even though there were only a few.

One person within the group, Frank, was the former CEO of the company I had recently left and who had been a very good friend of Randy's. Frank had recently experienced some serious business problems of his own, much of which were self-inflicted, and these problems were some of the major reasons the company had been doing poorly as of late. He had tried to take the company too far too fast, and it had seriously backfired on him.

Frank was a very financially intelligent man, and I had always liked his easy-going demeanor, but he was also a workaholic. He was the perfect definition of the high executive risk-taker whose major goal in life was to make it big. I have always admired this trait in people, but only to a certain extent and only when there was some balance present. Through conversations in the past, I had found Frank to consistently overstep the boundaries I had always tried to set for myself. His insatiable desire to become rich and successful had robbed him of irreplaceable time with his wife and two daughters for weeks and weeks on end. I remember talking with him on the plane once as he told me, "I haven't seen my little girls in almost a month and I really miss them, but I'm sure they'll appreciate all this when they're older." I didn't say a word, but I knew he was dead wrong. They couldn't care less about later, they cared about now. Through his recent actions with the company, Frank had lost it all. Frank was a memorial to all those who had sacrificed what meant most in this world for something of fleeting value...or no value at all.

Despite his current problems, Frank treated Randy and me to a delicious Mexican dinner at a restaurant along the water. As we parted that night, it was my hope that, just as I had been provided insights and newfound doors of growth by my marriage failure, Frank would see this period of time as an opportunity to put priorities back in order. Not achieving his goals of power and money may have been the best thing that had happened to him, but only if he would decide to choose the right path.

I slept soundly on Randy's soft spare bed and awoke to the sounds and smells of ham as Randy was cooking breakfast in the kitchen. *Perhaps this "roughing it" thing is a bit overrated.* "You're going to make someone a wonderful wife," I told him as I devoured the scrumptious meal of eggs, ham, and muffins.

"Is that a proposal?" he chirped back.

"Not on your life man," I laughed. "Harley image, you know." I could tell it was going to be a fun ten days.

After breakfast, we were feeling a bit on the lazy side, and the entire morning consisted of playing cribbage, a card game taught to me by Randy, whose sole goal, I am convinced, was to torture me over the next ten days by never allowing me to win a game. After lunch, I rode my scoot behind Randy's car and followed him over the border to his primary residence located in Burnaby, British Columbia, not far from the city of Vancouver. The weather continued its stubborn pattern of overcast and gray skies. I had hardly seen the sun in six days.

After the one-hour drive, we pulled up to his white tri-level house located atop one of the many hills in the Burnaby area. It was quite a beautiful home. He had named it "the house for wayward men," because it seemed that every man at work who had a falling out with his wife would end up living on the lower floor for a period of time. This worked out nicely because the lower floor was completely self-contained and worked quite well for apartment living. The second floor contained a spacious kitchen, large plush living room, and two spare bedrooms, one of which would be my sleeping area for the next week or so. The place was immaculately clean, and I was a little envious of Randy's housekeeping abilities, as this trait had never found its way into my gene pool.

As we climbed the plush stairs to the third level, we meandered through his larger-than-normal master bedroom and stepped out onto the balcony. Being at the top of the hill allowed the balcony's visitors a supreme view of the Burrard Inlet, a beautiful body of water whose frosty fingers disappeared into the bright green and thick-forested mountains to the east. Several tiny, tree-covered islands dotted this picturesque bay and the smooth water was disturbed only by an occasional boat whose subtle ripples flowed outward in their search for the water's edge. "Too bad you couldn't find a place with a view," I sarcastically remarked, puffing on the cigar Randy had so graciously offered.

Looking toward these mountains, my anticipation for the following day began to grow. Randy had managed to borrow a friend's Yamaha Virago street bike, and we would be riding to Randy's nephew's cabin, located just outside of Pemberton Meadows high in the British Columbian mountains. There, we would spend a few days doing...whatever. That's as much planning as I intended to do for this ride.

After a great night's sleep and tasty breakfast at a quaint cafe down the street, we headed out of town with high expectations of doing...well...whatever. It felt good to ride with another bike again, and I could feel steady waves of testosterone coursing through my veins. We were men riding motorcycles! Traffic was fairly heavy leaving the Vancouver area, but once the road narrowed to two lanes and we began to distance ourselves from civilization, the number of vehicles lessened and my thoughts became solely focused on the rhythmic leaning of my bike from one side to the other as I glided around the mountainous turns. Mountain roads...how I had missed them the past few days.

As we began to climb in elevation and away from the Pacific Coast, we were soon encompassed by an unexpected gift—sunshine. How I had taken it for granted! The warmth of the sun's rays reached deep within my face and seemed to fill my body with newfound energy. My mountainous surroundings suddenly came alive as the sun's magic unveiled colors previously concealed by the sky's dismal grayness. I felt reborn.

After lunch at the world-famous Whistler Resort, Randy and I were soon back on the road and not far from our day's final destination. The road past Whistler became much more desolate and secluded and infinitely more beautiful, nearly paralleling the winding roads of the Sierras. The forest here was much thicker than the California forests I was used to, and we rode between two ranges of mountains, the ones on the right definitely winning the prize in the height and beauty categories. The tall and craggy tree-less peaks seemed to extend an infinite distance ahead and looked as if they were standing in line at strict attention, waiting for inspection. They would have easily passed. The winding mountain road felt more like a magic carpet, transporting me to any place my mind wanted to go...and I went many places.

Suddenly, my serene thoughts became interrupted by something of a tickling sensation on my belly. It didn't take long to realize that I had an unwelcome visitor who had found his way inside my shirt and was now cruising along the bare skin of my stomach. I kept my breathing shallow so as not to alarm the little invader, and I calmly and slowly pulled over to the side of the road, wondering what kind of pain I may feel at any moment should it decide to attack. The moment my wheels ceased turning, I quickly but gently pulled my shirt out from my pants while chanting rapidly, "Don't sting me, don't sting me, don't sting me." Suddenly, one of the largest bumblebees I have ever seen fell out and plopped himself upon the seat, probably relieved he had been set free from the smelly jail. Oh, that would have hurt!

A short time later, Randy and I arrived at our objective and rode down the narrow gravel driveway that took us to the front of Al's cabin. Randy's nephew was in Vancouver that week and would not be joining us, but even though I did not personally meet Al, I soon began to strongly dislike him. This guy could obviously do anything with his hands. The one-story cabin was a handsome structure built on the side of a small hill, where the east side of the cabin hung over the descending slope, supported by miniature stilts. Randy told me that Al had completely reconstructed this building from a dilapidated "shack," using lumber he had personally cut from the trees on his own wooded property. The driveway and front-yard area had been dug out of the hillside and leveled with a non-operational bulldozer that Al had bought and then fixed. Al had built the water pump system down by the stream, including the pump shed and cement foundation, which supplied the cabin with fresh clean water. He had completely restored a vintage car that was sitting out front, built a storage room by digging and shoring up the room out of another hill, and completed a number of other projects I won't mention here. I'm fairly certain that the deer I saw in the woods was actually a robotic replica built by Al, but I can't prove it.

Once again, I was absolutely intrigued by a person's ability to begin and finish projects that I wouldn't think about doing. Al was living proof that things can get done if you just put some hard work into them. No wonder I didn't like him. This lesson was really starting to sink in with me. First Bruce, now MacGyver, errr, I mean Al. I was suddenly reminded of the many "home improvement" projects I had wanted to tackle around my condominium but had consistently put off. I thought of the challenges that I had always wanted to tackle in my life such as learning Spanish, playing the guitar, speaking publicly, working with kids, and even welding. Why had I not taken the time to attempt these things? I had to admit to myself that sheer laziness and lack of discipline had kept me from many of my desires for improvement. Although this was only the beginning of my second week on the road, the lessons were doing a fine job at exposing my weaknesses and challenging me in the areas where I knew I needed help.

Randy and I decided to spend two nights at the cabin and decided that the dinner theme for the first night would be barbecue. We needed food. We got on the bikes, hopped back on the road, and continued past the cabin for another twenty minutes until the blacktop came to an abrupt halt, dead-ending into Anderson Lake. What a view! A vast calm body of water laid out before me that glistened in the sun like glass, quickly narrowing several miles ahead, and disappearing through a gap between the two magnificent mountain ranges that were topped with patches of snow. The whole scene played back through the mirrored images reflected in the still water. The only civilization found at the end of this road was a general store, a campground, and a few boats moored near the water's edge. We bought what food and supplies we would need for the next few days, made small talk with the somewhat attractive cashier, and headed back to Al's self-made home.

As Randy volunteered for barbecue duty, I apathetically swung in the old hammock in the backyard, taking in my surroundings like they were a wine much finer than the cheap version that was currently in my glass. Towering jagged mountains gazed down upon us from both the east and the west, and the oversized grassy backyard was bordered on one side by a flowing stream just swift enough to provide a steady and soothing sound. A tree Al had sawed in half allowed passage across the mini-river and provided an entrance into the dense forest on the other side. The two neighboring cabins were nicely concealed behind thick underbrush and tall trees so they could barely be seen. I was constantly and pleasantly harassed by two of Al's dogs, whose sole goal in life was to chase a stick thrown by any human. If only my life were as simple as theirs.

After Randy and I took our seats around the picnic table, which I am sure was whittled by Al with a steak knife, we ate the last bites of our delectable feast consisting of barbecued ribs and pork chops, washed down with vintage red wine. I slowly tilted my head back and closed my eyes, suddenly becoming aware of the totally relaxed state of mind and body in which I now found myself. All that could be heard was the sound of water anxiously and noisily trying to reach its final destination to Anderson Lake, the wind rustling through the tree branches above, and unseen birds calling out to each other by name. How seldomly I had let myself become so still, both in mind and body, during my busy professional life. The peace was magnified with the knowledge this was not a short vacation but a long adventure with more to come.

The back roads were once again busily tutoring this willing student. Only in times of quiet and peace can we allow ourselves the gift of true rejuvenation and time for reflection. Letting our burdens go, if even temporarily, provides powerful healing for our overworked minds. How many ulcers, headaches, and heart attacks could be avoided if people would consistently embrace this one exercise? I vowed I would *make* the time when I returned home to allow myself to heal a little each week.

It had been a perfect day, and I was in a perfect place. Fitting that this day, June 21, should be the longest of the year. We didn't bid farewell to the sun until 10 p.m., and I squeezed out every precious minute of daylight that I was courteously provided. A rested mind brought restful sleep, and the night passed quickly to morning. My dreams went empty that night, as I am sure my mind could not conjure up anything that would best my current reality.

The next day was a lazy one and was mostly spent in quiet relaxation. As I was lying on the hammock, which had now become my second home, Randy walked out of the cabin and yelled, "Hey, check this out!" I went inside and saw that he had found a number of guns and weapons that had been stored away somewhere in the cabin.

"Let's take some pictures," I said, pointing at the arsenal. We parked the bikes on the lawn, slung guns over our shoulders, held revolvers in hand, and placed knives in anatomically strategic places while donning the proper attire of headbands and head scarves that only true militants would wear, then proceeded to take a multitude of pictures.

During our photo shoot, two of Al's friends decided to pay a visit and pick up some building materials Al had recently borrowed from them. Let's just say they were not feeling too comfortable, seeing two fully armed strangers on Harleys greet them at the gate. We quickly explained the situation, and although they didn't say it, I think they were quite relieved that we allowed them to live.

We went to bed that night after watching the movie *Planes, Trains, and Automobiles*, with Steve Martin and John Candy. It was the closest thing to a traveling movie we could find in Al's repertoire of video cassettes. We then watched a little satellite TV. Did I mention that Al installed his own satellite dish?

The next day was bright and clear, and we reluctantly set out at 8:30 that morning, leaving our little piece of heaven in the woods to return to civilization. I could have easily stayed there for weeks—no, make that years. We rode through more awe-inspiring mountain scenery via Lake Duffy Road and cruised through numerous mountain passes whose peaks were still white with patches of snow. The magic carpet had returned. We passed through Fraser Canyon and slowly began our journey back to Vancouver. As the number of cars began to increase, so did my appreciation for the solitude I had left. It was a long eight-hour day on the bikes, and we relaxed that night with a tasty margarita and a cheap cigar overlooking the water from Randy's upstairs balcony. I had traveled 2,200 miles to this point, and so far, every mile seemed to hold its own adventure.

After a day of just hanging around the house, we decided to switch gears, so to speak, and engage in some dirt-bike riding in the British Columbian mountains. Leading the off-road expedition would be Randy's friend Terry, a big jovial fellow who probably tipped the scales at around 300 pounds and who had worked with Randy at one of the regional correctional facilities. His big rosy cheeks, burly laugh, and gentle nature made me feel like I was with Santa Claus and I couldn't have asked for a nicer guy. We decided to meet at Terry's house the next morning.

As we sat around Terry's dining room table, eating breakfast, I looked over at Terry and asked, "So, where exactly are we going, anyway?"

"Granny's hot tubs," he loudly shot back just before taking another bite of scrambled eggs.

"This isn't some retirement home, is it?" I asked, unsuccessfully trying to be funny.

"Nope," he said, ignoring my futile attempt, "rode there quite a few years ago. It's way up there in the mountains, but as far as I can remember, the ride isn't too bad. Old lady had a claim up there and did some mining back in the early part of the century. They discovered natural hot water and somebody hauled up a few tubs and piped the water in. I think I can still find the place."

"Sounds interesting," I said, hoping this wouldn't be a bust.

Obviously, Randy had to score some dirt bikes for this ride. Randy owned an enduro motorcycle, which is a bike that can be used for riding both on and off the highway. Terry owned an older Honda XR500 dirt bike and had managed to round me up an old blue Yamaha IT175 which, coincidentally, was the same model and color of motorcycle that I had raced as a kid. It had to be a sign of good things to come, but these bikes were pretty old and who knew how well maintained.

"How long will it take us to get there?" I asked.

Terry looked at me with a raised eyebrow, probably tiring of my questions by now. "Probably an hour and a half of driving in the truck, then we'll unload. The dirt-bike ride shouldn't take more than forty-five minutes."

That didn't sound too bad. Well, except for one thing...he was wrong about everything! To begin with, we got a late start and didn't leave the Vancouver area until 11:00 that morning. The reasonable hour-and-a-half ride out of town turned out to be closer to three hours, an hour of which was spent on bumpy dirt roads. I soon found that spending three hours in the center of a pickup seat, between two men, tends to get a person a little on the edgy side.

Just before 2:00 in the afternoon, we were still in the truck, bumping down dirt roads high up in the British Columbian Coastal Mountains. Conversation had pretty much stopped by this point, but the silence was interrupted every so often with Terry repeating the same phrase he had just said ten minutes earlier, "This kind of looks familiar." I had to admit that the scenery was doing a good job of making up for the tardiness of the day. The fairly wide dirt road paralleled the long and beautiful Harrison Lake, which could be seen through an occasional break in the dense green vegetation to our left. It seemed as if we crossed a waterfall's path every fifteen minutes or so, as if the mountains were well aware of their important role in keeping the lake topped off.

Mercifully, after a few wrong turns, we finally found a dirt road that Terry thought to be the one. We pulled the truck over and quickly disembarked. I stretched my numb legs for all they were worth.

"So what's the trail like?" I asked, making small talk as I stretched my arms over my head.

"Well, like I said, it's been a long time, but if I remember right, it's no big deal, especially for someone who rides as much as you do."

Based on this "valid" information from this "credible" source, I made the decision to downsize my apparel a bit and wore only my Harley bike boots, my half helmet, my leather gloves, and a black tank top with jeans. Now, as I have some experience as a dirt-bike racer, my riding attire usually consists of enough riding gear to guarantee me a part in Star Wars. Suffice it to say, I felt just a bit on the naked side wearing only these bare essentials, not to mention that the gear I was wearing was designed for street cruising and not dirt riding. *Oh well, no big deal*, I thought. *Probably just fire roads anyway.*

We packed some sandwiches and three good-sized Asahi brews into Terry's backpack and headed down the first fire road in single-file order, with yours truly leading the way. Things went well for the first ten minutes or so, nothing real challenging, but fun. Then it got a little rocky. I was used to rocks— after all, I've raced in the desert, and the desert is full of rocks. Then it got a quite a bit more on the rocky side, plus a bit little steeper. Then it got real, real rocky. As the rocks grew in size, so did my regret for not dressing appropriately. Within twenty minutes, we found ourselves navigating through wet and slippery bowling ball-sized rocks while ascending at a significant vertical climb. To make matters worse, the runoff was now flooding down the rocky stream and we were riding straight up a river bed full of slick rocks and deep running water. I felt like a salmon.

Randy's enduro bike was pretty heavy, and the rear tire was not designed for this type of abuse. He was struggling with it as anyone would. Between the weight of Terry and his motorcycle, a total of about 600 pounds, the job of grinding their way up this "easy" run was definitely challenging and also very entertaining to watch. More than a few times, we found ourselves pushing our bikes over huge rocks and forging our way through water over our knees. Our cruise had quickly turned to a crawl.

I was pretty impressed with these two guys, considering how little they normally rode this type of terrain. The ride became so grueling that we were forced to create a structured plan. The ritual went something like this: Push bikes hard; yell, scream, complain; take a break; Terry smokes a cigarette; repeat. To be honest, I was becoming just a little concerned about Terry's condition. Whenever we would stop, he would gulp air faster than a dog on a hot day, his face sweating profusely, and if that wasn't bad enough, he was sucking smoke down his lungs. Not an ideal location for a heart attack. During these breaks, Randy would just sit there with his Beavis-and-Butthead laugh. I had long given up emptying my calf-high leather biker boots of their reservoirs of water and was asking myself if I could really give Terry mouth-to-mouth if needed. Luckily, I didn't have to find out. A fine mess we had gotten ourselves into.

During one of our many breaks, we met five guys coming down from the hot tubs in their dune buggies and motorcycles, and, contrary to our hopes, they informed us, it got worse ahead. All told, it took us about two and a half wet and grueling hours to make it to the tubs, a total distance of about three miles. We were exhausted when we finally reached the tubs, and all I wanted to do was have a beer and relax.

Granny's did not exactly look like I had envisioned. Frankly, there wasn't much to it. The trail ended at the top of a hill, where a large abandoned square wooden structure had been built. It looked more like a small barn than an old house and was absent of any furnishings. The tubs were located to the right of the building and consisted of one good-sized, ground-level wooden tub; an old-fashioned cast-iron bathtub to the side, the contents of which rivaled those in my tub at the Leggett motel; and one old-fashioned white tub up against the mountainside adorned with a myriad of red hearts all over it with the words "Love Tub" emblazoned in red lettering. Numerous black plastic pipes snaked out from among the dense mountainside underbrush, filling the tubs with an endless stream of the earth's warm fluid. We immediately shed our sweaty and unneeded clothing and slipped into the soothing warm water in the larger wooden tub. The water quickly pushed us close to ecstasy, and our tired muscles seemed to melt away as we eased ourselves downward. I believe the phrases "oh yeah" and "oh baby" were echoed countless times throughout the canyon during this process. While enjoying the soak cycle, we devoured our well-deserved meal of chicken-salad sandwiches and washed it down with still-cold Asahi beer. Suddenly, the pain of the journey was temporarily forgotten.

We took turns sitting in the love tub and taking pictures. We laughed hilariously when Terry got in, as most of the water was immediately displaced. After an hour of heavenly immersion, we put our clothes back on and talked with the only other people there, a small family camping down by the river. Suddenly, we realized the lateness of the hour, 6:00 p.m., and we knew there was not an abundance of daylight left for our trip home.

Sitting on my Yamaha, I bid the family good-bye as I raised my right leg upward and gave my bike a hearty downward kick, waiting for the familiar two-stroke sound to pierce the air. Nothing. I kicked again. Nothing. I kicked and I kicked and I kicked. As each kick ended with no hint of sound, the realization of pushing my bike back to the truck began to grow stronger. My bike absolutely refused to start, I believe, as a direct protest to the pain and torment I had inflicted upon it on our journey up the riverbed.

I checked everything I could check with the tools we had, which were few, and all seemed to be in fine shape except for the minor problem of the bike not running. The family just looked on helplessly, and I could feel their empathy for my situation. Looking at the bright side of a negative situation, I knew I would have gravity on my side for much of the way, but I knew there were also many flat spots, more than a few slight uphills, a couple of steep climbs, and a whole lot of big rocks. Well, enough whining, it was time to get going.

I jumped next to the bike, waved to our new friends with a big old smile on my face, as if this inconvenience didn't really bother me (it did), and started pushing. It didn't take long until I was knee deep in water, pushing my bike over stubborn rocks, and straining at any hint of an uphill. Because there was little Terry and Randy could do, they just stayed back, probably discussing how glad they were it was not them, and then caught up to me every fifteen minutes or so, saying the same thing, "How are you doing?"

"Okay!" I would yell back, then, under my breath, muttering, "How do you think I'm doing?" I was completely exhausted by the time I returned to the truck.

Once the bikes were loaded onto the truck, we began to head back home. We laughed at the whole experience, mostly at my expense, and I vowed that I would never believe a single word they ever told me again. I somehow found myself in the middle of the seat again, and the droning of the truck's tires upon the highway quickly lulled my aching body to a deep sleep. Appreciative of the sudden inactivity, my body remained comatose until we reached Terry's house at 1:30 a.m.

The next day was a time of healing for this 34-year-old. I was more than a bit sore from the previous day's events and felt ready for a change of pace. My wish came true when we returned to Randy's Birch Bay cabin and decided to play a round of golf at the nearby public golf course. Suffice it to say that my talents do not lie in the meticulous art of placing small white balls in slightly larger holes in an open field. I don't believe my score of 109 on a par-3 course will ever win me any prize money on the tour. It's a stupid game anyway.

After my exciting round of hell...umm...golf, we noticed that the ocean's tide was at its low point, exposing the bay's soggy bottom near Randy's house. Grabbing a couple of empty metal buckets and shedding ourselves of our footwear, we walked along the squishy and rocky bottom and managed to dig up about 40 clams for dinner that night. But the food shopping was not to stop there. Later that afternoon, with the tide at its maximum height, we borrowed Randy's friend's boat, complete with two oars and an arsenal of three crab traps. We were going crabbin'! (Randy told me that yelling the word "crabbin'!" at the top of my lungs would help heighten the experience. I think it just made me look silly in front of all the people on the shore.)

This was going to be fun. We picked the aluminum boat up with our hands, pulled it out from the bed of the pickup, and hauled the heavy vessel down over the rocks and into the water. As I soon discovered, setting three crab traps in a triangular configuration approximately one half mile off shore requires an incessant amount of rowing, much of which Randy brilliantly manipulated me into doing.

The bait we placed within the traps were plain, everyday chicken necks purchased at the nearby grocery store. The traps were simple inventions that resembled large basketball hoops and nets without the holes at the bottom. A large metal circular ring, about three feet in diameter, comprised the top, with nylon mesh hanging down from its cylindrical shape. A smaller metal ring adorned the middle of the cylinder to provide stability as the contraption was lowered to the ocean floor. When the trap would touch bottom, the netting and rings would lie flat on the ground, with the chicken necks nicely exposed as an enticingly quick and easy meal. The crabs simply walk over the netting and begin eating. Once we would return to the location of the trap, marked by large white buoys, we would quickly pull on the rope with mighty force, using gravity to keep the bottom-dwellers from crawling out of the netting before surfacing.

The placement procedure went something like this: We lowered the first trap down into the water, then I rowed about 200 yards, where we would set another trap. Then I rowed another 200 yards, to where we set the last trap, after which time I rowed back to the first trap and checked its contents for any tasty critters that might have wandered into our chicken-neck buffet. After unloading our prey and making sure they were of legal size, we would then reset the first trap and I would row to the second trap. Did I mention I had to row a lot? Like I needed the exercise after yesterday's events and 18 holes of golf!

Over a three-hour period, we ended up catching our limit of twelve crabs, and Randy did do a "little" rowing. I must say, it was extremely exciting to hurriedly pull up a trap, with childlike anticipation, and see three or four nice-sized crabs waiting anxiously to be measured and placed in our dinner bag—an experience I recommend to anyone who can try it.

Randy's large outdoor fire pit was waiting for us as we returned from the hunt, and would soon be used to cook our catches of the day. "How do you kill these things?" I asked as I gingerly picked them out of the bag and placed them on the grass.

"You turn them on their backs and hit them in their breastplate with a hammer. Kills them instantly," he said as he placed the black kettle of water over the fire.

I'll just let him do that, I thought. This plan immediately failed when Randy threw me a hammer and told me to "get cracking." I complimented him on his stupid pun, and after a quick demonstration, I overcame my hesitancy and was soon fulfilling my executioner duties in quick fashion. I then separated the deceased crabs' bodies from their legs, threw them in the large black kettle, and cooked them over the pit.

I had eaten lobster and crab on both the west and east coasts before, but I had never tasted crab this delicious and fresh in my entire life. The tender meat literally melted in my mouth, and neither butter nor shell crackers were ever needed. Randy ruined me for life, for I shall never enjoy crab again in a restaurant. I have also never eaten so much crab in a single sitting in all my life.

After our fill of fresh seafood, we sat outside, smoked cigars, and listened to the Eagles playing out over the speakers. When it was "Desperado's" turn to fill the air, I was once again reminded of that first morning of my journey. Much had happened since. I was about as content as I could get.

I gave Randy a reprieve from entertaining me the next day and spent it with another good friend of mine who coincidentally lived only a few miles from Randy's home in Burnaby. I had known Dan since I was 17 years old, and although he had been a brand-new friend at the time, he had been one of the first to visit me the night my father was killed. Dan has always maintained a remarkably positive attitude about life, even though he had experienced some very trying times in the past years. I have always tried to surround myself with people who like to laugh and make others do the same, and Dan is a master at this. Dan has always been there for me, and I felt it a privilege to visit with him during this ride.

Dan and I spent the day kayaking in the bay by Vancouver (more rowing), eating our fair share of food, and talking about a variety of subjects, including spiritual issues, his family, our past together, my trip, and, of course, women. The company he was working for was also on the verge of bankruptcy, and although he had done an incredible job in heading up the international sales department, they were unfairly withholding compensation—another story that illustrated my desire to take a break from corporate America.

Randy joined us later, and we all went out to dinner, Dan's treat. In the car, we began talking about relationships and women, which was pretty humorous because neither Randy nor Dan had ever been married. I piped in from the back seat, commenting on an observation that had become evident to me, "You know what's pathetic? Between the three of us, we have over one hundred ten years of life, and *I* have the most marriage experience." We all laughed at that one, but it was one of those pathetic kinds of laughs that people without women in their lives have. We all had a great time that night.

June 30 soon rolled around, and it was time to leave my good friends of Vancouver. I had thoroughly enjoyed my visit, but I was also getting anxious to skirt the blacktop once again and put some miles under my belt. As I sat on Randy's front steps, with my chin resting on my bent knees, I stared at the fully packed Harley sitting proudly along the street. I was about to begin a new leg of my journey that I knew would provide me with new challenges. Up until this point, my lodging plans had been fairly secure and I had never spent more than two nights in a row without staying in a comfortable home, in a soft bed, or with someone to talk to. Now, I had no one to stay with until I reached South Dakota, nine days away.

I knew I would have to force myself to meet people I did not yet know. I would be forced to find places to sleep. The doubts began to come fast and furious as I sat on those steps: How would I handle the loneliness? Would I have mechanical problems with no one to help me? Would I get in an accident with no one near to call? For the first time, nobody was expecting me. No one would call for help if I didn't show up. I had to admit to myself that I was feeling a little scared, but that was okay. It meant I was pushing the envelope a little bit. It meant I was stepping further out of my comfort zone.

Randy and I shook hands, and I couldn't thank him enough for the hospitality he had shown me. "No worries," he said with that familiar smile as I mounted my bike. I gently touched the shifter into first with my left foot, and with the twist of the throttle, I was on my own again. A pang of loneliness gripped me almost immediately, as I would miss my buddy. I rode eastward on Highway 3, the Crowsnest, a very scenic two-lane highway that winds its way through the Rocky Mountains and parallels the borders of Washington and Montana. The road reminded me somewhat of the road to Whistler as its constant turns through green forest took me up and down a wide range of various elevations. One minute I would be riding in the midst of a thick tree canopy, and the next minute, I would find myself breaking free from its green fortress and hugging guardrails that protected me from the steep and precarious drop to the valley below.

After about three hours, I noticed a couple riding behind me on a Harley Heritage Softail, obviously content in following my lead and pace. Although they were strangers, I still felt good riding with another bike for a while. After some twenty minutes or so, I glanced into my side mirror and noticed they had pulled off the road for some reason. I felt a little disappointed at their early departure, and once again, it was just me on the road. An hour later, I turned off into a gas station, gassed my bike up with the expensive Canadian fuel, and began to pull away. As I started to leave, I happened to look back over my shoulder and catch a glimpse of the same couple I had seen earlier, pulling in to the spot I had just vacated. I nodded that cool nod that bikers give one another and continued out of the parking lot. It looked as if he had wanted to say something, but I had left before he had the chance. As I was riding, I chastised myself for not taking the time to talk with them. I knew I needed to meet people, yet I had let this opportunity pass because I was too lazy or perhaps too fearful to turn around. I was experiencing a regret, and I vowed I would not let that happen again.

Thirty minutes later, a strange noise began emanating from the right side of my engine, and I pulled over next to a small lake to investigate. About fifteen minutes later, I heard the unmistakable sound of a Harley engine chugging up the gradual mountainous incline and, in looking up, noticed it was the same couple from the gas station. They immediately pulled over. "Everything okay?" the man asked.

"I'm not sure," I responded as I slowly walked over to where they had stopped.

They were riding a beautiful Heritage Softail with a pearl black tank and with leather tassels hanging from the end of the handlebars. Its windshield had been replaced by a rolled-up sleeping bag, balancing elegance and style with a rugged, outdoors look. The Heritage was one of my favorite bikes, as it was modeled after the throwback Harleys of old. Low and wide with the smaller sixteen-inch front wheel, fat fenders, and studded leather saddlebags, this bike was gorgeous.

Paul and Darlene were a thirty-something married couple whose friendliness was immediately apparent through wide smiles. Paul was not a large man, probably weighing in at 150 pounds soaking wet on his five-seven frame. His straight, thin hair was pulled back into a ponytail that fell below his shoulders. His chiseled face bordered on more of a drawn look than handsome and seemed slightly large for his smaller frame. He had traded his jeans and riding boots for shorts and tennis shoes because of the hot weather. Darlene was a bubbly blonde whose thin and wispy hair seemed to hang any way it wanted, finally resting somewhere upon her shoulders. She was also a bit on the thin side and exuded a physical attractiveness whose source came more from within than from without.

I explained my possible ordeal, and Paul and I looked over the bike, mutually concluding that the noise did not seem to be a serious problem and I could probably continue. "We're heading into Penticton for the weekend. Why don't you ride along?" Paul offered. The offer sounded good.

"I'll follow you in," I said. We rode together into the town of Penticton, British Columbia, which was about a half hour away. Paul and Darlene had reserved a campsite for the weekend near Okanagan Lake, and we pulled into the campground's office in the midst of one hundred-plus–degree heat.

Paul and Darlene generously offered to share their campsite with me that night, and I readily agreed, thankful that my first night after seeing my friends would not be spent alone. After a cooling shower at the campground's facilities, we rode around the region a bit, taking in winding two-lane roads through hilly terrain, and finished it off by gazing at a beautiful sunset that filled the sky with reds, yellows, and oranges. We then visited a local pub called Down Under and took in some great classic-rock music. Paul and Darlene's style was so easygoing and friendly, it was nearly impossible not to like them, and conversation lags were nonexistent.

Being on an adventure myself, I was fascinated at Paul's stories of hitchhiking across Canada for years on end. He recounted one story of finding himself in subzero weather and down to his last $20, which he spent during heavy negotiations with a local motel manager for a room and breakfast. Paul smiled as he remembered the story and said, "So there I was, sitting on the side of the highway, completely bundled up from head to toe in this giant blanket, and all you could see was my hand sticking out with my thumb up."

The most amusing story was about Paul's insatiable vice for cigarette smoking. Not just cigarettes, mind you, but Canadian brands only. Both Paul and Darlene were hard-core chain smokers, and I'm not sure I ever saw them without the tightly wrapped rolled paper protruding from their mouths. As expensive as tobacco was in Canada, I could only imagine the amount of money they spent every year. Paul was so particular about the Canadian variety that during one extended motorcycle trip in California, he remained on his bike, with Darlene on the back, for 1,000 miles absent of breaks, except for gas. The reason? He had to quickly get to the border because he had run out of Canadian cigarettes. Darlene at one point had gotten so upset that she got off the bike, left him, and hitched a ride with a truck driver. My mouth hung open as he told me the story. I couldn't believe anyone could be that picky about something smoked. I shot a glance at Darlene, and she just shook her head with a hint of disgust, as we were bringing up memories she was probably trying to forget.

That night, we returned to the campground. Several of their friends had shown up while we were out. I forewent the tent because of the heat and laid my air mattress beneath the open sky and bright stars. Paul, Darlene, and friends didn't skimp on the alcohol and marijuana consumption that night, and the noise rose proportionally to the highs they were reaching. I took advantage of my earplugs for the first time, and they worked like a charm. It felt good to forego any covering that would hinder my view of nature, and this serene setting seemed to bring slumber more quickly than usual in spite of the noise.

Morning greeted me softly as the heated rays of the sun warmed my face. Paul, Darlene, and I ate breakfast together and said our good-byes. The mysterious engine noise turned out to be a minor problem with the exhaust pipes that could easily be repaired at a local shop. The previous evening, the owner of the campground had told me that Mike, one of the campground's visitors, owned a bike-repair place in town. I had found Mike's location at the campground, and he had told me to come by his place around 10:00 in the morning. Perfect. After getting lost at least five times, I finally found his place around 11:00 a.m.

While they were working on the repairs, I heard the rumble of Harley engines off in the distance, and as I looked up, two nasty- and rough-looking guys pulled in on their bikes. They were wearing their colors, which simply meant they were wearing their vests with their gang emblems on the back. The large letters on the backs of their dirty and worn denim vests displayed the words "GRIM REAPERS," a pretty tough group of bikers, from what I am told. The owner of the bike-repair shop and his helper immediately helped these two guys as soon as they arrived, wanting them out of the way as quickly as possible.

By their looks, it was obvious these guys had been around. One of the men was heavyset, with long greasy hair and a scraggly thin beard. His clothes were filthy dirty with grease and road grime, and looked as if he had never washed his jacket in its life. The other man was a taller, handsomer man, with a muscular build. His hair was combed straight back with the aid of heavy grease and sported the always fashionable Elvis-like sideburns. His left arm was completely covered with tattoos, and in the midst of his forearm was a portrait of Hitler's face, which I immediately took offense to.

While they were talking, I glanced into my bike's mirror and stared closely at the figure looking back at me. My hair was long—well, long for me. I also had a beard, but it wasn't a long beard. I mean, it takes time to grow these things, and it had only been four weeks. I can't grow these things overnight, you know (I was getting more and more defensive). I was, however, wearing my Harley head scarf, which I felt made me look pretty tough. The realization began to slowly invade my dream world—compared to these Grim Reaper guys, I felt more like Barney Fife than a biker. This baby face could no more fool people into believing I was a bad dude than I could convince people that Elizabeth Taylor is committed to marriage.

It reminded me of a time three years earlier when my best friend John and I had taken our Harleys through Grand Junction, Colorado, on our way to Canada. Because it was our first Harley ride ever, we had figured we'd better look the part. We had become the ultimate wannabes. John had grown a mean-looking goatee, and I, although I really hate admitting this, had actually had hair extensions woven into my hair to give me that middle-of-the-back hair length. Hey, if rock stars can do it... We had topped it off with piercing our ears.

John and I had decided to visit a mutual friend of ours, Kathy, in Grand Junction, Colorado. We had picked Kathy up and given her a ride to a local pub where her husband was going to meet us. We cruised the side roads of Grand Junction, feeling and looking very "bad" with our skullcaps, black leather, and mean expressions. We were sure people would not dare take the chance of even glancing our direction for fear of their lives.

Our bubble had soon burst when a carload of elderly people had pulled up alongside our idling bikes at a stoplight, rolled down the window, and yelled, "Excuse me!" I had wanted to snarl back something like, "You talking to me?" but the woman had looked too much like my mother. She wanted directions to somewhere downtown. Kathy, not understanding our desire to be tough, graciously told them to follow us because we were heading that way. We were now the lead float in an elderly person parade. As they turned off a few minutes later, they looked over and waved at us while sporting giant smiles like we were their grandchildren or something.

I had looked over at John and said, "We're about as tough looking as a Girl Scout." Oh well, I guess there are just some things you can't change.

I sauntered over to the Grim Reaper boys with the coolest look I could muster and asked, "Where ya headed?" They mentioned some town that I did not recognize, but I nodded while donning my best Clint Eastwood squint as if I knew exactly where it was. We made small talk for a while, and they gave me a few bike tips and chastised me for not upgrading my stock exhaust system. In a half hour, they were back on the road. They're probably still laughing.

With my pipe problem now solved, I too was back on the road by late morning and decided to ride in the direction of Banff and Lake Louise. I had visited this place with my mom and dad as a very small child, and Lake Louise was the only memory I had of that trip. That would be my goal. A few hours later, I took a little rest and pulled out my British Columbia map to check out which back roads looked to be the most promising in helping me reach my destination.

Then I saw it. It was in very small print, but it jumped off the page and smacked me right in the face. Mabel Lake. The same name as my mother! It had to be a sign. I mean, how many lakes are named Mabel? I looked closer. If I visited the lake, it would not take me too far off course, but I would need to ride about ten miles of dirt to get there. I weighed the choices but decided that even though it would take a few hours out of my day, any son with a shred of decency would have to visit a lake with the same name as his mother.

The dirt road leading to the Lake of my Mother didn't turn out to be too bad as long as I kept the speed below forty miles per hour. When I neared the Mabel Lake sign, I stopped the bike and took a picture for posterity. I turned onto the lake entrance and found there to be more people enjoying its facilities than I would have imagined. It was a rustic place with few amenities and reminded me more of a city park than a campground. The lake was approximately twenty miles long and was completely surrounded by verdant forest and gentle, rolling mountains.

It had taken me about thirty minutes to arrive from the main road, and looking again at the map, I noticed that the dirt road where I had entered continued to parallel the lake to the north. It was also a fairly long road, about 40 desolate miles, that wound its way through the mountains, eventually terminating at

Highway 1. Hmmm, Highway 1 would lead me in the direction of Lake Louise. I had a decision to make. I could backtrack to where I had turned off the main highway and continue on blacktop as I had originally planned, or I could continue up the dirt road into seclusion and the unknown. Trouble was, I had no idea as to what the condition might be of the dirt road. Well, you can take the bike rider out of the dirt, but you can't take the dirt out of the bike rider. I decided to forge ahead and opt for the illogical choice. I would take my chances.

The fairly flat and smooth road of dirt I had ridden to the lake soon transformed itself into a mountainous, curvy, and rocky road, and my conscience would not allow me to accelerate over twenty miles per hour for fear that my bike would shake apart over the brutal terrain. In fact, my normal speed was usually around seven miles per hour. After about an hour, the road had taken me beyond the lake and veered left, crossing the river that gave Mabel life. I was now climbing steadily, and the road often provided me challenging U-turn–like switchbacks complete with the standard large-rock obstacle course. Every time I would cross a stream, I would pray that I wouldn't hit a slick rock below the surface and drop my baby in the water. By now, there wasn't a shiny spot to be found on my once-lustrous bike, but it didn't seem to matter. Our looks had become secondary to the adventure we were now experiencing. The solitude was a mixture of fear and exhilaration, and the only sign of life seemed to be the sounds from my thumping engine echoing throughout the forest.

After about three hours of this slow pace, I realized I was not going to touch pavement by nightfall. I took inventory. My food supply consisted of an oatmeal packet and two power bars. Good enough for dinner. I decided to find a place to camp. I wanted a place that was very remote, and it didn't take long for my wish to be answered. As the road made one of its many turns to the right, I caught a glimpse of an old two-track road disappearing into the forest. The overgrown branches and greenery at the entrance disguised it well, and at first, it looked as if no road existed at all. As a bonus, a running creek was about 200 yards up the road; I was in dire need of a bath.

I cautiously started up the trail with both legs sticking outward for support as my tires banged over large dead tree branches and foliage. I feathered the clutch to make sure not too much power was transferred to the rear tire. Several times, I was forced to dismount and bend branches back to continue. One hundred yards into the forest, I came across a small clearing among the fir trees and thick brush. This would be home for the night. The weather was hot and very sticky, and I noticed thunderclouds forming in the late-afternoon heat. The mosquitoes and gnats were more than plentiful, but nothing could spoil the serenity of this moment. I was alone as alone could be. I pitched the tent, blew up my air mattress, and unloaded my supplies.

Life was good except for one annoying problem, the smell. Time for a bath. I slowly rode back out to the road and cruised the half mile or so to the running stream that exited the upper mountain slopes and continued on under the road and down to the river 300 yards away. I surveyed the moderately sized running stream from the log bridge and concluded that the kitchen and bath area were more than sufficient to meet my needs. I walked down to the rocky creek equipped with oatmeal packet, power bar, small pot, soap, and a towel. I took my shirt off and gingerly placed my hands in the clear running water. Whoa...cold. I sucked it up and began the process of washing my grimy body. I was experiencing my first official in-the-woods-let-the-animals-watch bath of the trip. I really felt like I was roughing it now, and it was exhilarating. After my cold bath, I heated up some water using my miniature stove and added my raisins and spice oatmeal packet. To be honest, it would have tasted pretty bad if this were a normal setting, but this was no normal setting. It might as well have been filet mignon, because anything would have tasted delicious with this ambiance. I devoured a power bar for dessert, and although I wasn't exactly full, I was definitely content.

After returning to my base camp, I found a trail that led down to the main river. I spent an hour or so just walking along the rocky banks of the river, drinking in my surroundings—rolling hills expertly covered with a smooth carpet of abundant green foliage, its uniformity nicely broken up by an occasional cedar tree jutting high up into the sky. The river was perhaps fifty feet wide, but its low water level allowed me to easily walk along its shores and hop to small exposed gravel islands located in strategic places. Logs from long-deceased trees occasionally protruded out from the river's bottom, forcing the water to change course from its intended direction, the sound providing additional music to the already tranquil setting. I found myself once again in a state of deep reflection and peace. My communication with God and with nature seemed to be at an all-time high, and the absence of sound except for the constant rushing of never-ending water making its journey down the hill was deafening. Again, I was amazed at how relaxed I had become by simply being still and thinking, absent from all distractions and to-do lists. My solitude here seemed to take this feeling beyond even that which I had felt at Al's cabin. There was nothing or no one to break the silence of meditation this time.

During this time of walking and reflection, I noticed that a small pool of water had been cut off from the rapidly moving river by a slightly higher section of ground. It was no more than three feet across, and by the looks of it, it had obviously been separated for some time. The pool was thick with foam, scum, and algae, and numerous insects had made this place their permanent residence. I then noticed that only a few feet away was the river, which at one time had been this pool's source. The river was flowing freely and moving forward. Its water was clear as glass, healthy and inviting. I smiled to myself as the analogy hit home. Before this ride, my life had felt much like that pool. Like the flowing water, my ability to change my situation had always been close by, the only obstacle being my indecision to change. This journey was helping me break the dam that separated stagnation from activity. As I stood there, I could feel my life clearing up a bit, wanting to move forward. I would never forget this little lesson taught to me by these secluded waters of British Columbia.

I returned to camp just before sundown and immediately started a fire so I would have some light when night fell. As I sat on my small blue portable chair, taking in the fire's warmth, my peaceful and comfortable surroundings of the day began to change quickly with night's approach. Once darkness had taken full control, I felt as if I was sitting in the middle of Jurassic Park, waiting for the ripples in my cup of water to signal the coming arrival of the local Tyrannosaurus Rex. I looked around me. The flickering light of the fire barely illuminated the forest that surrounded me, and the overgrown trail that had brought me to this place looked as if it no longer existed.

Then I heard it! Noise in the woods. A sound definitely made by a fairly large animal, about twenty yards or so from camp. I was fairly certain it was not a dinosaur. My heart immediately began that aerobic thing, and being the survivalist that I am, I quickly pulled my knife from its sheath, ready to do battle against the demon just outside my fire's light.

As I looked at my six-inch–bladed weapon, I realized that if this were indeed an attacking bear, the only way this knife would benefit me would be if I killed myself with it before being brutally mauled and eaten.

I put the knife back in its holster and convinced myself that the mysterious noise in the woods was probably a deer, and the thought of Bambi attacking a lone camper made me feel a bit more at ease. Of course, when I would tell this story upon my return, it *would be* a grizzly bear that I fended off, using only a spark plug wrench from my tool kit.

In fact, I had contemplated bringing a gun on this trip precisely for this reason and had actually gone to the trouble of buying a .38-caliber snub nose, but it hadn't worked out quite the way I had hoped. I thought back to my handgun ordeal of only a month before and just had to laugh as I threw another log on the fire.

I had been unsure that buying a handgun was a good idea because my total experiences at shooting handguns could be counted on one hand, although I had grown up with rifles and shotguns as a boy. Despite my apprehension, I had figured my deep love for Clint Eastwood movies would certainly get me through any problems I might encounter. So, one week before departure, I had decided to get a little target practice in and had taken my gun to the indoor firing range along with a box of 100 bullets. I just knew I would eat up the targets for lunch. If it was too easy, I could make it a little tougher by firing behind my back or perhaps using a mirror.

I've heard if you can hit the target consistently at twenty-five yards, you're doing pretty well. That didn't sound like much. I donned the fashionable headphones and fumbled with the switch that would transport my target to the specified distance. I found the sign with a "25" on it, hit the button, and watched my target sail down to that line.

I loaded my piece, raised the gun in my best Dirty Harry imitation, and fired while muttering something like "man's gotta know his limitations." The target didn't move an inch. *This thing really recoils*, I thought as reality slowly began to invade my dream world. I continued shooting at the helpless target, and with each firing of that gun, a piece of my ego fell to the floor.

I pressed the button to retrieve my target and witness the damage. I found that only about one-third of my bullets had hit the paper at all, and those were arbitrarily scattered around the target like pimples on a teenager. Only one errant shot had managed to come anywhere near the intended center.

My survival instincts had taken over, and I had immediately began to rationalize. "Hey, it's my first time, and that's still not bad for twenty-five yards," I said to myself. I looked over at the man standing next to me and asked if the line I was shooting at was indeed twenty-five yards, hoping to confirm my beliefs. He pulled his safety glasses down and, looking over the top of his goggles, said in quite the condescending tone, "No…that's twenty-five feet." Big chunks of ego were now hitting the floor.

Although I had continued to practice for an hour, I did not get any better. I then made the very wise decision that, for the safety of all concerned, it would probably be to my advantage to leave this particular weapon at home. I figured that shooting at a charging bear and killing the owl in the tree above him would not save my life anyway.

Luckily for me, the creature in the woods eventually made its way to other places more exciting, and I was alone once again. I reflected on the unexpected events this day had brought, confirming my belief that this kind of day can be the best of all. I took one last look at my camp spot and, with a smile, saluted my bike in recognition for service beyond the call of duty...for bringing me to this place. I zipped the tent door closed behind me, and sleep came swiftly.

I awoke the next morning to the sound of rain. No, make that the feeling of rain. It had been such a pleasant night that I had chosen not to put up the rain fly, which was a piece of tent fabric used to cover and deflect any water from entering the large mesh fabric at the tent's top. I was now receiving a very unwanted morning shower while still half asleep in my sleeping bag. I quickly ran outside in my trendy and stylish BVDs and did the best I could to untangle the rain fly from among its many bungee cords and hooks within the tent bag, and placed it securely over the tent. I looked at my watch and grimaced. It was only 5:30 in the morning.

As I returned to my warm but slightly damp sleeping quarters, I thought of all the packing I would need to do. Those things that had been left outside were sufficiently wet, and the thought of driving on a dirt, or should I say mud road for another fifteen miles in the rain was more than discouraging, yet my desire for sleep overpowered my wish to start early, and I fell back asleep again until I awoke at around 7:30.

No change in the weather. I patiently waited for the sound of rain drops to temporarily cease as they noisily pounded the top of the tent, and finally, they did. Knowing this was probably only a temporary condition, I rolled out of my bag and got moving. As I unzipped the door, the heavy fragrance of the forest immediately filled my nostrils as the rain seemed to intensify every smell, almost making me forget the tasks at hand. The sky was chock full of dark clouds, and I could not be sure how much dry weather I had to work with. It was still quite warm, and the gnats and mosquitoes were almost too much to take as I busily packed my gear. They seemed to take great delight in their torturing process of flying into my eyes, nose, and, most annoyingly, ears.

Forty minutes later, everything was finally packed and loaded. As I reached for the starter button, my thoughts traveled back to that morning in Bandon, Oregon, the last time I tried to start my bike in the rain. This time, however, there would be no one to help. I held my breath, hoping for the best, and pushed the little button that said "start." She fired right up with a loud roar. Yes! Music to my ears.

The rain continued to fall sporadically, and in the periods when it would really start to pour, I would quickly seek cover under a nearby overhanging branch and wait it out. I wore wet clothes instead of rain gear in the warm weather because the thought of wearing a fully self-contained sauna was just not a pleasant thought. The muddy and slippery rocks proved a challenge and required steady concentration as I slowly worked my way back to the highway.

Two hours later, I was only three miles from the pavement when the clouds decided to open up and dump buckets of rain all around. I sat under a tree for the better part of an hour, waiting for a break, never seeing a car or a human being. This was really starting to get old, and I had to work a little harder at staying positive. It didn't take long to see the bright side…it could have done this to me the previous night, and I would not have had the incredible evening I'd had. It proved again that we have the power to be content in all things, because it can always be worse. The clouds finally gave me an extended reprieve, and I rode to a town called Revelstoke, staying relatively dry in the process.

At lunchtime, I pulled into a family-type restaurant just off the main drag in good old Revelstoke. The food would have been only passable under normal conditions, but because I had only consumed about 500 calories in the past twenty-four hours, it tasted great.

I swaggered out to my bike, having thoroughly disgusted myself with my own eating habits, and ready to continue eastward. As I prepared myself for the journey, two guys on Honda Gold Wing motorcycles pulled in, fully clothed in the latest rain-gear fashions. I asked them what the weather was like east from town, and they pretty much summed it up with one word: rain. Actually, this was followed by four more words: "And lots of it."

In my continuing and infinite stupidity, I made the intelligent decision to not believe these two gentlemen. Why? Because the weather looked pretty good at the moment, which we all know is very helpful in forecasting weather conditions many miles away. I completely ignored the fact that these two men had just come from where I was going. It's okay to be an optimist, but when one is given hard-core facts from people who have just been there, wisdom dictates that one should listen to them. Yeah, well that's what one should do. I chose to go with the half helmet, Harley scarf, leather jacket, and jeans.

Those guys pretty much knew what they were talking about. Twenty minutes later, it rained and rained hard. Not only was it raining water droplets that felt like peas being thrown on my face, but the temperature took a mean dive southward and things were getting mighty cold. Within minutes, I was completely drenched and decided to forego the rain gear at this point and gut it out.

I received quite a number of stares from the cars I passed, as I had pulled my head down against my shoulders to keep the rain from running down my neck and sported a scowl on my face that would have made the Grim Reaper boys back in Penticton proud. When I arrived at the town of Golden a few hours later, I decided to get a cheap motel and dry out. I was numb and wet and knew it would take at least three hours for the grimace on my face to slowly melt away, hoping it wouldn't stay that way forever. I found a dumpy little motel that provided all needed services.

The next day proved no better. It was raining hard, but the rain gear decision was an easy one this time. I reluctantly suited up and headed down the road. When I arrived at the turnoff to Lake Louise, I realized that it would be useless to head in that direction because the clouds were hanging far too low, completely hiding from view the majestic mountains surrounding me. I was very disappointed, as my primary reason for making this northern trek into British Columbia had been to see Lake Louise and the surrounding country.

Fortunately, my disappointment did not last too long. I quickly gave myself an attitude adjustment, putting into practice my philosophy of not focusing on the result but on the process. Although Lake Louise had been the goal, the process of getting to this place had been absolutely incredible. I thought back to my friends at Penticton and my adventures at Mabel Lake, and I knew those were experiences I would always treasure. Suddenly, it was not such a big deal anymore. How much simpler my life could be if I embraced that attitude every day for the rest of my life. I decided to continue on to Fernie, British Columbia, and get a motel there. I was starting to get pretty cold.

I was beginning to hear some new engine noises out of the left side of my bike, and that kind of worrying can ruin a ride. I found myself continually lowering my head to the left as I rode, trying to understand if continuing on might be making things worse. The rain picked up its intensity as I was making my way down a mountainous back road, and suddenly, my bike just quit. I couldn't believe it was happening today of all days, in the pouring rain. I dismounted and looked over the engine visually, looking for something obvious, but I saw nothing wrong. "I couldn't be out of gas, could I?" I asked myself. Because my bike does not have a gas gauge, I was forced to estimate my fuel consumption using my odometer. According to my calculations, fuel should not be the problem. Then suddenly I remembered that I had not filled up where I thought I had and my calculations were actually off this time. I *was* out of gas. I was temporarily relieved, although I did not know how far the next gas stop would be. I flipped the lever below the tank to reserve, and to my relief, the engine fired back up again. I rode into the next town on fumes.

I arrived in Fernie, British Columbia, that afternoon and paid for a very nice motel room for about $28 U.S. Although things are more expensive in

Canada, the buying power of the American dollar was about 30% stronger, which certainly helped me out. For the second day in a row, I unloaded my supplies in the rain and spread everything out on the motel floor to dry out until the next day. I turned on the weather channel and saw that the story was a sad one: rain for the next several days. It made me a little depressed because the areas I would be riding through would provide me with some of the most spectacular scenery of the trip. I didn't want to miss it, but I didn't want to spend my money on a motel for three days, either. Little did I know that these problems would soon be solved.

I awoke to my country's birthday, July 4, and I must admit that I felt a little disappointed that I couldn't have been somewhere in the USA to celebrate this great holiday in small US town instead of in a cold and damp place in Canada. Fernie, however, was a breathtakingly beautiful ski resort town nestled in the Rocky Mountains of British Columbia just north of the State of Montana. Majestic mountain peaks rivaling those of the eastern Sierra seemed to completely surround the small town, and in those brief moments when the clouds would vacate their positions around the mountain tops, the true rugged beauty of the peaks, many still white with the snows left over from winter, was unveiled.

I had not ventured out the night before, and the full night's rest had left me refreshingly awake. It was midmorning and the rain was still coming down in occasional spurts. I waited for an "off" period, then quickly hopped on the bike and went downtown to grab something to eat. The town was quite small and was bordered by a small river that one had to cross to reach the downtown area. After several wrong turns, I finally found the right exit and found the heart of Fernie, which resembled something more out of the early thirties than the nineties.

The word quaint certainly fit the bill here. First item on the agenda…cash. Unfortunately, I was out of the colorful Canadian paper and had recently discovered that my ATM card did not use the same network as did the local Canadian banking system. The motel manager refused to advance me money on my credit card, and I was getting a little desperate trying to figure out how I could get some money. It finally dawned on me that I could get a cash advance on my credit card at the nearby bank, and I was thankful that I didn't have to resort to plan B, charging people fifty cents to hear how I had killed a grizzly with my spark plug wrench.

As I entered the bank, I immediately noticed a , "squirrely looking" guy standing in line to do some bank business. He had a bit of a buck-toothed grin, and his hair was pulled back into a stringy ponytail that barely made it to his shoulders. This look, combined with his black leather jacket and dirty jeans, provided an indication that he probably owned a Harley. I walked up to him and said, "Hey, you ride?"

He looked at me and, with a big, buck-toothed grin, replied, "Yup, that's my Sporty outside. She's a beauty, ain't she? Just got her not too long ago." He was busting with pride. I immediately took a liking to this fellow. I asked his name, and he told me that everyone called him Meeker. I never did ask how he got that name. I didn't get to know him real well, but I just knew he had been a Fernian his whole life. We engaged in a little small talk, and I learned that the warm grin that I had first noticed was truly reflective of his genuine personality.

After eating a Reuben sandwich at one of the local diners, I decided to walk down the main street and replenish my diminishing supply of film. As I strolled out of the store and toward my bike, a very large, bearded, "biker-looking" fellow started walking in my direction, leaving little doubt that his sole intention was to make contact with me. He was about six-foot-one and probably weighed about 250 pounds. High, rosy cheeks were barely visible through his untrimmed thick and mostly gray beard, and his head was roofed with long, stringy straight hair, reflecting much less gray than the hair on his face. His hair hung loosely, lying close to his features and resting on his broad shoulders. Looking down at his large arms, I noticed a surplus of tattoos, at least four or five on each arm. I figured he was either going to be really cool and ask me where I was from or he was about to call me Deputy Fife and beat my head in for impersonating a biker.

He moved in closer, looked me up and down, and asked if the FXR was my bike...and where I was from. Okay, so far so good. We talked for a while about my trip, and during the conversation, I happened to glance over at an old truck parked along the main street, with the easily recognizable Harley eagle covering a good portion of the back window. I asked if that was his truck, and he said it was. "What's your name?" I asked.

"Ma name's Fred," he responded with a big old grin while simultaneously sticking his hand out. I enthusiastically grabbed it, and my hand seemed to disappear into his huge paw.

Just then, a cute and bubbly girl came bouncing into the scene and introduced herself as Ruth, Fred's wife. After about five minutes of active chitchatting, Ruth cordially invited me to their place for a sudsy brew. I put on a little act as though thinking intensely as to my reply and said, "You know, I only have about three months left on this ride, so yeah, I think I can probably squeeze you into my schedule." Their surprised expressions and smiles made me feel pretty good, and I knew they would give anything to be given that much time to ride.

I followed behind their old pickup truck as they led me to their quaint little home located on the outskirts of Fernie. While I rode, my thoughts worked overtime, unsure of what to expect. Was I getting myself into a nasty situation or was this a good move? *I have no idea what they are in to. Maybe I should have politely declined the offer. Well, that would have been the easy way, wouldn't it?* No, regardless of the outcome, I was stretching my boundaries by saying yes. I had made the right decision…I hoped.

Their house looked like your everyday *Leave It to Beaver* home, but in dire need of a few external repairs. They invited me into the kitchen, where we sat around the old-fashioned Formica dining table and talked about the details of my journey, their various Harley adventures, the annual toy run that they sponsored every year, and so on. This was certainly the last place I had thought I would be this time of the afternoon. The best part was, I was having a great time. I had been invited to my first stranger's house of the ride.

Then, who should walk in but my close and personal friend Meeker and his wife, Rose! I had only been in town one day, and I already had friends stopping by to say hi. As we continued to share stories, I found that Meeker had recently been in a serious truck accident in which he had fallen asleep at the wheel and crashed head-on into a giant tree stump. By the sounds of the injuries, he had been in really bad shape and had not been discovered for hours after impact. He suddenly turned very serious when telling me his story and said, "I never realized what incredible friends I had until this happened. People visited me, they cared for my place, they were there for me. I didn't know I had so many friends. That's what life is about, friends who care." His genuine character showed brightly, and I detected a little mistiness in his eyes and his voice. It was evident that if Meeker liked you, he would be a friend for life.

Somewhere in the next three hours, we transitioned to the subject of tattoos, and the inevitable question was asked as to whether I had any. I replied that I had none but, to save biker face, told them that I had always thought about going under the needle at least one time, which was true. As it turned out, Ruth's dad had been in the tattoo business for more than 30 years. Wouldn't you know it? I hate it when people call my bluff. I was suddenly feeling the pressure of conformity and feeling it in a big way. Meeker was standing across the table from me and said clearly and loudly, "Hell, you ain't no biker if you ain't got no tattoo!" Thank you, Meeker! I promised them I would think about it.

"Hey, Fred, how many tattoos you got?" I inquired, trying to divert the subject from yours truly. He started pointing out all the different emblems and designs on his shoulders and arms and then tore his shirt off and showed me his back. It was completely covered with a picture of a giant tiger with wings, mouth wide open in a snarling expression, jumping toward the viewer in an attack position. Below, in huge bold letters outlined in red were the words "Harley Davidson Motorcycles." He turned around with a big old smile, his rosy cheeks busting out over his beard, so proud of the artwork on his back.

Although Fred was a formidable sight, I had come to know him a little better in the past few hours and discovered that in actuality, he was a very gentle man. He reminded me somewhat of Santa Claus in his biker days, before Santa had traded his Harley in for the reindeer and sleigh. He worked where many of the locals worked, in the local mine, currently on the night shift. I could tell that he was the type who worked hard and played hard.

That night, they took me downtown to the Northern, one of the local biker bars. Because of the rain, we had decided to take Fred and Ruth's elderly Oldsmobile in lieu of the bikes. I'm not sure what year she was, but I'm guessing that disco was all the craze when she rolled off the assembly line. We all piled into the personable old car and headed for downtown Fernie once again. I laughed to myself as I sat in the backseat. The outsider had been accepted and was now being taken to the local hangout. We had a great time as I hung out with the gang and played pool most of the night.

While we were inside talking, the rock music emanating from the jukebox was suddenly broken by the sound of an ambulance's siren, and Ruth's expression turned from a face of fun to a serious expression of concern. She looked at me with down-turned mouth and said, "I hate hearing that. In a town this small, chances are, it's someone you know. I hope it isn't anything serious." As it would turn out, a friend of theirs was in a car accident that night, but fortunately, the injuries were not life threatening.

At one in the morning, it was time to go home. Fred had the next few nights off, so he didn't hold back a whole lot that night. He and Ruth weren't exactly in any condition to drive, so I volunteered my services for chauffeur duty. My second night in Fernie and I was already the designated driver. It was still lightly raining, so Fred and Ruth had me drop them off at their house and gave me unlimited use of the car for the night.

I shook my head in wonder with a big old smile as I found myself driving someone else's car around the town of Fernie. Before this trip had begun, I had really wondered if I would indeed meet strangers on this ride who would actually take an outsider in, trusting them with their belongings or their homes. I had heard other people's stories of such events, but I had been unsure if this would really happen to me. Now it had, and it felt really good. I now owned at least one great story to tell of such an experience simply because I had taken a chance and said yes. Comfort zones rarely provide experiences like that.

I drove the cruiser over to Fred and Ruth's the next morning, and they informed me, in no uncertain terms, that I was to vacate my premises at the motel and stay with them that night. The offer was too good to pass up, and the weather was not supposed to clear up for another day anyway. That same day, a friend of Fred's had checked out the noise on my Harley and made the comment that Harleys make that noise once in a while and that it was nothing to worry about. I was very relieved.

After moving my possessions to Fred and Ruth's house, we rode our scoots out of town about five miles, to another biker bar, where I met a few more of their friends. Once again, we had a great time. Len was the ponytailed owner of the place, probably in his sixties, who, I soon found out, possessed a very dry sense of humor. The table where we began to take our positions was made of wood, but the top had been carved out to fit different pieces of biker memorabilia such as patches and badges. A thick coat of clear plastic of some kind covered the top to keep them buried for eternity. As I began to sit down in the first available chair, all eight faces looked at me in almost a horrified expression as if I had just insulted someone's mother. "What?!" I asked incredulously.

Fred gave me a concerned look, leaned over toward me, and said, "You're sitting in Len's chair."

"And this is not a good thing?" I asked, knowing the answer.

Ruth chimed in, "Nobody ever sits in Len's chair." I looked up and caught Len looking down at me as a vulture would eye a carcass.

"Why don't I just sit over there?" I volunteered as everyone, except Len, began to laugh at my expense. I knew Len liked me, but he wouldn't let on.

I also met a man named Sugar, Ruth's dad. He was originally from England and had received his nickname from his younger days when he had competed in bare-knuckles boxing. His fighting style apparently resembled that of Sugar Ray Johnson. He often talked with a half-cocked smile with a hint of a British accent, and confidence seemed to exude from his voice. Individual tattoos left little room for bare skin on his arms, and his face was home to long, powdery-white sideburns leading to long white hair that protruded sideways from under his baseball cap, which was used to cover his bald dome. Sugar was about my size, but perhaps a little stockier. One thing was for sure, you just felt like you wouldn't want to mess with him.

The stories were flowing from everyone that day, and some of the best came from Sugar. A story that seemed to stick out in my mind was one that Sugar had to tell in his English-tinged accent. "I was a member of the Royal Navy and worked part time as a tattoo artist's assistant," he said. "One day, the owner wanted to take off early, so he let me finish up a tattoo he had been working on. When he saw the good job I did, he told me to go ahead and work the rest of the day and he would be back around 5:00. I did a good number of tattoos that day, and when my boss came back, he told me to keep most of the money. It was no small amount. So one night, a very drunk and not-so-friendly U.S. Marine comes in and tells me to tattoo a giant picture of Old Glory on his back. I tattooed a flag, all right, but it was a British Jack instead. I didn't like his attitude much. He didn't check on my work when he left, but the next day, they had to restrain a very angry marine who wanted to see me in a pretty bad way." I shook my head from side to side and had to take the marine's side on this one. Sugar hadn't gotten his name because he was sweet.

We spent that afternoon in the Northern. My desire for a tattoo had been growing steadily since that first conversation around the dining room table. I nudged Sugar with my elbow and showed him a design I had drawn on a napkin. It was a symbol of my Christian faith, which portrayed an empty cross with a banner hanging from the arms displaying the word "Victory" in Victorian-style letters. We went back and forth on different design ideas and finally came up with one I liked. "So how long would something like this take?" I asked.

"Ahhh, thirty, maybe forty minutes," he replied, never taking his eyes off the drawing.

I thought about it for about two seconds and said, "Let's do it," looking around and wondering who had said that. Fred and Ruth were so excited, you would have thought I was their son and had just said my first word.

We jumped on the bikes and roared off to Sugar's place, up on the hill, for my virgin arm-piercing ceremony. As we entered the side door, we continued downstairs to his all-purpose workshop and "tattoo parlor." The "parlor" was actually a tiny room set aside in his workshop. Covering the wall hung colorful pictures of all the tattoos he had done. The needles and colors all sat on a paint-stained bench, and two chairs were all the furniture this room held.

Sugar set me in "the chair," and Ruth offered me a screwdriver drink as cheap anesthesia for the pain I was apparently about to endure. Hey, this guy did not need alcoholic beverages to numb any pain. How bad could it hurt? I had been in a number of nasty dirt-bike crashes, not to mention a few street-bike wrecks, and I've learned that I can take pain pretty well. Nope, I would take this the natural way, like a man.

To prepare me, Sugar issued a warning that the outlining process would hurt the most because of the thick needle he would be using. "No problem," I said emphatically. "Use a jackhammer for all I care." Sugar drew the outline on my right shoulder, grabbed the needle of torture, and went to work. Now, I didn't yell, scream, or pass out, but the pain shot through my shoulder, across my chest, up my neck, and directly into the inner depths of my brain in about two nanoseconds. It was far worse than I had ever thought it would be. I immediately ordered a double screwdriver on the rocks and told Ruth she could have my motorcycle free and clear if she got it to me in the next fifteen seconds. I tried to make intelligible conversation during the process, but my words came out slowly and deliberately through clenched teeth. Another tough-guy failure. I am sure everyone present was doing their best to hold in their laughter.

Through earlier conversations, I had discovered that big Fred had a few of his tattoos in some *very* sensitive areas (and I mean sensitive), and sitting there, feeling this pain, I wasn't sure whether I should respect him or think he was the biggest idiot in the world. I did know one thing, that once the needle hit the old shoulder, there was no turning back. *Mom's going to love this one,* I sarcastically thought to myself.

When it was finished, I really must say, I liked it. Little had I known when arriving in Fernie like a cold wet dog, I would be leaving with an inked arm. Being a tattoo novice, they informed me that the tattoo would soon scab up and would require about a week or so to heal and would need to be kept out of the sun. I was very relieved that I held no regrets about this permanent decision.

The next morning, I bought Fred, Ruth, and Sugar breakfast as a token of my appreciation for all their hospitality. The weather had finally cleared, and it was time to move on. It would be hard leaving new friends I had not even known only two days earlier. Ruth looked at me and, with sincere tears in her eyes, remarked, "I wish there was something you could take with you that would remind you of us."

I looked at her a bit dumbfounded, rolled my shirt sleeve over my sore shoulder, and said, "You're right, I wonder what that could be?" We all laughed at her Alzheimer's moment and agreed that we would all stay in touch. It was hard to leave.

The Fernie experience provided an invaluable lesson that fortified a principle I have always tried to live by, although not always successfully: When events in life don't go according to plan, move forward and accept it. In the past, I had found myself getting very upset if things had gone "wrong" or simply had not gone the way I thought they should go. Fernie was a great example that this thought process is nothing but an exercise in futility and a waste of energy. Three days earlier, the rain had been perceived as a problem, a negative condition that had kept me from realizing my goal of seeing Lake Louise. Out of the negative, however, had came positives and new windows of opportunity. Had I worked myself into a frenzy over not reaching my intended destination, I would not only have wasted my energy on events that could not be changed but may have missed the positive opportunities that crossed my path because of my positive attitude.

After four days of rain, I was reveling in the beautiful sunshine that surrounded me. The sky was cloudless, and the previous days' fall of rain had again intensified the fragrant smells of the land. This is when the open road is not only ridden but is consumed.

I wasn't on the road twenty minutes before a mile-long line of cars were at a standstill, waiting for a road construction crew member to mercifully turn the stop sign around and let them continue on their individual journeys. It is usually permissible, in this type of a situation, to let motorcycles move to the front of the line, because they take up little space, and I immediately took advantage of this wonderful privilege. I could feel the icy stares from the people who had been sitting in their cars for more than forty minutes burrowing into the back of my skull as I slowly putted past them. I love motorcycles!

As I arrived at the front of the line, I began a conversation with the lady holding the red stop sign. As it turned out, she was a Fernian herself and knew Fred and Ruth very well. I told her about our little party with the neighbors the night before, and she commented that she was very aware of it because it had kept her up most of the night. "Sorry about that." I said.

"No need," she replied, "I wish I could have joined you guys." I felt like a local, a Fernian.

She finally swung the sign around to let us pass, and, with a wave of her hand, I led the one hundred cars or so through miles of road construction. There were several places where I was forced to ride through deep, rutted sand and a few times when I came very close to falling. Wouldn't the cars have loved that?

Once the mountainous road opened up, so did my soul. The temperature was sheer perfection. I would soon be making my way through Waterton Park and on to one of my favorite places in the States, Glacier National Park in Montana. I leaned back heavily against my black tee bag and once again comfortably extended my legs forward upon the chrome highway pegs at the front of the bike. The cares of this Earth passed by me like the warm wind, and my spirit comingled with every vision and scent that came before me. I couldn't stop smiling as I glanced into the mirror every few miles, still not able to believe who was staring back. I still couldn't believe I was actually doing this.

Every once in a while, my sore tattooed shoulder would twinge a little and I would instinctively move it around a bit. My head slowly nodded as I replayed the past few days in my mind for about the twentieth time.

I had a feeling that experiences such as these were only the beginning.

Randy and John in Washington cabin (Nice hat)

Randy and John heading to Al's cabin

Al's creations (Including dog)

Looking stupid with guns

Big Terry fall down in creek

Randy doing a little better (steeper than it looks)

Complete water displacement

View From the 'Love Tub'

After pushing for two hours, tow strap comes in handy

Crabbin!!

Saying goodbye to a good friend

Paul & Darlene

Lake Mabel (It's a) sign

Lake Mabel dirt road

Mountain campsite - British Columbia

Washing up outside Lake Mabel

Fred, Ruth & Sugar in Fernie (Real Harley people)

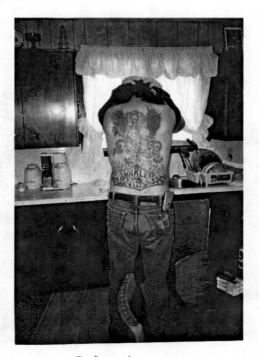

Fred's very large tattoo

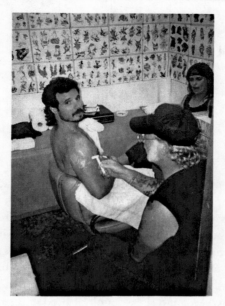

Getting prepped for a much smaller tattoo than Fred's

Post tattoo and Fernie family

CHAPTER 4

Roughing It

The moment my tires crossed the border from Canada into Montana, I immediately pulled over to the side of the road, took off my helmet, and stored it away under the red cargo netting located behind the bike. For the first time since this trip began, I had the legal freedom to ride without the protective covering adorning my head. Although I think anyone who doesn't wear a helmet while riding a motorcycle is taking some real chances with his or her life, I must confess that I love the feeling of the wind blowing through my hair, the lack of added weight on my head, and the extra bit of freedom I seem to feel when the headpiece is absent. Of course, for every upside there always seems to be an opposite downside, and for me, the downside is the Don King look, which my hair tends to emulate after all forward progress has terminated. Not a pretty sight.

My excitement was quickly mounting to an eruptive level as I neared one of my favorite locations in the world, Glacier National Park, one of the most awe-inspiring parks on the North American continent. What makes this park so memorable, aside from the breathtaking mountain scenery, is the fifty-two–mile stretch of narrow highway called the Going-to-the-Sun Road, carved within the park's steep mountains. This road cuts directly through the heart of this stately park. Its creation took more than twenty years during a time when horses, steam shovels, and a man's sweat were the predominant tools of moving earth.

This narrow and winding path reveals portions of the most romantic western landscape imaginable as it passes through virgin forest; deep, clear, glacier-carved lakes; vertigo-inspiring cliffs; and luxuriant meadows of delicate alpine flowers. Logan's pass, named after the man who oversaw the building of this park, reaches its maximum height of 6,664 feet directly below the Going-to-the-Sun Mountain, whose square-like rocky peak explodes behind the tourist center to a height in excess of 10,000 feet.

The highway begins and ends with its own large crystal-clear and glacier-fed lakes: St. Mary Lake to the east and Lake McDonald to the west. It is a must to travel this highway in an open vehicle, eliminating any hindrance between the visitor and his or her surroundings, allowing the park to embrace the visitor as one of its own instead of limiting the person to being only a spectator.

The history here is intriguing as well. One of the highlights, during the road's opening ceremonies on July 15, 1933, was marked by the smoking of the peace pipe by the Blackfeet, Kootenai, and Flathead Indians, traditional enemies who had hunted in and followed game trails throughout the mountains. Representatives of the three tribes placed a bent stick at the pass, signifying that the Blackfeet desired peace. The Indians knelt, faced one another, and passed the pipe from right to left, marking an end to years of enmity between them. It was fitting that such a peaceful place would be the site of peace among men.

As I neared the eastern entrance to the park, a modern wooden building, built to look older than it was and created to provide gas and food services to its customers, came into sight. As I slowly turned the handlebars toward the parking lot's entrance, I suddenly became immersed in overwhelming emotions of the past. I parked my scoot and slowly swung my leg over the seat, then stood there, staring at the wooden door that served as the store's entrance. For the first time since Lodi, I was standing at a place that was once again familiar, a place I had stood almost three years earlier, in September of 1992. A place where another dream had been fulfilled and where I had first truly experienced the feelings of ecstasy while accomplishing a childhood fantasy. The same bike I was now riding had been here with me then.

John Fergason and I had been best friends since we were five years old, and we had shared many an experience as we had grown up in the small town of Lodi. Over the years, we had discussed many dreams together, but one that particularly stood out was our desire to travel across the country on motorcycles. Although we had given it great lip service, nothing had seemed to come of our dream to travel the open roads, even though we both owned street bikes for a short time. Life's circumstances soon separated us, and before we knew it, we had been in different parts of the country, I in Southern California and John in Texas. Another lifelong ambition seemed destined to die before ever being given a chance to live.

In March of 1992, I called John just to say hello. Little did I know that that phone call would end up costing me over $11,000...and start me on an adventure I would never forget. Somehow, we found our discussion detoured to the subject of the ominous street-bike trip that had never come to pass. As we discussed the reasons why we had not achieved this long-held desire, we began to realize that we were unable to come up with any good ones. We simply had not made the choice to do it. Could it be that simple? I don't remember who made the life-changing statement, "Let's just do it." Just that quickly, we agreed to take the plunge.

Looking back on that night, I have come to learn that many times, the only difference between doing and dreaming is simply the decision itself. Although this is an obvious statement at face value, taking a closer look at my life revealed this to be one of my major obstacles. I like to use the analogy of own-ing a huge ranch with numerous horses who are given free rein on the open prairie. Although the rancher may own them, they are of no use to him if they are only allowed to roam free. Similarly, I had always given my dreams the freedom to ride the open range of my mind, free and limitless...and numerous, but I had never taken the time to rein them in, put them in the corral, and make use of them. Eventually, they would wander out of sight, like horses over the next hill, never to be seen again. They were missed, but instead of searching them out and retrieving them, I would only replace them with new ones. After all, that is much easier. The trouble was, I was becoming content with having a full herd but an empty corral. I discovered that having the dream is not enough. The mind must be the first to accept the challenge, and that requires a conscious decision to move forward.

Now that John and I had made the decision to herd this dream into the cor-ral, we needed to work out a few minor details, like what type of bikes we would use for our momentous journey. After discussing it for a short time, we came to the conclusion that they had to be Harleys. Bad to the bone, that was going to be us. Our goal would be to reach the Canadian border...somewhere. We set the date for September of that year and set aside twenty days for the trip born of our childhood...one day for each year it had taken us to get to that point.

When September finally rolled around, we rode our Hogs from Southern California up through the Rockies, through Glacier, into Canada, and then back home. I will never forget the feelings of exiting Glacier and stopping at the store where I was now standing, knowing the Canadian border was only a half hour away. We were as punchy as two school boys going out on our first date, acting completely irrational, stupid, and immature...and just not caring. We had finally made it! We had made it together!

As I stood in this place by myself, every emotion that had touched me so deeply that day returned home as if it had only happened the week before. I longed to have John with me right then, to reminisce and share our feelings regarding our personal triumph of the past, to laugh at how similar his would be to mine. It was ironic that I felt so alive and happy yet, in missing my buddy, felt so incredibly alone.

I entered the park from the east on a cloudless and crisp day, wearing the widest and goofiest grin imaginable. Man, I felt alive! As it turned out, the park had only been open for a few weeks because of the high elevation and snowpack left over from the late spring storms. Perfect timing for the observer. I was so glad I had stayed in Fernie those few days and waited out the rain and clouds. As I rode the narrow and winding road, large valleys of red cedar and hemlocks opened up before me, coming to rest against sloping rocky ledges that continued upward, disappearing into the snow. These expansive valleys, sculpted by the age-less work of glaciers throughout time, seemed so open, so inviting. Rivers and waterfalls seemed to be all around me as they made their way downward from the heavy snowpack, providing a panoramic view of crooked white fingers careening over the valley's ledges, forcing viewers to pull off to the side of the road as if some magnetic force was at work. What a gift I had been given to view such a place. It was a glorious ninety-minute ride.

By the time I left the park, it was time to find a home for the night. I located a cheap campground within the moderately sized town of Kalispell, Montana, and set everything up. I had only worked out at a gym once dur-ing the entire trip so far, and I was in fear that someone would soon mistake my biceps for a bad case of acne. I had the energy, I had the will, it was time to work out. Using the phone book, I located a gym downtown and figured I could get not just a good workout but a nice shower as well. As it turned out, I received my shower, all right. There was not a cloud in the sky when I left the campground, and I made the executive decision to forego fitting the rain fly over the tent...which could be the reason I was never an executive.

I followed the directions the campground director had provided but didn't pay an exorbitant amount of attention to the many turns required. After get-ting lost several times, I finally stumbled upon the correct address, more by accident than by intellect. It was a small place, with only two other guys mak-ing use of its facilities, but that was the way I liked it, down and dirty.

About an hour into my workout, I heard a noise that sounded like either a sonic boom or a loud clap of thunder. I was praying for the jet. "Don't tell me it might rain," I whined to the guy next to me as he curled another forty pounds up to his chest.

"Yep, happens a lot this time of year," he grunted breathlessly. Then I heard it. Raindrops the size of Volkswagen Beetles hitting the sidewalk. I thought back to all my possessions, which were safely stored inside my tent *with no rain fly.* After I let my workout buddy know of my predicament, he graciously vol-unteered his phone number and a place to stay that night if my possessions were indeed floating in my tent when I returned. Nice guy.

I grabbed my clothes and rushed out to my very wet motorcycle. Night had fallen, and I was motoring through town with nothing more than a tee shirt and pants—no eye protection whatsoever. I rode through the heavy rain, using my hands as makeshift goggles and not exactly enjoying the massive show of lightning and thunder that was bearing down on the small town. It didn't take long before I was completely lost and wandering through Kalispell's residential area.

It took me about twenty minutes to finally locate the campground, and by then, things were more than sufficiently wet inside. The lesson had been taught well. From this point on, I would always put the rain fly on no matter what the weather was like at the moment. Fortunately, the water had not completely soaked through my sleeping bag and I had only a semi-soggy night's sleep.

July 7 was another clear and perfect day, and except for the fragrant smells of the damp earth, evidence of the previous night's storm had all but disappeared. After reclaiming my previous night's wet clothing from the campground's dryer, I packed the still warm clothes in my tee bag and was soon back on the road. I enjoyed my ride immensely as I cruised along the edges of Flathead Lake and penetrated deeper into Montana's southern interior. Once I crossed Highway 90, the backcountry of Montana really began to open up and come alive. I rode atop the two-lane road known as Highway 93, which seemed more than content to simply follow the path of the tiny river that ran along its border rather than to forge its own way. My eyes would systematically glance at the rushing water cascading over rounded rocks and ledges as we both descended the mountain. Every mountainous turn was like opening a Christmas present as I wondered what gift nature would provide me around the next corner. I was never disappointed.

After a few hours, I veered off Highway 93 and took a thin gray line on the map called Highway 43, which transported me over the continental divide and into an expansive valley between two large Rocky Mountain ranges. I was now in the Big Hole Valley. Traffic was nearly nonexistent as I rode the straight two-lane road that cut through infinite miles of the darkest green and yellow pasture I had seen to date. Thousands of cattle grazed on the sweet grass, and this landscape painting was perfectly framed on all sides by snow-covered peaks. It was a matchless snapshot to back up Montana's claims of wide open spaces.

I planned to rest my bones in a small town called Wisdom, Montana, toward the end of the valley. I figured with the constant infusion of insight I was receiving on this ride, it only made sense that I should stay there one night. As I entered the town's limits, I quickly discovered there weren't many limits to this town. Not much Wisdom here. I looked at my watch and saw that it was around six in the evening. I really needed to find a place to stay. I found the ranger station just outside of town and stopped one of its employees as he was just getting off work.

"Any campgrounds around here?" I inquired.

He furrowed his brow a bit beneath his wide-brimmed Yogi Bear Ranger hat and said, "Got a campground, but it don't have any showers and the mosquitoes are going to eat you alive." As if on queue, I immediately noticed about five of the little boogers taking their dining positions upon my bare arm. It didn't take much convincing to realize that Wisdom was not for me. "Your best bet would be to head up to Dillon, about seventy miles east," he added.

By the time he had finished providing his wise counsel, the five mosquitoes had multiplied into a swarm, as word must have gotten out that there was bare skin nearby. It was obviously time to get the heck out of there. I thanked him for his advice and returned to the road that would lead me toward Dillon. The moment my tires touched pavement from the ranger station's dirt driveway, I looked to my left and noticed a female road crew worker, adorned with her trendy yet stylish orange vest, holding a giant red stop sign. Construction again! Out here!?

She informed me that I had just missed the last group of vehicles and that it would be about twenty minutes before the pace car would return to allow us controlled passage across the open land. I begged her to allow me to continue on and catch up with the last group. I gave her the best "puppy dog" look I could muster, but to no avail. She, herself, had been there all day in the humid heat, battling the mosquitoes, and was not exactly in the mood to be persuaded by anyone. I don't believe one part of my body remained motionless for the next twenty minutes, as at least one hundred bloodthirsty demons seemed determined to find the one patch of skin that would provide sustenance for their short, meaningless lives. Life on the road is not always glamorous.

I don't believe I have ever been so happy to see a road construction pace car in all my life! I led the parade of cars behind me at a miserably slow 30 mph over 17 miles of dirt and gravel. I glanced at my watch, and the digital readout showed 7:00 p.m. It was really getting late. I finally rolled into Dillon around 8:30 and cruised the small Old West-like town for a while to scope things out. Finding a cheap KOA camp just outside of the town's limits, I set up my tent and grabbed a much-needed shower. Now that I was presentable, my stomach reminded me, in no uncertain terms, that it had been neglected for far too long. Dinnertime! I found the street that was home to all the bars and restaurants in town and bought myself a nice little steak dinner at one of the local establishments that reminded me more of an old-fashioned saloon than a modern bar and restaurant.

While waiting for my food, I moseyed on over to the jukebox, perused the selections, and sneaked a dollar's worth of quarters into the slot. The air was soon filled with the song "Hotel California," followed by "Stuck in Lodi Again." Ahhh, pieces of home in a faraway land.

It was a Friday night, and, looking over at the waitress, I asked, "So what's happening in the metropolis of Dillon tonight?"

"Blues band playing over at the hotel. They're really good," she shot back. Good answer. I love blues. After finishing my slightly tough but edible steak dinner, I excitedly went out to unlock my bike and cruise over to where the band would soon be playing, anxious for a little entertainment.

As I crouched over my lock, three women began rushing toward me, like a linebacker blitz, yelling, "There he is!" I didn't know what I had done, but I knew I was about to find out.

"We saw you ride in," one blurted out, "but didn't know where you went to."

I smiled back at the matronly woman who seemed to be in her early fifties. "Well, I've just been here eating." Wow, good comeback. They began to compliment me about everything imaginable until my head was easily the size of my Harley gas tank.

One of the ladies, an attractive African American girl, looked at me and said, "We could tell you weren't from these parts by the way you dressed."

I looked down and humbly relied, "I'm wearing a white tee shirt with a black leather vest."

"I know," she came back, "but it's a *clean* white tee shirt." Okay, that was funny. The other girl asked if I was one of those Los Angeles Chippendale dancers. Now that was really funny. I, of course, said yes. I have to say, though, I was definitely enjoying the sudden attention, although I knew deep down that any stranger on a Harley would have been given the same attention.

Deanna was definitely the youngest of the three women and offered to buy me a drink if I would stick around a little longer. I agreed, and we sauntered inside the local bar where all the locals had been congregating for some time already. Deanna was not overly beautiful but definitely had a cuteness about her. Her straight brunette hair hung loosely upon her shoulders, and she wore a type of halter top that completely covered her very shapely figure with the exception of her lower stomach. I would guess she was somewhere in her mid-twenties, and she seemed genuinely friendly. It felt good to be talking to someone after riding alone for the past few days, and didn't hurt that it was a woman.

We talked for a while as we leaned against the bar, and it didn't take much time to discover that her family life had been more than a little confusing. I soon found out why. An older lady in her mid-fifties staggered over to us as we were talking, and Deanna quickly introduced me to her as her mother. By this time, I had already been told that Deanna's mother had been married nine times and was currently engaged to number ten, who was also there at the bar. It was also obvious she had been there for quite a while. She was feeling no pain.

About five minutes after being introduced to me, Deanna's mother and one of her mother's friends began a very loud discussion about the numerical value that should be attached to my butt. Her friend loudly claimed it was a ten, but the mother claimed it couldn't be a ten unless the "feel" test was administered. So as not to come across as egotistical, I want to point out that in the condition these ladies were in, Marlon Brando would have had a ten rating that night.

While this intense philosophical debate was going on, I was standing up and facing the bar, ignoring this discussion as best I could until I heard the "feel test" remark. I hung my head, closed my eyes, and just hoped it was only drunk talk. Just then, two hands grabbed my Harley rest area and squeezed hard. I couldn't believe I just got felt up by the 55-year-old engaged mother of my new friend. Her fiancé didn't exactly appreciate this gesture a whole lot, and they proceeded to get into a huge fight over the issue. I'm sure they will have a long and happy life together.

This provided a perfect opportunity to exit stage left and check out the band. I felt very bad for Deanna, as I could tell she was extremely embarrassed. This scene certainly made me appreciate the moral upbringing and family values my parents had demonstrated to me over the years. An upbringing I had often taken for granted. It was fairly obvious that Deanna probably had never had a decent role model when growing up.

The band turned out to be surprisingly exceptional, and I had a great time closing my eyes and listening to the blues guitar filling the hotel lobby as my body swayed to the soulful rhythm. As midnight approached, the band began to pack up, so Deanna and I put on some warm clothes and went for a brisk night ride under the huge Montana sky. The heaven's boundaries were limitless that night, and every star ever created seemed to be out in all its glory. We sat on the bike on a deserted dirt road and talked about life, why I was taking this trip, and her desires to break out of her own self-made boundaries. She had been married twice already in her short 25 years and seemed destined to follow in her mother's legacy. She was not a happy person. I couldn't help but wonder why certain people must start out in life at a disadvantage and others don't. It didn't seem fair. It was evident she yearned for somebody to look up to who could help her through life's trials.

After dropping Deanna off, I idled into the campground around 4:00 a.m., trying my best to keep my loud Harley engine as quiet as possible. It didn't work. I made no friends in the campground that morning. Around 10:00 a.m., the sunlight's glow illuminated the inside of my bungalow to a degree that sleep became impossible, and I slowly rolled my lazy "ten" butt out of my sleeping bag and out into the open spaces. As I put the final touches on my packing ritual, Deanna showed up in a beat-up car, looking as tired as I felt. We had breakfast together and delved a bit more into her life as I continued to provide her with whatever advice I could. She was a great young lady, and I have fond memories of my night in Dillon.

After a few hours of gliding through Montana's rolling green hills, I again found myself in familiar lands, at a place where John and I had visited three years earlier, Nevada City, Montana. This was a small ghost town that contained many of the original buildings and artifacts from the 1800s and had been laid out perfectly along the two-lane road. This place was so convincing that several scenes from the movie *Return to Lonesome Dove* had been filmed there. Grocery stores contained actual cans of food from that era, and the schoolhouse was stocked with straight rows of old wooden desks with ink-well holes in the upper right hand corners. It was like taking a step back in time.

On the other side of the highway sat several old passenger trains dating back to the nineteenth century, patiently waiting for visitors to gaze through their windows, transporting their imaginations back to a time of journeys from the east coast toward the west. I peered into the window of the church car, where the old-time organ stood at the head of the rows of wooden bench seats. I looked into the passenger train, where old wallpaper was hanging from the ceiling in strips, its glue no longer able to battle the forces of gravity and time. I remembered how John and I had run around this town like little children in a new playground three years earlier and how we had taken a picture of a mock gunfight down one of the old town's main streets. This place had been one of the highlights of our trip, and although I didn't stay long this time, I enjoyed the pleasant memories this place held for me.

My ride that whole day was saturated with beautiful scenery and relaxed winding roads. It was a day when my heartbeat seemed to lose its desire to pound at its normally driven pace but instead settled at a more carefree rate, where I felt as one with the highway and the beauty around me and time seemed to stand still. I must say, I will never forget those times and those feelings for as long as I live. As the day was nearing its end, so was my time in the beautiful state of Montana. There is no doubt that the Big Sky state will always be one of my favorite places to ride.

As the sun hung above the western horizon, I knew I needed to reach my destination fairly soon. I had planned to stay near the small town of West Yellowstone and then continue on through the park the next morning. I always became a little nervous around touristy areas because finding a remote campsite seems consistently more difficult thanks to the increased forest regulations and influx of inhabitants around the areas. I also knew that finding a vacant campground with no reservation could be a problem because of the number of tourists this time of year. After much searching, I finally found a campground on the outskirts of the park, about ten miles north of West Yellowstone. I made a left-hand turn across the oncoming lane and followed the tiny ribbon of asphalt through the tree-studded campground. I was overjoyed that few spots had been taken. This was good. I finally settled on a secluded spot near the back, against the forest known as Yellowstone Park.

I proceeded to unload all my equipment, lay my tent down upon the ground, and begin the ritual of threading the poles through the tent pockets. As I was about to raise the tent to life from its flattened condition, the campground's manager drove up in his red pickup truck and stopped in front of my little patch of ground. "Didn't you read the sign when you came in here?" he asked. This was not going to be good.

"Nope," I squinted, giving him my best perplexed look.

"No tent camping here. We got too many bears in the area," he replied.

"You've got to be kidding," I whined back. This was definitely not conducive to my previous good mood.

"Sorry," he yelled as he stepped on the accelerator of his Ford truck and rolled away. I looked down at my little space and dreaded the task of loading everything up again only to have to repeat the ritual a short time later. I didn't even know where I would go. I practiced my positive-attitude speech but must admit that I had a hard time convincing myself of my own wise words at that moment. I literally could not find anywhere to camp that night and was forced to settle for a KOA campground that charged me more than $20 for a little piece of grass. I resentfully paid the ridiculous amount and vowed that, after this night, I would not stay in campgrounds again.

As I was setting up, a couple of older gentlemen came by my plot of land and quizzed me a bit on what I was doing and why I was there. They were owners of a couple of Honda Gold Wing motorcycles pulling small tent trailers. Now, I don't want to be disrespectful, but I define Honda Gold Wings as sports cars with two wheels because they are so plush—it's pretty much like riding a convertible with the windows down. Too plush for this purist.

At the end of their interrogation, they politely invited me over to their campsite to meet their better halves. They were extremely friendly and made feel like I had known them for years. My initial plans had been to head into town and see what was up, and my first instinct at their invitation was to stay the loner and forego the neighborly visit. Well heck, they had taken such a liking to me, I would most likely disappoint them if I didn't show. Better make an appearance, you know, for them.

I tracked down their tent (which looked more like a motel room) among the many small camping areas and yelled in through the large wall of mosquito netting. They looked up, a bit startled, and my warm reception soon turned a bit cooler than I had expected. They invited me inside, more out of obligation, it seemed, than out of hospitality, and I quickly discovered why my presence was not being greeted with great excitement. I had made the mistake of invading their abode in the middle of a bridge game. Well at least it was a good reason (heavy sarcasm here). I might as well have been a mosquito...no, at least they would have tried to kill me were I a mosquito. After about five minutes of "making their day," I decided to excuse myself and head into town. Hey, it doesn't always work out.

Once I had ridden the eight miles into West Yellowstone, I inquired of some locals as to the location of the local biker hangout. I was in the mood to mingle and tell my story to whomever would listen. I found the place, but it was nearly empty, with only two motorcycles parked out front on the sidewalk. I went in anyway and found only one guy who was barely half interested in listening to my story at all. I tried to make conversation with the bartender, and he acted very interested...for about ten seconds. Tough room.

The next morning fell on a Sunday, and I decided to attend the morning service at a small church in West Yellowstone. It was the first time I had decided to do this. I don't know why I picked this particular church, but its square, white wooden structure reminded me of the old-time churches I had seen on "*Little House on the Prairie*. There were perhaps a total of thirty people in attendance, and I received more than one stare as I began to take off my leather chaps and black leather jacket in the parking lot. I certainly won the award for the most underdressed person in the congregation.

Regardless of my looks, however, I was received warmly by the parishioners and sat in one of the small wooden benches toward the back of the tiny white church. The pastor had recently been hired from a former youth-pastor position, and his sense of humor and natural way of speaking were right up my alley. His message that morning was an excellent one, not to mention pertinent.

I had been struggling with the decision of whether I should involve myself with the youth group at my church back home and had been putting this decision off for some time...for years, in fact. This minister's entire message was geared toward each adult taking responsibility in reaching today's youth. His words provided me the motivation I had been looking for, and I made a commitment to myself that I would exit yet another comfort zone and get involved with the junior high group when I returned. Now that would be adventure! I never would have dreamed that a small church in West Yellowstone would give me the answer to a five-year question. Funny how God works sometimes. I would end up spending two years in the junior high program of the now famous Saddleback Church in Lake Forest.

As I began to ride through Yellowstone Park, I tried to make it a point not to travel roads that John and I had ridden in our earlier trip and concentrated my travels on the northern part of the park. An hour into the ride, I stopped near one of the main intersections and pulled out my map from the inside pocket of my black leather vest to make the vastly important decision of which way to turn. You know life is good when that is one of your major decisions of the day.

As my eyes scoured the Yellowstone section, I noticed there was something called the Yellowstone Grand Canyon. I nodded my head in a decision well made and began folding the map to return it to its rightful place. Just then, I began to hear an intense rumbling that seemed to shake the very ground on which I was standing. My mouth began to turn upward in a half grin, and I believe I started to salivate just a bit out of the corner of my mouth as the realization of what the noise was became evident. Moments later, about fifty loud Harleys of all shapes, sizes, and colors passed me, their riders raising their hands in a salute of solidarity, which I quickly returned. I felt extremely proud of my bike at that moment. She wasn't the prettiest of the bunch, but I was fairly certain she would be taking me farther than any of the bikes I had just seen. She was in a class by herself.

On my way to the Grand Canyon of Yellowstone, I took a slight detour to view one of the many waterfalls that has made Yellowstone the famous park it is. As the sound of rushing water began to intensify, I knew I was getting close. As I exited a left-hand turn around a rocky mountain wall, the wide and cascading falls 200 yards away to my right met my eyes. I pulled my bike to the side of the road and looked downward at the beautiful scene before me.

The falls were probably fifty yards across, and their steep descent was drastically slowed by hundreds of rocks barely submerged below the white torrent of water, reminding me of a giant water slide. I pulled off to a dirt turnout, exited my bike, and slowly and meticulously crept onto a precarious rocky overhang located about twenty feet from the road. Hanging my legs over the rocky ledge, I found myself perched fifty feet in the air over sparsely laid trees and rocky boulders. I slowly retrieved a cigar from my vest pocket, placed it in my mouth, and lit the torpedoed end. As the first white puff of smoke exited my mouth and hung in the air, everything in life seemed to be in order, the silence broken only by the soothing sounds of water making its own journey through the woods. With each exhale, my body and mind relaxed just a little more. It was a memorable fifteen minutes in which I just enjoyed the moment.

Now tranquil and content, I continued on my way. Although still not of Grim Reaper stature, the face that peered back at me from my bike's mirror was making progress. I had shaved my beard in British Columbia and now sported only the mustache and goatee. My head was completely covered by a red, white, and blue head scarf complete with an eagle perfectly positioned at the forehead level, wings spread. To further accentuate the look, I firmly held my two-inch stub of a cigar between my teeth. I may have still looked like Barney Fife, but definitely a much meaner Barney Fife.

The Grand Canyon of Yellowstone did not disappoint me as I had thought it might. Although obviously not as impressive as THE Grand Canyon, it was surprisingly vast. I'm not exactly sure just how many feet separated me from the river that flowed through the canyon's bottom, but I would guess far more than one thousand. The sunlight glistening off the canyon's sheer rocky walls produced a reddish tint to its surface, and the enormity of this natural wonder made the detour more than worth the time. Good call. Okay, enough standing around, it was time to get some more miles behind me.

Forty-five minutes later, immediately after cresting a long mountain grade, my bike suddenly began to cough and sputter. This was not going to be temporary. The further I traveled down the hill, the worse her condition became, until eventually, when reaching the bottom, the pistons stopped moving. Fortunately, I was able to coast to a busy tourist stop complete with phones, store, and food. A silver lining!

I found a shady spot beneath a tree and began the arduous task of unloading my supplies and diagnosing what the problem might be. It didn't take long to discover that I had no electrical power whatsoever. I soon found the reason...the battery was as dry as my dating life had been recently. I had religiously checked the battery at different times during the beginning of the trip but had lately been lax in performing this most basic ritual. I reprimanded myself for my neglect and knew that I had to get the battery filled and charged. In looking further, I also noticed that the plug from the regulator (a unit that regulates the amount of current sent to the battery) to the alternator was very loose and worn and that it too would need to be fixed or my problems would only get worse. I was guessing that the regulator was probably on its way out and that it was allowing my battery to be overcharged, causing its water to boil out. Great.

I meandered into the busy grocery store and used the office phone to finally track down a battery charger located at a gas station ten miles down the road. I looked pretty pathetic as I asked visitors which direction they were heading and if they would drop my battery off at the station. More than one inquisitive stare met me as I explained my story, and one German couple flat out said no. I almost took this opportunity to practice my German phrase and call him a donkey but thought better of it.

I finally found some people heading that direction who were receptive to my plight. I waited around for three hours, reading my repair manual, making small talk with a few visitors, and trying not to blow my budget by eating my problems away as my battery was in the process of being charged. At least I hoped it was being charged. It was time to call the station. Over the next hour and a half, I must have called that place twenty different times, and found that no one was picking up the phone. My bad mood was increasing by the minute.

Finally, one of the station's attendants pulled up in his pickup truck with my battery in tow. I suddenly forgave the world at the sight of the electrical storage unit and installed the square box back under my seat. Bad mood over. After I pushed the starter button, the engine cranked slowly and then suddenly roared to life. It was obvious the battery was not charged to its potential. I prayed the bike's charging system was still working and that it would complete the process of charging the battery over the next hour. The whole ordeal cost me $20, and I was back on the road around 5:15 p.m.—a somewhat wasted afternoon, but when reflecting on how much worse the incident could have been, it suddenly didn't seem so bad.

I left Yellowstone through the northeast entrance and headed for Bear Tooth Pass, a route that several bikers had told me not to miss on this trip. As I left the park, I saw that the heat of the late afternoon had created massive, black thunderclouds all around me and faraway dark funnels of rain touched the ground in at least five different locations. *I'm going to get soaked*, I thought as my bike and I passed the "Thank you for visiting Yellowstone Park" sign.

As my ascent up Bear Tooth Pass began, the temperature started to plummet in direct relation to the increase in the wind's speed. So far, I had mercifully been bypassed by the various spigots of rain around me, but the chill of the air had forced me to don my black leather chaps and jacket all the same. I was also low on gas and was uncertain if there was even a gas station on this very remote road.

As I topped a mini-summit of the range, just before the pass really escalated into the heavens, I noticed an old gas station sitting alone on top of a small hill. I kept telling myself to be sure and not turn the bike off for fear that the battery would not have the juice to start her again. With the short time I had been riding plus the intense chilly weather, there would be good chance she wouldn't fire up. I pulled onto the gravel yard that would lead me to the pumps and slowly passed the owner chopping wood in the thirty-mile-per-hour icy wind. I pulled next to the pump marked "Supreme" and immediately turned the motor off. I'm an idiot.

As I pumped the obscenely expensive petrol into the tank, the owner ambled up and said, "You riding the pass?"

I made sure I didn't snicker at his hat with the ear coverings when I replied, "Sure am."

"You take it easy out there," he warned. "I've picked up a bunch of bikers like you off the cliffs." It seemed as if his concern was far more directed toward his inconvenience than toward my safety, and I simply told him he would have nothing to worry about. His condescending look was unmistakable, as if to say, "Yeah, I've heard that before."

Fortunately, my motorized buddy roared to life, and a wave of relief washed over me at knowing the alternator was at least doing its job.

It didn't take long before the massively curvy road began its steep climb toward the 10,947 foot summit. I was relishing this road as I would a fine wine as I negotiated hairpin turn after hairpin turn, slowly working my way upward, past the tree line and into a land which seemed barren and absent of living things, wondering when I would crest this bad boy...and hoping I never would. With each turn, I slowly rose above the majority of peaks all around me and consistently opened my mouth wide to force my ears to pop. Finally, I found myself at the pinnacle of this mini-adventure, the summit of Bear Tooth Pass. I couldn't believe it was July as the cold wind whipped through my hair and as my panoramic gaze picked up cold rocky peaks still heavily blanketed with snow. No cars, no people, just me and the sound of the wind blasting over the summit of this desolate yet beautiful place.

I sat on my bike a while, just experiencing the moment, and again consumed the scene around me. I wondered where I would be right now had I not made the decision to leave. Probably in an office, sweating out the next sale and looking forward to the weekend, wondering why I wasn't as happy as I should be. There, my soul was bound by time and schedules, but up here, the birds of the air had nothing over me. My soul seemed to float on the swirling wind, and I felt as if I could command its journey to any peak visible to me. Everyone should feel this way at least once in life. I will never forget it...and these moments were becoming more frequent.

My descent from the pass was as exhilarating as my recent ascent had been as I negotiated the tight hairpin curves with gravity now on my side, working the brake instead of the throttle. An hour later, I entered the limits of Red Lodge, another quaint small town like so many others I had passed through. It was getting late, and I grabbed a quick dinner in a local cafe whose walls were adorned with black-and-white photos of the real western days. Looking closely, I recognized the cafe's building in several of them. It hadn't changed much. It had been a long day, and the meat and potatoes I consumed quickly renewed my energy and motivation. I needed a place to sleep, and campgrounds would not be an option tonight. It was time to start roughing it!

The sun was low on the land as I rode the secluded back roads that took me from the Montana to Wyoming. My anxiety level was on the rise as I kept looking but just couldn't seem to find a safe place to pitch my tent. Finally, about twenty miles north of Cody, and with more than a little uncertainty on my part, I discovered a small dirt road off to my left that showed some potential. Although there were farmhouses and green pastures on the other side of the highway, the dirt path allowed me to camp behind a small hill, which protected me fairly well from the view of a few nearby ranches. My first squatter campsite.

Although I could see mountains in the distance to the west, my current location was fairly flat and my home would be located in a dry grassy bowl with desert-like bushes and weeds sporadically placed about. The brown landscape certainly was a poor replacement for the green, luxuriant mountain meadows I had witnessed over the past several days, but I was not to be choosy this night. I was happy for a place to sleep. I eagerly set up camp while sheepishly glancing over my shoulder, hoping nobody would discover my home before morning.

Once my homestead was fully constructed, my concerns began to melt away as the beautiful full moon slowly crested the hill to the east, kindly illuminating several deer prancing by in the distance. Any anxieties I held close were suddenly transformed to peacefulness as I realized how special these "free" camping spots had become to me, providing me with solitude and a sense of adventure that campgrounds could not fulfill. I sighed to myself as I realized this was the first full moon since Mono Lake. It had already been a month. Where had the time gone? I felt a slight tinge of pride in knowing I had made it this far, and I secretly wondered where I would be laying my head when I would gaze up at the next full moon.

Fortunately, my campsite went undetected throughout the night and my journey continued on through Cody, Wyoming, where I would consume my morning meal before continuing on toward my final day's destination of Sturgis, South Dakota, about 400 miles away. For the first time since Vancouver, I had someone to stay with planned.

I found a small family restaurant just down the street from the Buffalo Bill Museum in Cody and pulled in to one of the few available parking spaces. I was always intrigued by the different responses I would receive from the families parked around me as I entered the parking lots of these small family-type restaurants. Some would enter their cars by walking to the other side, away from the "bad man on the motorcycle", while others would strike up conversations or throw me a smile.

As I began to dismount, an older couple in their seventies walked toward me with such direct eye contact that it was obvious I was to be their point of destination. "Where ya going?" the old man asked with a hearty and strong voice.

"Just going," I replied, returning his gracious expression.

After I had provided him a little more information, his response was unexpected. "I have two boys," he said, "and I would give anything if they would do what you are doing. They're so blame busy with work and getting ahead, they don't know which end is up. What you're doing is a great thing. If you're ever in Tennessee, you look us up. You got a place to stay for as long as you want." With that, he handed over his business card, waved good-bye, and walked away. By the looks of it, his wife definitely did not share in his enthusiasm, but I thanked him all the same and appreciated how wonderfully this day was beginning. The friendliness of a stranger can do much to brighten one's outlook on life. I'd have to remember that.

Leaving Cody near the noon hour, someone had decided to turn the thermostat to the high position. The blistering 100-plus–degree heat soon forced me to trade my black leather vest and boots for a white tee shirt and tennis shoes. Normally, this would be tantamount to an act of treason, but being "cool" and being cooler were two very different things. I was dying.

I rode flat valleys and plains most of the morning and early afternoon, with little break from the constant heat bearing down upon me. Earlier in the trip, while checking the battery's water level, I had inadvertently twisted off the top of one of the fragile yellow plastic screws that secure the water in one of the battery's cell and needed a new one. Although not as handy as Bruce and Al, I had managed to find a stick that fit the hole quite nicely. It needed to be replaced. As I cruised along the Wyoming back roads, I noticed a sign to my left that read in large, hand-made black letters, "Motorcycle Salvage." I stuck my left hand out to let the driver behind me know of my intentions, and I made a lazy left-hand turn onto the gravel driveway. As I made my way toward the white ranch house, it became obvious that someone had simply collected a bunch of bikes, stacked them in their pasture, and decided to make a business out of it. Not a professional place, but they would surely have the part I was looking for. The man of the house and his two boys came out to greet me, and after exchanging pleasantries, he quickly retrieved the simple plastic screw from one of many old batteries stacked in the garage and handed it over, refusing my attempt to pay.

I immediately noticed his face reflected a dark bronze color, directly contrasting with his white shirtless body. This usually means only one thing. "Been riding?" I asked as I turned the new screw into the battery.

"Just got back from California yesterday," he replied. As it turned out, he had just toured the eastern Sierra range I love so much, and he quickly sang its magnificent beauty's praises.

"You're preaching to the choir on that one," I told him. I would guess the two boys were somewhere in the sixth grade or so. They couldn't stop looking at me with a kind of open-mouthed stare. In their eyes, I was some rugged biker whose home was the road and whose path they'd better not cross...or maybe I just really smelled bad. I don't know. Either way, I sure wasn't going to tell them I was an ex-computer software salesman.

After several more minutes of shooting the breeze, I found myself back on the road and again feeling very hot. Gazing ahead into the distance, I noticed a good-sized mountain range lazily waiting for my arrival, and I knew it would be on my agenda within the hour. I considered this very good news because the rise in elevation would surely give me a temporary reprieve from the scorching heat.

As I began to ascend the Powder River Pass in northeastern Wyoming, my wishes were indeed granted. The temperature dropped from 100 degrees to around 60 in a matter of minutes. The heat from the valley mixing with the cooler temperatures of the mountains had formed some nasty-looking thunderclouds, and I just knew I was not going to escape an unwanted cold shower this time. This would have been a fine idea on the valley floor only moments before but was not a welcome gift in these conditions. My fears were soon realized when the clouds opened up and poured out their watery load upon me.

I had chosen to wear my cloth skullcap in lieu of my helmet, and the combination of the cold air and rain inflicted an intense I-ate-the-ice-cream-too-fast headache that seemed to reach down into my shoes. The downpour was so intense that I could barely see each turn in front of me. At one point, I came treacherously close to missing a steep downhill hairpin turn when the slippery conditions did not allow me to apply all my available braking power and my downhill momentum carried me into the opposite lane, bringing me within a foot of hitting the guardrail on the opposite side. Luckily, no cars were coming from the other direction and I was spared a very nasty accident.

Once I was over the 9,666 foot pass, it took nearly an hour to descend the mountain in my wet and cold state, stopping every so often to warm up a bit. When I hit the valley on the eastern side of the range, it didn't take long for things to dry out as the valley's temperature quickly soared back to above 100 degrees. My body was not happy with these constant fluctuations in temperature, and I was hoping I wouldn't get sick.

Because it was getting so late, I made a rare exception and traded my cherished country road for the interstate. I needed to make my destination of Sturgis before nightfall. Three weeks later, this same small town would host over half a million Harleys at the famous Sturgis Rally, the largest of its kind in the United States. I would have loved to be part of this event but could not possibly rationalize spending three weeks in waiting.

My stay would be with a lady named Mickie whose phone number had been given to me by the same friend who had given me the name of Bruce in Washington. Both that friend and Bruce had stayed at Mickie's during previous Sturgis rallies, and she had agreed to put me up based solely on his reference. It would feel good to stay with a living, breathing person again.

After several hours of hard 70 mph driving, I exited the highway at the Sturgis off-ramp and pulled into a small grocery parking lot to call Mickie for directions. The friendly voice greeting me over the phone did much to ease my concerns that I was being intrusive. The underside of the sun was just beginning to touch the Earth's edge as I pulled onto the street whose name Mickie had given me over the phone. Six houses or so on the left, it sat. I just knew I had found it as I noticed no less than five people congregating at the front steps, intense in their discussions.

As I slowly leaned my bike into a tight U-turn to park in front of the older white one-story home, all eyes were upon me. I inched my bike backward until my rear tire rested against the street's curb. The turn of the key returned the neighborhood back to the quiet they had enjoyed before my rude interruption. Taking in my surroundings, I felt more like I was on a street in Lodi than in Sturgis. Older, simple homes lined the streets, each with its uncomplicated yard and unadorned porch. I expected to see Norman Rockwell any minute, busily at work with his brushes and easel, capturing a stellar yet everyday scene in Small Town, America. "Ya finally made it, huh?!" Mickie yelled from the porch as I stiffly pulled myself from my seat.

"Perfect directions," I shouted back, then slowly walked to the small gathering of people.

Mickie was probably five foot four, in her fifties, predominantly gray, and a bit on the stocky side. She had an air about her that let you know she didn't take any guff from anyone. I liked that. As tough as she appeared, however, she turned out to be equally caring and sweet, with a definite motherly side to her. I knew the second she opened her mouth, we were going to get along just fine. Her house doubled as a home for the elderly, and there was plenty of activity going on both outside and inside her place. As I had expected, we hit it off immediately.

Glenn was a very friendly sort who just happened to be passing through as he was returning from a trip to Colorado on his BMW motorcycle. He was a shorter, stocky man with young-looking features, his gray hair the only attribute giving away his true age. He was on his way home to Indiana and would be spending the night at Mickie's as well. This chance meeting proved valuable, as he would provide me a place to stay at his Indiana home a few weeks later.

Koreen was an attractive, shapely girl in her twenties who turned out to be Mickie's part-time assistant and had no trouble keeping her end of the conversation going. Glenn quickly offered me a not-so-cold beer out of his ice chest, and we spent the next few hours sitting on the old white wooden steps and talking about everything imaginable. After the many nights of solitude I had spent on the road, it felt good to talk with people again beyond shallow pleasantries.

Glenn had spent many years cruising on his bike alone, and his suggestions for creative sleeping locations intrigued me. I was still a little new to this game and appreciated any helpful advice. Even though Glenn was in his late forties or early fifties, he still slept on picnic tables, in RV parks, in city parks, or in or on whatever else he could find. "Tell you a little secret," he said in a lowered voice, as if somebody might be listening. "You enter a town, find a cop, and ask him where you can sleep for the night. They'll usually tell you of a place in the park or something and let you stay there as long as you are up and out early." His boyish smile reflected a sincerity and innocence that was engaging, and I found myself shaking my head in amazement at stories I would expect to hear from a risk-taking teenager rather than from a grandfather.

Glenn was truly an inspiration to me at this juncture of my ride, and he confirmed my own feelings that I would never let age or "maturity" slow my quest for adventure. Glenn was living proof that you can act like a kid at any age. We turned in around 12:30 in the morning, and the answer to my usual camping dilemma of finding a suitable location was an easy one this time, Mickie's front yard. I had covered a lot of miles that day and was ready for a good night's sleep.

I awoke uncharacteristically early the next morning as my dry lips smacked together, searching for any hint of moisture. As I traversed from deep sleep to reality, I soon realized that I was completely soaked and a bit on the sticky side. As I slowly moved my limbs within my sleeping bag, I quickly realized that the moisture was my own sweat. My humble abode had transformed itself into a self-contained sauna, and the fact that it was this hot at seven in the morning meant a blistering hot day ahead. Little did I know that this would be the beginning of an extended hot spell throughout the Midwest that would claim a number of lives.

I drug my sticky tail out of the tent, hopelessly searching for a breeze that wasn't there, and stiffly worked my way up the wooden stairs where we had visited late last night. Mickie had been up for a while and was busy running around doing chores. She pointed the way to the bathroom, and before long, I was the recipient of cool fresh water pouring over my face, wiping the sweaty slime from my body.

I treated Mickie and Glenn to breakfast that morning as a way of thanking them for their hospitality. Downtown Sturgis was only a half mile or so away, and the diner we chose in which to eat reminded me of a typical small-town cafe, complete with torn padded bench cushions and Formica tables. I fully expected our waitress to be called Flo and to yell to the cook over the counter, "Eggs down and dirty and slap a little pig on the side" or something like that. It was hard to believe that in only three weeks, this diner would be packed with hundreds of bikers.

We drove back to Mickie's home, where my bike sat packed and ready to go, anxious to discover what new adventures lay ahead that day. We took a few pictures for posterity, and I hugged Mickie good-bye, knowing I had made a great friend. "You're welcome here any time. You know that, don't you?" she said. I smiled and nodded. She had definitely made me feel that way. I told Glenn I would stop by if I were in the area, and with that, I roared down the small city street of Sturgis.

Before exiting the city's limits, however, I had a few errands to run. I had come to discover there were certain items I had brought on this trip that I was simply not using, and it just made no sense to haul this extra weight around. When I had left home, I had been confident I would be a regular Julia Child out in the woods, cooking everything from oatmeal to squirrel quiche. Well, the truth is, I'm too lazy to cook at home, and I was far too lazy to cook in the woods. The cooking utensils would have to go, along with a few other selected items. I ventured over to the post office and shipped home approximately seven pounds of the unneeded stuff. I then ventured over to the local civic center, got a quick workout in at the gym, and jumped back on the road.

Much of my ride this day would be within the boundaries of the famous Black Hills of South Dakota, a place chocked full of history. Where Indian treaties had been ignored and tribes had been ruthlessly slaughtered. Where gold fever had brought tens of thousands of men looking for that one rich vein and where Wild Bill Hickock had been killed while gambling in the town of Deadwood. I would also make it a point to visit the world-famous landmark of the Black Hills, Mount Rushmore, a place which I had viewed many a picture of since I was a little boy but had never had the chance to actually see in person. I always had a strong desire to witness this incredible monument and to see how a man's dream had been turned into reality. I had never expected to experience it while living a dream of my own. How fitting.

After an hour or so, I could see the sign that let me know I would soon be entering the Black Hills National Park. This would be another needed photo opportunity. I was a member of the Harley Owners Group, or HOG, which is an international club of Harley enthusiasts. Membership to this organization provides several benefits, including the ability to join local HOG chapters, purchase cheaper insurance, a great traveling atlas with great information needed by a biker, and much more. The group published a monthly magazine called *Hog Tales*.

Hog Tales provided a little challenge to those who wanted to travel. They set up 12 destinations around the country, and, depending on how many of those places you could prove you had visited in a twelve-month period, you would be awarded touring pins for your vest or jacket. The way you normally proved you had been there was to take a picture of you, your bike, and a current issue of HOG magazine. Well, the Black Hills was one of those destinations. I pulled my scoot next to the Black Hills park sign, snagged an unaware tourist nearby, and had them snap my picture. One more off the list.

Unfortunately, I had gotten a very late start on the day, and it was taking much more time to reach Mount Rushmore than I had originally intended. To add to the delay, my "enjoy the journey" philosophy had completely kicked in, and I decided to take a scenic route in lieu of the direct path to the famous mountain. The decision was not necessarily a bad one, but it did turn out to be incredibly slow. After a few hours of sub-30 mph speeds due to a combination of slow-moving vehicles and tight turns, I could feel a hint of stress entering my life, an emotion I had not experienced for some time now. I knew I needed to make up some time because I really wanted to reach the South Dakota prairie by nightfall.

It was midafternoon when I finally realized my primary goal for the day and entered the Mount Rushmore parking lot, obeying the parking attendant's gestures as he pointed me toward my parking place. Before coming to a complete stop, I glanced upward and sneaked a peak at the majestic mountaintop, which now loomed above the visitor's center. I must say, any pressure and stress I had been experiencing melted away as I marveled at the masterpiece before me.

I placed my padlock through the holes of the bike's steering column and could only hope that no one would help themselves to my gear as it innocently sat on my seat and rear rack with no way to adequately protect its contents from a dishonest soul. It was times like this when I had to place my trust solely in the goodness of mankind.

I made my way up the procession of cement steps that transported me from the parking lot to the large visitors' center, which partially blocked the base of the mountain but did not completely obstruct the rocky faces, which were partially visible through the trees. With every step, the rocky faces in the distance seemed to grow a little larger and more real. I took advantage of the visitors' center and read the history of this magnificent piece of work while scanning through photographs that chronicled the slow transformation of rock to human form.

I meandered through the various gift shops, amazed at the number of ways people could make money off Mount Rushmore paraphernalia. After passing up the strong desire to purchase a Mount Rushmore ashtray, I headed toward the viewing area to witness this site firsthand. About one hundred yards later, I was standing with an unobstructed view of the mountain whose pictures I had seen for so many years. Its grandeur was humbling. I had read that the presidents' pupils, within the eyes, actually consisted of long and narrow cylindrical pieces of rock, purposely giving the viewer the feeling that the stony faces were looking directly at them, no matter where they stood. It worked.

I really had no lofty expectations of being overly affected by this attraction. I had figured it would be one of those things that were "kind of neat to see." But my ride thus far had probably placed me in a much more introspective state than usual. I tried to look beyond the finished product and imagine the setbacks and obstacles that Gutzon Borglum, the creator, had endured during his fourteen-year creation. I had read how his idea at first had been met with skepticism and downright hostility. He had waged a "one man war" in raising hard-to-find funds during the depression years. In fact, only six and a half years had been spent on actual sculpting; the rest had been spent on fundraising.

As I descended the steps to the parking lot, my eyes searched for my red companion, and I was relieved to see that my equipment was all present and accounted for. This was always an anxiety-ridden ritual, as I would hold my breath, praying all would be as I had left it. As I departed the Mount Rushmore parking lot, I unknowingly took a wrong turn and suddenly found myself behind a string of very slow motor homes with nowhere to pass. The temperature had passed the century mark by now, and the lack of wind was not helping my severe overheating condition. I was getting miserable fast, and my introspective nirvana had been replaced with ugly old grumpiness. I actually found myself looking forward to the long straight roads of the prairie. I needed wind. After about an hour of 20 mph speeds, I finally was successful in passing the long procession of vehicles. When looking to my left, I noticed, through the trees…Mount Rushmore! I had driven in a giant circle! I was now officially in the worst mood since my trip began.

I not so gingerly pulled the map out from the red cargo netting, put myself on the correct path, and, two hours later, finally left Black Hills National Park, descending its eastern slopes onto the open prairie of South Dakota. The lack of any elevation made the heat even more stifling, and I was thankful for the 60 mph wind now doing its best to defray the blistering warmth. I had once again traded my black biker boots and vest for tennis shoes and a white tee shirt, and the straight two-lane road stretched out before me for what seemed to be an infinite distance. Mountain riding would not again be on the agenda until New York…a sad thought.

After forty-five minutes of cruising, it was time to find a place to lay my head for the night. I had perhaps an hour of sunlight left. The prairie was beautiful in its own way, with infrequent small rolling, tall, grassy covered hills that seemed to appear just often enough to successfully break up the monotony. Glancing to my right, my eyes picked up a small dirt road that disappeared over one of those little grassy mounds. It was probably private property, but no fence was in sight. I slowly made the transition from blacktop to dirt and carefully crept over the rough and bumpy path. The first hill offered perfect protection from the road to the north, and a second hill provided protection from some fields that were being farmed to the south. I was fairly confident that the little depression I found myself in would suffice in keeping me from being discovered for the night.

With the turn of the key, everything became amazingly silent. I always felt a bit lonely when I found myself in such a secluded place, when quiet would so abruptly fill my ears. Lonely, but invigorating all at once. The prairie mosquitoes were partying hearty and were out in great numbers as I began to unload my supplies. I was beginning to hate them even more than usual, especially because I was still scratching old bites I had received from my previous nights in Canada.

I finished setting up my tent and was preparing myself for the dreaded ritual of blowing up my air mattress when I realized that I had left the mattress
plug on Mickie's front lawn in Sturgis. This day was just not going according
to plan. The thought of sleeping on hard, rocky dirt was not a pleasant one,
and I really needed a good night's sleep that night.

Hey, I'm resourceful, I thought. *I'll figure something out.* I believe this was
the point of the journey when I was actually starting to believe the illusions I
had been creating over the past month...or were they illusions? Hey, perhaps
not. After all, I had survived a little more than a month on the road and I
hadn't turned around when things had gotten a little tough like the Alaskan
man I had met that first day. Perhaps my illusions were slowly being transformed into reality.

As I realized what I had accomplished so far, I began to feel a wall of confidence build within me. I was conquering little problems daily, and each time
I made it through, I felt a little bit better about myself and my abilities. I have
always had a tendency to focus on my faults and ignore my successes, no matter how small they might be. Self-assurance has a difficult time finding a
home when we concentrate on only our failures. I began to realize how vitally
important it is to recognize my accomplishments, to give myself some credit
when due, so that confidence may be nurtured within while keeping pride at
bay. I had always struggled with confidence in the past, and self-doubt had
seemed to be more of a steady and willing companion.

This revelation alone was worth the price of the ticket. Facing my fears was
the only way I could help eliminate the self-doubt that seemed to plague me
daily. I had to be willing to change. As I thought about this, I asked myself,
"So why didn't I do something like this sooner? Why didn't I challenge myself
before this ride?"

I was once told at a seminar that many of the decisions we make in our lives
are, in fact, not made by us but by the programs we have grown up with. When
faced with a challenging task or decision, we often and immediately respond in
the negative. "We could never do that," we automatically say to ourselves as we
pass on yet another possible opportunity to grow. Something or someone has
programmed us to react this way, and we mindlessly succumb to those events as
if that is the normal thing to do. It isn't. We risk living our lives on automatic
pilot, with little input from ourselves, allowing others to control our des-
tinies...driving the interstates of life, afraid to take the side roads.

My ultimate challenge was to change my programming, my inward thinking, and break out of the comfortable box I had been living in all my life. I

wanted my life to be the center of a circle with no circumference. No self-imposed boundaries to limit my potential. It was becoming clear that the boundaries that now surrounded me were there because I had placed them there or had allowed someone else to place them there.

Well, here I was in the prairie with one of those little dilemmas. It was time to test my creativity. What would Al do in this situation? Probably build a new air mattress from tree bark. No, I needed something a little simpler. If I could only find a cylindrical section of timber that would be directly proportional to the air mattress orifice. Yes, I needed to find a stick that would fit. Okay, so this dilemma wasn't that challenging. However, surveying the dry, grassy prairie around me, I saw there was not a stick to be found that would solve the problem. I placed my hand on my forehead to shade my eyes from the setting sun and scanned my surroundings for answers. The only trees I could see were those by a creek about a mile off. Well, a man's gotta do what a man's gotta do.

I grabbed my knife and, in my best Daniel Boone imitation, trekked through the knee-high grass and weeds while constantly shooing mosquitoes away from my sweaty body. I could tell I was nearing the creek, as the rancid and disgusting smell provided me with plenty of warning. The water was low and unmoving, and the thick brush and trees crowding its banks provided a perfect habitat for trillions of insects who were relishing the high heat and humidity. I found some low-hanging branches of a tree and quickly cut off four twigs of varying thickness, hoping one would be the right size.

I triumphantly returned to base camp with my spoils and tried each twig, hoping for a perfect fit. I was getting a little nervous as the first three candidates fell short, but fortunately, the last twig I had cut fit the hole fairly well. I blew the mattress up and twisted the branch into the hole, and to my relief, the air seemed to be holding. I poured water over the makeshift plug, hoping it would expand the wood just enough for an airtight fit. My two-mile, insect-infested walk now seemed well worth the effort.

Earlier, as I had set up my tent, I had personally guaranteed myself a mosquito-free night by being extremely careful to not let any of the torturing insects enter as I placed my possessions inside. The process was a simple one: open the flap, throw my stuff in, and immediately zip up the mesh door. As night would overtake the prairie of South Dakota, I would fall asleep secure in the fact that all the little blood-sucking varmints were outside gazing in, thinking of what might have been.

The air was heavily laden with moisture and heat as darkness fell, and falling asleep was becoming a serious challenge, one I had not experienced in the past month. The heat forced me to lie atop my sleeping bag wearing nothing but my underwear. It was stifling. After an hour or so of tossing and turning, my eyes eventually grew heavy and rest overtook my tired body. Yes, it would be a gentle night of dreams and utter peace.

Then it happened! I was awakened at 2:00 a.m. by the worst sound any human being can hear during complacent slumber—the buzzing of a mosquito in the ear that rivaled any F-18 fighter jet! As the numbness of sleep began to leave me, I began to feel an intense itching sensation...and not just in one place. A mixture of fear and anger began to invade my once-tranquil world as I slowly reached down and began to feel numerous, huge swellings all over my body. I had been an unknowing human smorgasbord for the past few hours. I was furious!

I ripped open the door to the tent in a frenetic and out-of-control fashion while talking very loudly to...nobody. I tore open the right saddlebag cover on the bike, thoughtlessly threw out those innocent items that found themselves perched on top of the flashlight, and raced back into my tent, cursing the flying leeches. I flicked on the light and saw not one but SIX fat mosquitoes sitting on the roof of my tent, gorged with my blood.

Events from this point on are a bit hazy. I believe I actually left my body for a time as I embarked on a murderous rampage of meticulously popping each insect with my finger, making a nice little red circular stain on the white mesh fabric that made up the ceiling to my tent, forever reminding me of the bloody battle that took place that night. I tried to fall back asleep, but the constant itching all over my body was almost too much to bear. I finally managed to doze off around 4:00 a.m. but was suddenly awakened by a loud clap of thunder followed, almost immediately, by a bright flash of lightning. Soon, I heard the familiar sound of rain pellets hitting the tent. I had been tempted to forego putting up the rain fly when setting up camp because the sky had been absent of any clouds at the time, but my Kalispell lesson had been a strong one, and I had put the rain fly on regardless of current conditions. I was glad I had.

Sleep was neither sound nor plentiful that night, and I awoke just a tad on the cantankerous side. I was hoping the previous night's events had all been part of a horrible dream, but the lumps on my legs and chest along with the blood stains above confirmed that it had not been a subconscious battle. This day would turn out to be the hottest of the entire ride. It was before 8:00 a.m., and the temperature was already nearing the mid-80s. Before the day would end, the mercury would hit 110 degrees in the shade with high humidity. I also realized the riding that day would not exactly provide extreme excitement because the road I would be traveling would be straighter than a Baptist minister. Oh well, time to pack up. The mosquitoes seemed bent on revenge for the ruthless killings the night previous, and they took great delight in performing fly-bys in my ear and watching me slap myself into oblivion while stuffing my gear into bags and strapping them on my bike. Get me out of here!

It felt great to have wind in my face again as I accelerated to a steady pace of 60 mph. I hadn't showered in more than 36 hours and I was feeling pretty ripe. When cars stop tailgating you, you know it's time for a cleaning. Late that morning, I ventured into a small Indian town called Pine Ridge and decided to take Glenn's advice and ask a policeman where I might find a shower. He looked at me with a very inquisitive look, and I couldn't tell if he was put out with me, was not in the mood, or thought it was a stupid request. Probably all three. He pointed to a large square brick building up on a hill. "Try that" he said.

"What is it?" I asked. He mumbled something about a hospital, police station, or something. I really didn't feel like asking him again, so I decided to give it a shot. I was still a little new at this "bathing on the road" thing.

I found a vacant parking place out front and pulled on the glass door that looked as if it hadn't been cleaned in forty years. No reception area, just a hallway. I was feeling a little uncomfortable. I soon found myself aimlessly wandering down one of the white-walled halls in search of water. I felt like an idiot when I stuck my head into one of the offices and asked if I could take a shower somewhere. A man and a woman looked up at me with an expression that seemed to say, "What kind of a loser would come into this building and ask for a shower?" After I had informed them of my police friend's advice, the nice lady graciously took me around to the police station portion of the building and showed me the men's locker-room door. This was now becoming *very* uncomfortable. I really didn't feel at ease showering with the local cops. As it turned out, both showers were out of order. "Thanks anyway," I said, grateful for an excuse to leave. As I walked out onto the blazing parking lot, I rationalized that I stunk so bad at this point, eight more hours wouldn't make a huge difference anyway. My shower finding technique definitely needed work.

I hit the blistering asphalt once again, looking forward to getting a cheap motel at the end of the day. There was no way I could sleep in a tent again. I decided to pace myself and rode an hour at a time, pulling off for a half hour or so to let my body and bike rest in a shaded area somewhere. I had no desire to be stranded on the road in these conditions.

Around 4:00 p.m., I was crossing the Missouri River and noticed a cattle truck coming at me from the opposite direction. I was so hot. Soon after the truck passed, however, I suddenly felt a cool mist hit me that at first felt refreshing. At this point, anything wet felt refreshing. My "sharp" intellect quickly wrested control from the emotions department as I looked into the sky and confirmed my suspicions. No clouds. Reality began to set in as I looked at my small windshield and viewed a multitude of sporadically distributed brown splotches over it that had definitely not been present a minute before. I slowly lifted my left hand to my nose, smelled my fist, and, with a frown of disgust, realized I had just been showered by cow crap and pee. How low can you go?

I immediately shot a piercing gaze over my left shoulder at the truck, which was slowly fading from view, and I swore I saw two cows high-fiving each other. I was thoroughly disgusted with myself and immediately found a motel room in Pickstown, South Dakota, for twenty bucks. The lady at the front desk was a sweet, frail, old woman who was extremely pleasant when she asked me how I was this day. My reply came quickly and without emotion. "How's my day? I'm on a motorcycle, I haven't showered for two days, it's one hundred ten degrees out, I'm full of mosquito bites, and a cow just dumped on me."

I could tell she was holding her laughter in a bit as she smiled and said mat-ter-of-factly, "Sounds like you might like to take a shower." I complimented her on her perceptiveness.

The twenty-dollar room was gloriously cool, and the shower was as close to a spiritual experience as any earthly thing could be. It felt good to lie in a bed that I didn't have to blow up, and I realized I had actually missed watching television. I spent the evening just relaxing, wrote some letters, and simply enjoyed not being miserably hot. I slept like a baby.

The morning came much too quickly, and starting my day seemed to require much more discipline than usual. I rode to Sioux Falls, where I per-formed my ritualistic oil and filter change at the local Harley dealer's store. The rest of the day's riding was uneventful and straight. It was still unbearably hot, so I conceded once again and rented another cheap motel room in Spencer, Iowa. At $20 a night, I couldn't go wrong.

The next day would be an interesting day. I would be visiting distant fam-ily—uncles, aunts, and cousins, many of whom I hadn't seen for twenty-five years or hadn't met at all. I was nervous. After being on my own for so long, could I slow myself down enough to enjoy kicking back and just talking for several days? How would they react to me? Would I spend the entire time searching for things to discuss? I just didn't know what to expect. It wouldn't be so bad if I had someone else to keep the conversation going, but the emphasis would be on me, and I knew I would have to carry the load. A part of me wanted to ignore this portion of the ride, to continue on, make time, and see new things, but I knew that was really not an option. This was important. This journey was exposing all kinds of new frontiers; until now, I had not thought of family as falling into this category, but I guess they did.

I was about to challenge myself once again.

Glacier Park

Yellowstone Grand Canyon

Bear Tooth Pass in July

Be vewy vewy quiet - House over the hill

Hidden campsite in Wyoming

Mickie & Glenn in Sturgis

Downtown Sturgis - 2 weeks before the annual rally

Breathtaking - Always wanted to see this

Not your typical Southern California traffic jam

South Dakota prairie - Infamous mosquitoe battle

CHAPTER 5

Nothing Like Family

I slowly rolled to my back as my eyes began the reluctant process of letting the morning's light invade my once-dark domain. A few blinks later, with my chin resting on my chest, I found myself focusing on the tawdry yellow and red rose pattern that was embroidered on my bed covers. Why must all cheap motel linens utilize ugly floral patterns? I tossed the covers aside, lazily swung my legs out from beneath the sheets, and staggered toward the window to make certain my transportation was in the place I had left it the night before. Still there. A smile quickly came to my face, as I had forgotten how good she looked. I had taken her to the car wash the night before and spent some quality time shining her up. It had been a while. The beautiful vision before me immediately kick-started my adrenal glands and flooded my body with an awakening unmatched by the strongest of coffees.

My swelling enthusiasm soon waned, however, as my day's agenda came to mind. This was family day, the first day of seven when riding the open roads and experiencing new lands and adventures would be replaced by the quiet interaction with distant family. The loud and rhythmic rumble of my 1340 cc engine would soon be replaced with talking and sharing...and mostly with people much older than myself. I couldn't immediately recall watching any episodes of *Renegade* or *Easy Rider* where they sat around a country dining table and talked about...well, whatever distant family members talk about. I'm ashamed to say that the thought of the next week made me feel a bit dispirited.

Don't get me wrong, it's not that I am anti-family. In fact, I have always placed a strong emphasis on the importance of immediate family and on how the foundational love and support I received throughout my growing years had much to do with the person I have become. I am a firm believer that if a home provides strong family values, regardless of the family's economic level, the odds of raising upright and responsible members of society are so increased that many of our social ills would be drastically reduced...without the need for government programs or psychiatrist sessions.

Even though I have always held these views close to my heart, however, I did not seem to practice what I preached when it came to my more distant relatives. My mother had tried for years to interest me in the lives of our family who lived in the Midwest, but I had exhibited only moderate regard for what they were doing, and for the most part, they were simply familiar-sounding names. I was just too busy living life in my world to invest the energy in learning about people I would probably never meet anyway...no immediate benefit. What shallow thinking. I was not only brushing aside the lives of people who were of my blood but also ignoring a place from which I had come, ignoring my roots, forgetting those who, in some cases, were indirectly responsible for my existence on this earth...out of sight, out of mind.

There was also one heck of an age gap. Because my unplanned entry into this world came late in my mother's life, most of my cousins are around fifteen years older than me and all of my aunts and uncles are in their seventies and eighties. As I began to get dressed in my swank motel room, I began asking myself, "What the heck am I going to do with these people?" I thought back and strained to remember what they looked like, thinking back to a time they had visited us in Lodi many years before. I remembered bits and pieces, but it was a time when Mom and Dad had been responsible for the ongoing conversations and all I'd had to do was make my guest appearance, smile big, make a few witty remarks, and exit stage left. This time it would be up to me to keep the old tongue wagging.

My first family stop of the week would be the town where my mother and her three sisters were born and raised: Elgin, Iowa, population under 1,000. The last time I had been in this town, I had been about nine years old and on my way to the famous Hodel reunion in Quincy, Illinois. All I remember of my stay in Elgin was shooting a sparrow at my uncle's farm with my brand-new BB gun and proudly showing my uncle my recent kill, expecting high praise for my marksmanship. Instead, what I believe he said was, "Now what did that little sparrow do to you?" Ouch. No wonder I hadn't been able to shoot that .38-caliber gun—repressed sparrow guilt.

At about nine in the morning, the temperature had already climbed close to ninety. After five minutes of strategic bungee wrapping, my cargo was in place and I was ready to roll. I had spoken to two of my mother's sisters the night before, Aunt Margaret and Aunt Millie, and made sure they knew I was coming. My first stop would be with Aunt Millie, Uncle Paul, and their son Tim. I wolfed down some eggs and sausage at the local Spencer Diner and hit the road around ten.

As I cruised through one small farm town after another, three things became very evident about the Midwest: cheap gas, cheap motels, and the friendliest people I've ever met. On my way to Elgin that day, I must have experienced fifteen people waving at me from their cars going the other direction. Similar scenes had taken place over the past two days. Of course, this was nothing new to me, being from Southern California and all. People would wave all the time...just not with the whole hand. It felt good to wave back at the locals, and I am sure my two-wheeled motorhome was a welcome change of pace from the John Deere variety of transportation they were used to seeing. It's funny, it seems like any time you lift your hand to a stranger, a smile involuntarily comes to your face. We should try that more often.

At around two that afternoon, I passed the sign that let me know I was entering the town of Elgin, and a nervousness began to creep up within me. *Here goes,* I thought as I pulled a sheet of paper from my vest pocket to glance at the directions written down the night before. I received more than my share of stares from the townspeople as I loudly putted through their downtown area wearing my black Harley garb. It was funny how nobody was waving at me once I was going under fifty miles per hour.

I hadn't really thought about it until now, but wondered how my own family would receive this tattooed, shaggy-haired, goateed family traveler. Unbeknownst to me, I later found out that my mother had been busy the previous few weeks warning the family of what her wayward son may potentially look like at this point of the trip and had been diplomatically apologizing in advance for anyone I might offend. She had done such a fine job of setting negative expectations that I am sure they envisioned someone just short of Charles Manson.

Somehow, I had managed to screw up the directions and found that I was lost in Elgin, which is pretty hard to do. Millie and Paul's last name is Butikofer. I figured with a name like that, it would not be a difficult chore to ask someone if they knew of a Butikofer in town and find who I needed. How many could there be? While trying to find my way, I had passed a downtown warehouse about five times and finally pulled up to an old feller loading up his truck with some farming supplies. He was probably in his sixties, a bit on the skinny side, with hardened wrinkles dug deep in his face from many years in the flatland sun. Everyone in the Midwest seems to wear a baseball cap with some kind of wording associated with seed, and he fit the role to a tee.

He looked at me with a suspicious eye as I pulled alongside to ask directions. He slowly walked my direction after my motor was shut down to signal my desire to talk to him. "Do you know a Paul and Millie?" I asked.

"What's their last name?" he asked with a hint of suspicion.

"Butikofer," I stated.

He gave me one of those squinty, bordering-on-disgusted looks and said, "You gotta be more specific than that son."

"There's more than one Butikofer?" I asked incredulously.

"Nothing but Butikofers around here," he fired back, tiring of this useless conversation. After I mentioned that Paul used to be an Apostolic Church pastor, we finally narrowed it down, and within three minutes, their house was in sight.

The neighborhood was simple Small Town, USA, all the way. Millie and Paul's house was a single-story, blue-paneled home with white shutters and tightly trimmed hedges out front just high enough to touch the bottom sill of the large family-room window. It was just as I had expected it to look. They must have heard me coming a good thirty seconds before I pulled in, because there they were, standing in the driveway, awaiting their nephew from the west.

Uncle Paul is one of those men who always seems to be smiling, and you just know he would never hurt a fly (definitely not a sparrow). You can't help but want to hug the guy. He stood probably five foot eight and was more slight of build than thin. His large wire-rimmed glasses lay lightly on his nose, and his thinning gray hair smartly accented the gentle face that lay beneath. His wide smile quickly displayed the years of dental work he had experienced, reflecting the days when taking care of the problem had been more important than making it look good.

Millie had not changed much from what I remembered. She had my mom's round face and build, and her abundance of gray hair was pulled up into a bun, which is the way the Apostolic women wear it. She reminded me a lot of my own mother. Before I knew it, the nervousness had disappeared. I was home.

I turned the key to the off position, stiffly dismounted, and opened my arms wide to receive the first of my distant family. As I hugged my aunt, it was the first time I had felt truly safe since my journey had begun. I hadn't expected that. We walked inside their small country home and began to talk about my ride, what they had been doing, and the town of Elgin. Their son Tim was also coming over for a visit. He lived just a few houses down.

Millie had a great sense of humor and was as sharp as anyone I've met. I felt myself opening up, and we shared with each other about family and life, and every once in a while, loud laughter would permeate the room. It didn't take long to realize that the conversation was not only not lacking but thriving. They seemed genuinely interested in who I was and what I was doing, and in turn, I became more interested in them. Tim showed up an hour or so later. His appearance had not changed from when he had visited me in Southern California a few years earlier. Tim was a definite doer, and, in my mind, bordering on the line of being a workaholic. He maintained several businesses, including selling seed to farmers and leasing dairy cows, the latter of which still sounds really funny to a Southern California boy. I keep picturing a Hertz rental car lot where new Ford Escorts are replaced with Jersey cows waiting for a renter to come by and milk them.

Tim's wife, Kathy, met us at Tim's office later in the day, as did his two beautiful daughters, Amy and Meg, both in their teens. Both girls had long dark hair and olive skin and would cause any boy their age to look twice. This family and several of my relatives had been raised in the Apostolic Church, which had a more legalistic approach to the Christian faith. Women didn't wear jewelry, traditional women wore their hair in buns, television was absent from the home, and many marriages were arranged by the elders. Although I have some disagreements with this view, every person I met was high caliber.

It was a Friday night, and the girls were going out on the town with friends. They politely offered to have me join them later, and although I was tempted to say yes, I quickly remembered what I had thought of thirty-something people when I was their age. I could just imagine all their friends staring at the guy who was going through his midlife crisis. It would be far safer and emotionally beneficial to stay with the old people.

After returning to Paul and Millie's home, I awaited the next item on the agenda, praying it would have the word "food" in it somewhere. I was starving. Aunt Millie, sensing my need for nourishment, glanced my way and said somewhat excitedly, "We decided to treat you to pizza tonight!" Her eyes were wide in anticipation of my response.

I stared at her, put on a little show of frustration, and, while rolling my eyes, said in a discontented voice, "I have been traveling the hot and dusty roads of this great land for four weeks, eating at greasy spoons and filling myself with ninety-nine–cent Whoppers, dreaming of the day I can eat an incredible home-cooked meal at my aunt's house, and you're taking me out for a pizza?" I stared at her, knowing she would regain her senses and exit to the kitchen.

Never losing her original expression, and without skipping a beat, she said, "Yup." Guess I was eating pizza.

Of course I couldn't let her forget this little event, and it turned out to be an ongoing joke that night and for the rest of my trip. On the way to the pizza parlor, Tim mentioned that some friends of his had erected multiple storage units in the local area and that he should probably help them out by giving them some business. I quickly suggested they place Millie's kitchen in there because she obviously didn't use it anyway. Throughout the next week as I visited other aunts and uncles, I would make it a point to snap little pictures of the many plates of home-cooked food they provided me and to send Aunt Millie a copy. I figured these helpful photos could act as a guide for the next time a long-lost relative would visit so she would not make the same mistake again. She was a good sport about it, and it should be noted that she did provide me some wonderful home cooking the next morning and that evening. Guilt can be a wonderful tool sometimes.

Saturday provided an unbelievable coincidence that turned out to be one of the most special days of my journey—an unexpected inward road that would transport me to some very deep feelings...down to my very soul. Paul informed me that the lady who had been living in the house where my mother had been born and raised could no longer manage the place herself. She was selling the house and her possessions through a public auction, to be held...that day. This house had never been opened up like this to the public in any of its eighty-plus years of existence, and here on the day I showed up, I had free reign to walk around. The lottery should give me such luck.

Paul, Millie, and I piled into their car, and soon, we made the transition from pavement to dirt road, cruising through the small rolling green hills of Iowa. I didn't realize that any part of Iowa would include hills, or forests, or streams and lakes, but this area had all of the above. *What a great place to grow up*, I thought as I imagined my mother frolicking through the knee-high grass as a little girl. I found out that many immigrants from Switzerland had migrated to this area in the 1800s, as it reminded them of their homeland.

After ten minutes or so, we pulled onto a tiny dirt road where old pickup trucks and cars were parked haphazardly along the side of the road, allowing just enough room to drive by. Off in the distance I could hear the amplified voice of the auctioneer selling everything from old rusty tools to a Model T Ford. At the center of the commotion stood an old two-story white house that was about as plain as a house could get. But this particular head was turning as Paul turned the wheel to the right, gradually bringing us to rest at the side of the road, keeping company with the many American-made vehicles already there.

The three of us began our walk toward the house, and the volume of the auctioneer's oratorical chants began to rise. I walked passed the group of farmers bidding on an old plow and found myself facing the door that provided entrance to the kitchen. Off to my left stood a large red barn that had certainly seen better days. The roof was sloping inward, and the barn seemed to lean a bit to the left. Wood planks were missing in various places, and the smell of musty hay permeated the area.

The cement walkway to the kitchen door was uneven and cracked from years of tree roots working their way underground to trip the next unwary visitor. Off to the left was an old horse trough where my Aunt Rose had nearly drowned as a child. In the foreground was the clothesline where Aunt Rose had nearly decapitated herself as a little girl, running recklessly and obviously, blindly. Rose is Mom's older sister, and because of a serious infection in her early teens, she was not expected to live to see twenty. Rose passed away in 2003 at 88 years old. I don't think she got the memo.

It seemed a bit surreal that I was now standing in the place my mother had stood hundreds of times. I could almost picture her little feet running over the walkway as her mother yelled, "Dinner's ready!" or "You get in here right now!"

I think Millie sensed my nostalgic wanderings and with a smile said, "Let's go inside." The kitchen was a step back in time—small, with the old-style green Formica tops and gas-top stove with three burners. It was very tiny compared with today's kitchens.

We ventured from room to room as Millie shared tidbits of what had gone on here and there decades before. The unusually narrow stairs leading upstairs were off limits to visitors, but Millie and I quickly rationalized that we indeed, were no common visitors and justified our trespass as we climbed the very steep stairway to the second floor. I soon found myself gazing upon the room where my mother had played and slept as a little child more than seventy years before. The stories flowed from Millie's lips, and I took them in as a thirsty man would a cool glass of water.

On our way out the back door, Millie pointed out the original outhouse they had used as children, and I learned just how important the Sears catalog was in that day, if you know what I mean. The green rolling hills speckled with forested trees provided the perfect backdrop to the drooping barn where my mom had milked cows in the morning. I stepped back in time as my imagination took over and transported me to another era, to see another generation when families had had to be tough to survive the harsh winters and the pressures of keeping a farm alive and a family fed from season to season.

I began to gain a new appreciation for my parents and where they had come from. To be standing in the place where my mother had once crawled as a baby made her more real to me, more human, perhaps. I had never thought of her as an infant, as a person who had grown up with daily chores, or as a young woman learning about life on a small Iowa farm. I was touching a place that had only been described to me by limited words in the past...words that had meant little but now meant everything. The little girl who had used a Sears catalog in the outhouse had grown to be a woman and one day given me life.

For me to be here on the same day as this auction seemed much less a coincidence now. I felt as if God had allowed this divine timing to take place so I may be taught a valuable lesson regarding family. Family is incredibly important, yet I had treated it with indifference and cast it aside as I would a gum wrapper. Coming face to face with this realization opened my eyes to a place within me I had kept unintentionally darkened. Another inward road discovered. I had been in Elgin for only twenty-four hours, yet I had already learned so much. My hunger for my past had been awakened, and my appetite began to grow.

Suddenly, I wanted to see everything. Paul showed me the grave of my grandfather, a man I had never met but who had been the relative for whom I had been named. He had died in the 1918 flu epidemic when my mother was only six weeks old, and my grandmother had suddenly been abandoned on an Iowa farm with four children. Her father had come to help but had soon died of an illness as well. I can hardly imagine the struggles my grandmother had had to overcome to survive such a tough time in life.

That afternoon, we returned to Paul and Millie's home. Tim was already there waiting for us. I asked him if he wanted to take the bike for a ride, and after a very slight hesitation, he agreed. He mounted the heavy Big Twin with surprising confidence and quickly accelerated my pride and joy beyond earshot. After about ten minutes, he returned with a wide smile on his face and proceeded to take his daughters out for a ride of their own. I later discovered the reason for his slight hesitancy.

Tim had ridden bikes since he was fourteen years old and had probably spent up to ten months out of the year on his two-wheeled friends. He loved motorcycles. Tony had been his best friend in the world, and they would do everything together, including riding bikes. Tim told me that they were so close, the one friend would know what the other was thinking before he said it.

When Tony was 18 and Tim was 20, Tony had stopped by Tim's place and told him he was going to town to wash his bike. Tim had told Tony he would meet him there and that he would leave in a few minutes. Tony had nodded and headed off to town. Tim was soon on the road, and not a few miles later, he noticed several cars pulled off to the shoulder. To his horror, he had seen the bent and broken motorcycle that was Tony's. Tony had passed a car on the left just as the car was turning into a driveway. Tony had died that day and Tim hadn't ridden a motorcycle since.

My Harley was the first bike he had ridden in twenty-four years. I guess he felt it was time to let go of the old emotions and enjoy the things he loved. The smile on his face told me volumes, and I knew he missed that feeling. Maybe my bike did a little healing that day, I don't know.

As the end of the day approached, I was pretty mentally drained. Nothing that morning could have prepared me for what I had experienced. I had truly and literally touched my past. I also couldn't help but feel a slight sense of accomplishment that I had successfully interacted with my family on my own merits. I did not have to rely on others to keep the conversation crisp, ask the probing questions, or give the right answers. It was just them and me, and it had not been hard at all. I had learned more about me by learning more about them. The fear of a communication gap between seventy-year-olds and this thirty-four-year-old was no longer a concern. There was no gap.

It was difficult leaving the following day, but I had a date with Uncle Mark and Aunt Margaret, another one of my mother's sisters, Millie's twin. Mark and Margaret lived in Wapello, Missouri, which only required about a four-hour ride. I reluctantly left the little town of Elgin around noon, a different person than the one who had entered it thirty-six hours earlier. Until now, Elgin had only been the name of a town somewhere in the Midwest to me. Now it was a place with real people, real family, and real love.

Aunt Margaret's daughter Beverly was planning to have dinner for us around six, so when I got a bit lost on the country back roads, I was a little concerned I would be late. I was. The riding was fantastic that day as I drove through the hills and farmland of eastern Iowa.

I finally arrived at Mark and Margaret's ranch-style home in the outskirts of Wapello, exchanged hugs, got cleaned up in due order, and piled into the car to head to Bev's for dinner. As the door opened at Bev's, I found myself facing eleven smiling faces, all family, who had gathered for one purpose...to see me. How cool was that? I felt like the prodigal son being welcomed home after a long absence. I didn't know half of them, but it didn't take long to feel like I had lived there my whole life. We ate a bountiful meal and later gathered in the family room and laughed until our sides hurt. We had such a great time together that evening, we decided to have dinner at my cousin Wayne's place the next night. I was all for it.

Uncle Mark had four sons who had started a very successful plastics-molding plant, and we toured the facility the next day. The place was huge, and I am guessing they employed more than 100 people. Huge machines were everywhere, and as Mark explained how it all worked, I was dumbfounded by the complexity of it all. The one thing that particularly struck me was that they had accomplished all this on their own and they had done most of the work themselves. They had set up the huge pieces of machinery, they had constructed most of the building, they had personally made the sales, and they had put the business together using their own hands and the brains God had given them.

My thoughts went back to my cousin Tim, who had managed three separate and successful businesses. I thought of Bruce in Washington and Al in British Columbia, both of whom had accomplished incredible tasks of their own. "What drove these people to accomplish such things?" I wondered. What gave them the drive to succeed and the ability to overcome the failure along the way? Was their fortitude stronger than mine, or was my unwillingness to commit the time to live my dreams holding me back from reaching my potential? Was I paralyzed with the fear of failure? I wasn't exactly sure, but what I did know was that this was how I wanted to live my life, a constant process of learning, trying, and doing…and yes, failing and then doing again.

My cousin Kent, who was one of Mark's sons, told me how he had built his first house himself with absolutely no idea of how to do it. He said, "I remember going down to the building supply store and showing them the blueprints. The house had been framed, and I needed heating ducts. They loaded me up, and when I returned, I spread all the heating equipment on the ground, looked at it, and had no idea what to do with them. I just kept asking questions and getting advice until the job was done." I was intrigued with this.

"That's what I want to do someday," I said, "but I just don't know if I can."

He assured me I could but stated, "Nothing will get done until you start it." He was proof of this. Why did it sound so simple yet seem so impossible to place into action?

That afternoon, I spent some real quality time with my uncle Mark, fishing at his personal lake and talking about life and family. Let it be known that

fishing is not on my top ten list of things I love, but I must admit that this particular fishing trip was quite different and more enjoyable than most I had tol-
erated before, due solely to the fact that I was sitting in that tiny boat talking
to my seventy-plus–year-old uncle. It gave me time to really get to know him
in a way you can only get to know someone when your world becomes a rec-
tangle of two feet wide by eight feet long. As I continually threw my hook in
the water, praying that a fish would at least touch the hook and provide me
with a hint of excitement, my uncle was reeling in fish after fish, shooting me
a snide wink every time he pulled the hook out of his current catch. Somehow, he always managed to pick the "good side of the boat." Those winks
were starting to get on my nerves.

Mark had been a "wheeler dealer" throughout his life and had traveled all
over the world investigating business ventures. His smile was infectious, and
his gray wavy hair certainly didn't reflect the youthful mind found underneath.
He was one to jump in without necessarily knowing all the facts, and I liked
that. In fact, the day before, we had been discussing how difficult it was to
buy a new Harley from a dealer, and I had told him that sometimes folks were
waiting up to a year or more. He hadn't believed me.

I had said, "Then call the dealer in Bloomington."

No sooner had I said it than he had called information and had the dealer
on the phone. Without having all the facts, he'd said, "Yeah, you got any of
them new Harvey Davidsons? What? Yeah Harley, that's what I meant. What
size? I don't know...the big ones. What? Really? Okay, thanks."

"What did he say?" I'd asked, already knowing the answer.

"Up to a year" he'd said. "I'll be darned." I liked that though—you don't
need to have all the facts to get something started. That stuck with me.

Before I left the next day, I gave a few of my relatives the opportunity to do
something they probably would never have a chance to do again...ride a
Harley. This sounded good in my head, but I feared I made a terrible mistake
when I half jokingly asked my uncle Mark if he wanted to take it for a spin.
This, the man who does not need all the facts...nor the experience, to try
something.

He looked at me, glanced at the bike, and matter-of-factly said, "Sure."

"Oh", I said, very surprised and without enthusiasm, and we walked over to
where it was parked on the smooth cement driveway. The long road to his

farm from the main highway is 100% gravel, and I was more than a little nervous about letting a man in his seventies handle a bike that weighed more than 600 pounds on such a loose surface, but I had already committed myself to the offer.

The family was there, and we dressed Mark up in full Harley garb, including fingerless gloves, sunglasses, and head scarf. He mounted the bike with a half-cocked smile as I pressed the button and started it for him. He asked me about the shifting pattern, and I told him that it was one down and four up. I felt this was a good motorcycle question, and I began to breathe a little easier. That is, until I saw his foot start to press the gear shifter without reaching for the clutch.

I quickly yelled, "Pull in the clutch!"

His foot immediately pulled away as he shot a puzzling look in my direction, replying, "Oh, it has a clutch?" I'm not sure if he actually saw my lower lip quiver, but I'm pretty sure everyone else did. This was NOT a good answer.

Five thousand miles without a hitch, and my uncle is going to total my ride and probably put himself in the hospital, I thought. He pulled in the clutch, pressed the shifter down with his foot, and shakily started the bike rolling forward as I held my breath. It wasn't pretty, but he made it out to the highway. I was relieved, until ten minutes had passed without a sound. I was thinking what everyone else was thinking…he's in a ditch. After about fifteen excruciating minutes of making small talk, I heard the glorious noise of a big V-twin motor. He made it back safe and sound but had been having so much fun, he'd felt the need to elongate his experience a bit. That's my uncle.

Next stop was to see my cousin Marvis that afternoon. Marvis was my mother's brother's daughter, and I'd had very little, if any, real contact with her in the past. Once again, I felt a little intimidated, but my confidence in conversing with family had been given a great boost over the past few days. I was looking forward to it. After an uneventful ride through Missouri, I arrived at Marvis's farmhouse in Luray, Missouri, around 5:00 p.m.

Marvis and Harold Trump…farmers all the way. They owned thousands of acres of land and leased thousands more and worked it the old-fashioned way, through hard work and long hours. Marvis was a slender woman with short brunette hair and glasses. She was probably ten years older than I and wasn't one for excessive conversation. I had to work at it a bit, but her dry sense of humor and no-nonsense style appealed to me. You knew just what she thought. Harold was a short, stocky man who reminded me of a Marine drill sergeant…without the loud voice. By contrast, he made Marvis look like a fast-talking salesman. Answers from him were usually no more than three words in a low monotone drawl, and he felt much more comfortable with his nose in the paper or a book rather than engaged in active conversation.

I remembered Marvis's mother, my aunt Francis, vaguely from when I was a kid, but much had happened since then. She'd had a number of medical problems and surgeries over the years, including cancer for which half of her stomach had been removed. She was a tough one, though, and had come through all of her infirmities amazingly well. I remembered Francis as a heavier-set lady—partly by memory, but mostly by pictures I had seen. I was taken aback a bit when she came out to meet me. She looked much older than I had expected. Her frail frame probably didn't weigh more than 100 pounds, and the fullness of her face had been replaced by sunken cheeks and deep wrinkles. After her husband, Elmer, had died seven years before, she had begun living near Marvis and Harold, in a trailer that was a stone's throw from their house. As she came up to me, I was preparing myself to speak twice as loudly as normal and slowly so she could u-n-d-e-r-s-t-a-n-d w-h-a-t I w-a-s s-a-y-i-n-g. It didn't take more than five seconds to realize that she was as sharp as a razor blade with a wit that would cut metal. In fact, dinner was at *her* house that night.

Marvis mentioned that she had old black-and-white photographs that dated back to the early 1900s, and I jumped at the chance to see them. We moseyed over to the house and spent the next several hours gazing at pictures of my parents and grandparents that I had never seen before. My hunger to know more about my past had continued to grow, and this night only fueled that desire more. I was looking at pictures of unknown grandparents who were younger than I was. It seemed that every day that passed brought me closer to my heritage and new meanings to the word "family."—words like tough, hard-working, loving, Christian, humorous, caring…words representing the genes that were in my brothers and me.

The large country breakfast on the farm was incredible the next morning, and I made sure I snapped a picture of my plate for Millie before I devoured the scrumptious food. We picked up where we had left off the night before and continued my journey through the black-and-white photographs of years past. It seemed I couldn't get enough.

The regulator connection on my bike was really beginning to worry me now, as the semi-solid connector was becoming more "sloppy" and I feared that the charging of the battery would soon be compromised. I worked on it with Marvis's son, Mark, to come up with a way to fix it. It wasn't pretty, but I was hoping it would hold me till the end of the trip. I just wasn't prepared to spend the $100 it would cost me for a new one. As it would turn out, I should have spent the money.

Mark was a miniature Harold. He was in his late twenties, had red hair, was slender, but had a solid build and was only slightly more outgoing than Harold when it came to conversation. He took me around the farm and into the nearby town in their old pickup truck, and we spoke of this and of that, but mostly about the farming of soybeans and corn. He was ready to find a girl, but it isn't easy when you're a farmer in the country working long hours. I let him take the bike out for a spin and snapped a picture before he left. His wide grin and display of emotion seemed uncharacteristic for him, so I knew they were genuine. He loved riding that bike. This was the picture I would give to him five years later in a Mexican hospital bed, just weeks before he would die from cancer. I'm sure glad he had a chance to take that ride.

It was early afternoon once I got back on the road. My new destination was Quincy, Illinois, where my aunt on my dad's side had lived most of her life. I remember Aunt Loida from when I was a small boy but had had little contact with her over the past two decades. She had stood out among the relatives when I was young because she had been very faithful in sending me birthday cards every year. She had lost her husband about six months before I visited, and I knew that this had been a powerful blow to her, as they had been married more than fifty years. I remember being at her house twenty-five years before, during a family reunion, and spending most of my time with her youngest son, Kevin, who is one of the few cousins who is my age. He now lived in Bloomington, Illinois, where I planned to visit the next day.

I arrived in Quincy around 6:00 p.m., and Aunt Loida and I just spent time catching up and getting to know each other. Once again, this "old" relative surprised me in her youthful conversation and genuine interest. She was also an Apostolic and therefore wore her gray hair high in a bun. That's the only way I had ever seen her. We just sat there in her kitchen and talked. She asked me if I wanted to go for a ride, and I said sure. She drove me around the area and showed me where my various cousins were living, where her husband was buried, where my dad had purchased some land to farm but had failed at it. I was now touching my father's side of the family.

While meeting many of my cousins for the first time, one thing had become fairly evident: I seemed to be the only guy in the family who, by his thirties, did not have a family of his own. Heck, I hadn't even been able to handle the wife piece of the puzzle more than ten days. I knew that to be truly happy in this world, I had to be content with where I was in my life, but I must admit that seeing so many happy families the past few days had made me feel a bit out of place and perhaps a little envious.

The next day, I left for the last of my family reunions, at my cousin Kevin's home. Kevin and I had been about eight years old the last time we had laid eyes on one another, and all I could remember of my visit to Quincy in 1969 was a song on the radio: "Bertha, Bertha Butt, she was one of the Butt sisters." He and I would play pool at their house and crack up every time that song would play. In fact, we had called the radio station and actually heard our pre-pubescent voices talking to the DJ, requesting the Bertha Butt song. Pretty sad when that's all you remember of your family vacations.

I pulled into Kevin's driveway around six o'clock in the evening, and when I saw him, I felt like we hadn't been apart at all. The garage door was open, and he was inside, putting away a few things. He had heard me coming up the street and was facing outward with a huge old grin as I pulled into the drive-way sporting a pretty healthy smile of my own. He looked somewhat like yours truly, with the exception of his bald dome, and I quickly swung my leg off the bike, walked over, and said, "Hey, cousin, been a while." We gave each other a huge hug, and I immediately felt close to him.

After about five minutes of trip and Harley talk, I mentioned that I had been thinking of a song we had heard as kids about twenty-five years earlier. Before I could finish my sentence, he immediately replied, "The Troglodyte song? You mean Bertha Butt?" I couldn't believe we both remembered this one event in a lifetime. We laughed long and hard over this ridiculous memory and enjoyed the time of getting to know each other again.

Kevin and his beautiful wife Robin had had twins about four years earlier, a handsome boy named Reuben and a beautiful daughter named Emily. Unfortunately, Reuben had been born with cerebral palsy and was wheelchair bound and unable to speak. His glasses were conspicuous because his face was so tiny, his head tilting from side to side as he seemingly tried to understand what was going on around him, his mouth often opening and closing for no apparent reason. My heart broke. Why children? He would never experience a normal life. It wasn't right. I suddenly felt small and ashamed for those times I complained...about anything. I could communicate, I could walk without a wheelchair, I could take a trip like this one. What in the world did I have to complain about?

After dinner, I went outside and sat in lawn chairs in a circle with Kevin's family, his brother Ron and Ron's wife, Donna. I was deeply moved by the love Reuben received from his family. They treated him no differently than anyone else in that circle. When his face would show a reaction, they would smother him with attention and praise. I found that Kevin would often take Reuben on trips, knowing full well it would be easier to leave him at home, but that wasn't the point. Love does not choose the easy and convenient way. I was inspired by all the love that was surrounding this place. I was proud of this family. I was proud to be related to them.

Kevin and I both felt a bond that I hoped we could continue to nurture, although I knew that distance and hectic schedules would make it challenging. Ron and Kevin had to fly out the next day, and I could tell that both Kevin and I wished we had more time to talk. I prayed it wouldn't take us another twenty-five years to see each other again.

The week spent with my family was as important to me as anything else on this pilgrimage. The lessons learned were so many and so unexpected. As Ebenezer Scrooge had been taken to Christmas past, I had been taken to my past. I had been shown that I came from good, tough, and loving people who are willing to reach out if I do the same. I was provided a second chance in life to care about those who are my family. The message from the ghost of John's past was clear: Change your ways.

This week solidified my beliefs that life is not fulfilled through money, material things, or power but through relationships. Without relationships, everything else is temporary, empty, and meaningless. The relationship of family turned out to be much more important than I had ever imagined. Like an Illinois crop of corn, these relationships would need to be nurtured and cultivated for me to reap the true harvest of love and caring, but if neglected, they will wither and die. I knew the crop I would try to nurture and hoped it would harvest bountiful rewards.

Cousin Tim, Meg, Amy & friends

Iowa Family

Uncle Paul (right), his brother, and lots of avon bottles and tractors

The grandfather I never met

The room where mom was raised as a child

Fishing with Uncle Mark - Unhooking a snapping turtle

Mark Trump - A life ending far too young

Aunt Loida - Her husband of over 50 years (my dad's brother) Hank had just
passed away 7 months earlier

Hodel Kin in Illinois

CHAPTER 6

Women, Horses, and an Island

During my brief stay with Bruce the previous month, he had provided me the phone number of a seemingly attractive woman named Cindy whom he had met on a cruise a few years back. At the time, he had told me that she lived in Lincoln, Illinois, and that I should give her a call if I found myself in the area. I had written the name and phone number down on a piece of paper and shoved it in my journal, not really thinking I would ever retrieve it. But, you never know, I'm always willing to go the extra mile to visit an attractive woman.

While unpacking at Uncle Mark's, I had come across Cindy's phone number and decided to pull out the old map and see exactly where Lincoln, Illinois, was located. As it turned out, Lincoln was only forty minutes or so from Bloomington, where my cousin Kevin lived. The traveling plan was to head north to Wisconsin from Kevin's home, and seeing that Lincoln was due south, I had to weigh my options: ride north to nowhere specific or turn south and take the chance.

I called Cindy from Kevin's house, just before dinner. Now, I get nervous enough asking women out at home who actually know me, but I had never called somebody for a date with the opening line of, "you don't know me...but." As it turned out, I didn't have much time for butterflies, as she answered the phone after the very first ring. This, as I would find out, was a miracle in itself, as I have *never* been able to reach her by phone at home since (hmmm). The voice on the other end quickly degraded from giving a cheery and musical hello! to wary and tentative one-word replies as I explained who I was and what I was doing. She did have a cute way of saying "uh huh," though. The fact that I knew Bruce afforded me some credibility, but there was still more hesitancy than even I was accustomed to when asking someone out. I went for the close and suggested we have lunch together the next day. There was a bit of a pause followed by a somewhat surprising answer of "okay." Now that was selling.

Cindy provided me with directions to the restaurant where the blind date would take place and conveniently covered her bases for an early exit by stating that she had a party to go to afterwards and that it would have to be a short lunch. Hey, I hadn't been on anything that resembled a date since Montana, and the only women I had spoken to lately were related to me. A little time was definitely better than no time at all.

The next morning, dark, rain-filled clouds covered the skies to the south, and I began wondering if my decision to head in the opposite direction from my goal was a wise one. Too late now. My cousin Ron and his wife, Donna, had graciously put me up at their place, and I hugged them good-bye. The family portion of my journey was now officially over.

I hit the road and steered my two-wheeled date machine toward the bustling little town of Lincoln, named after our sixteenth president, who had worked at the courthouse there. As it turns out, he had been the attorney for both the owners of the pre-town land and the railroad company for whose right of way the potential town had been surveyed. While writing up the paperwork to officially set the land up for a future settlement, Lincoln had stopped, settled back in his chair, and inquired of his constituents what they were going to call the town. "Lincoln" was their reply, and the future president replied that anything named Lincoln had never amounted to much. I love that guy.

The moment I entered the town's outskirts, the rain began to fall—and not too gently, I might add. I found an old train overpass nearby and remained under its damp but dry shelter for about twenty minutes, hoping that the sudden downpour would subside. Fortunately, it did, and after taking one more look at the directions I had written on a piece of paper, I found our meeting place at the local restaurant within ten minutes. I smartly parked the bike across the road under the overhang of an abandoned building, figuring this would be the perfect place to keep my scoot and possessions dry. At least it seemed like a good idea. I snapped the padlock into place and somewhat nervously walked across the road and into the restaurant's parking lot.

The restaurant was an older building, in need of some cosmetic repair here and there, and was split into two sections, the one being a basic coffee shop and the other, a more "upscale" place to eat. I was about a half hour early, so I sat myself down in the lobby, picked up a newspaper, and began to read while waiting for my new friend. After what seemed to be some time, I glanced at my watch. The digital display let me know that she was ten minutes late. I started to get that uneasy feeling, but hey, anybody could be ten minutes late. Maybe she had hit the Lincoln rush-hour traffic...hmm, not likely. I held my place and continued to wait. Forty-five minutes later and still alone, my mood had understandingly changed. I was berating myself for going out of my way for nothing and wasting an entire day in a Lincoln coffee shop in the rain. The young teenage hostess seemed genuinely concerned about my emotional state, but it really didn't help when she kept checking on me every five minutes as if I might try something drastic. "No, she *still* isn't here yet, but thanks for asking," I would say with a huge fake smile.

I called Cindy at her home and left a courteous message in a forced pleasant tone, stating that I just couldn't wait any more and would soon be on my way. After I hung up, I was on the phone with some other friends back home, letting them know where I was (not mentioning that I had just gotten stood up, of course) when the hostess motioned to me that I had a phone call. I don't think anyone else in the world knew where I was except Cindy. This had to be a good sign. As it turned out, she had arrived at the restaurant a little early and, not seeing my motorcycle in the parking lot, had waited outside, in her car. We had been waiting for each other for over an hour, about 100 feet apart. I was suddenly quite happy that I had not let the tone of my voice leave an angry message that might have made her think twice about calling back.

Cindy once again agreed to come by but added that the time would have to be fairly short, about fifteen minutes or so. Hey, better than nothing. I captured a table by the window and waited for anyone who might look like a Cindy. A few minutes later, I saw her walking along the sidewalk, taking a left toward the glass doors of the lobby. She was in her mid-thirties, about 5'6", with shoulder-length brunette hair and small wire-rimmed glasses. She looked more professional than I had anticipated, and it was quickly evident that her pictures did not lie. I rose and quickly met her by the lobby. Of all her features, what struck me most about her was her smile—one that radiated an aura of warmth and included not just her mouth but her whole face.

Although I am certainly not God's gift to women, I am sure her smile was an involuntary one as she realized I was not a 5'7" 350-pound Harley man with greasy long hair and beard who hadn't showered in three days. We broke the ice by talking about my trip and the circumstances that had led me to this point in my life and about her life in Lincoln. As single people have a habit of doing, we spoke of past relationships in our lives, and she was surprisingly open about her feelings. She was also very intrigued about my ten-day marriage story. That story is always good for a solid twenty-minute discussion. We lost track of time, and those original fifteen minutes lasted more than an hour. Although she had to leave, I could tell that she didn't really want to go. The detour had already been worth it.

Cindy was late for another engagement (translation: date), and she invited me to go horseback riding the next day, weather permitting. Although I had not planned on spending the night in Lincoln, it made me feel good that she offered. I decided to plant my roots for the night and splurge on a motel, looking forward to an enjoyable time the next day.

That evening, I decided to give my mother a call for only the second time since I had left our home. She seemed to share my excitement about all that had happened over the past weeks. She had also spoken to a number of my relatives whom I had visited, and had received very favorable responses regarding my recent visits. I guess her boy hadn't made her look too bad after all. For the first time, my journey had provided my mother with a benefit that was personal to her. Her son had built relationships with members of her family, those whom she had wanted me to meet for so many years. This was no longer a son taking his chances in Vietnam in 1968, it was another son learning about life and his family in 1995. Perhaps it was no longer a pointless venture to her...maybe it never had been. We had a good talk.

The next morning, I woke up full of anticipation of a great day, only to be greeted by the sound of rain. "Ahh, not today," I muttered under my breath. My hope for a romantic gallop in the fields on horseback was quickly sinking into the mud with every raindrop that fell. I tried calling Cindy all morning, but the line was busy. By 10:30, I was getting a little frustrated because I had only planned to stay the day, and that day was quickly passing by. Finally, I broke through around eleven in the morning, and Cindy apologized for being on the phone so much and getting such a late start. "Oh, it's okay," I replied, adding just a touch of disappointment to my tone. She said she would be right over, and within the hour, we found ourselves at a local sports pub, having lunch.

As expected, things were just too wet and muddy for horses, but during lunch, the weather transformed itself into a clear and beautiful afternoon. Illinois boasts a plethora of narrow country back roads that wind their way through the endless corn fields, and I asked her if she had ever gotten lost in the country. She looked at me a bit quizzically and slowly replied that she hadn't, not exactly sure what I meant. I smiled and asked, "You want to get lost?" She quickly flashed that wide grin I had already come to love, and she nodded. I had her wear my helmet as I quickly tied my headscarf into position and just started to ride, making random turns on every little road I could find. What a great way to ride! We did manage to get lost for a while and discovered some incredible roads she had not even known existed. At various times during the mini-trip, she would give me a back rub as we rode through the Illinois cornfields. It felt great to feel the gentle touch of a woman again.

During one stretch of desolate road, I felt the rear brakes begin to squeeze on their own, causing the bike to "drag" a little bit. I had had this problem before the trip began but had thought I had fixed it. I was disappointed to find that, after all these miles, the problem was reemerging. For whatever reason, the brakes would not release completely after rear braking and would stick just a little. The friction between the rotor and the pads would create incredible heat, thus heating up the brake fluid and causing the pads to close even more, continuing the vicious cycle. I pulled the bike over near a country bridge full of medium-sized oak trees and with just enough water to qualify as a brook, and I let the brakes cool, a little concerned how this might affect me the rest of the trip. As it turned out…it would. Cindy and I talked near the bridge, ate some snacks she had packed, and laughed some more. I felt that if I made the move to kiss her, she would definitely kiss back, but I chickened out. What a wimp.

Three hours later, we returned to Lincoln and stopped by the house of Joanne, one of Cindy's coworkers. Her house was one of those homes you found on "Elm Street" in Small Town, USA. It had the trees, the large front porch, the friendly neighbors, the whole *Leave It to Beaver* backdrop. We sat on the front porch in one of those old-fashioned wooden swings made for two and just talked while sipping lemonade and gently rocking back and forth. Once again, I was in a completely relaxed state of mind, swinging on that swing and just taking time to talk to people—no to-do list, no guilt for not doing things that should be done, no running around trying to commit to my overcommitted schedule.

It was getting late in the day, and it was time to go. I wasn't sure what my next move would be. My stuff was packed, and I didn't know if I would ride on that day or stick around. I certainly didn't want to spend money on a motel again. By this time, Cindy had come to trust me and somewhat sheepishly offered her place to me for the night. I'm sure that was a risky thing to do, but I think she knew my intentions were for good. I smiled and accepted the offer.

After a good dinner at a restaurant called Daphne's, we went to Cindy's place and watched *Legends of the Fall*, which we had rented at the local video rental store. We snuggled up on the couch, and it felt good being there. When the movie was over, I kissed her for the first time, and although the evening became quite romantic, we didn't let it go too far. She was a lady, I was a gentleman, and we both knew that. I slept on the couch that night and wished I could have spent a few more days in Lincoln, but she had to work and I needed to move on. I was very glad I had made that phone call.

The next morning, we awoke around seven, and after grabbing a quick shower, I began the now unfamiliar task of loading up my belongings. I wouldn't be enjoying many more friendly accommodations in the future, so I had better get used to roughing it again. I took a shot at getting Cindy to take Monday off from work, but she couldn't swing it. I guess I wasn't THAT impressive. She walked me to the front yard of her modest home, and I gave her a hug and a kiss and told her that she had provided me a great memory. I left with a somewhat heavy heart, as I had become accustomed to being with people who enjoyed my presence. The love of family and the company of a sweet woman had softened me. Leaving, I felt a tug of loneliness as I loudly gunned my Harley out of her driveway and pointed the bike toward Interstate 55.

My next destination was the Harley-Davidson plant in Milwaukee, Wisconsin, and I really did want to make it there by the end of the day, so I decided to employ the dreaded interstate for a while. I stopped for lunch at a trucker's restaurant called Dixies, which is where the famous Route 66 highway began (or ended, depending on which way you were driving). It was somewhat ironic that I had stumbled upon this place seeing how the other end of that highway was at Santa Monica, California, only an hour from my home. I spent about thirty minutes at the Route 66 museum and then moved on.

Because Interstate 55 would take me far too close to Chicago, I decided to leave the interstate and embark on a thin, squiggly line on the map that would take me toward my destination for that day…Highway 47. The land was unchanging, flat, and unexciting as numerous thunderclouds began to form over the Wisconsin border. This type of weather was always the most difficult to figure out because the sky could look completely menacing and never rain a drop or it could open up and drench you in thirty seconds. The one strategy I had come to trust was to closely watch the cars coming at me. If I saw their windshield wipers on, I would know there was rain ahead and I would stop and put my leathers on, hoping it was not raining hard enough to require the dreaded full rain gear.

Moments after I crossed the Wisconsin border, the sky had transformed itself into the blackest color I had seen to date. That didn't look good. I kept a close watch on those cars, and sure enough, I saw windshield wipers blazing. Not a moment later, rain droplets began pelting my face. Ah, the plan had worked well, and I quickly turned around, accelerated away from the wetness, and put my leathers on along the dry shoulder of a side road. I was proud of myself for being so wise and figured I had completely outwitted Mother Nature once again in her attempt at soaking this biker. Pride is definitely one of the seven deadly sins.

After dressing out in my Johnny Cash outfit of black leather, I turned back and continued down the road from whence I'd come. Within a half a mile, the rain hit me so hard that I couldn't see past my front fender. Cars in front of me immediately began braking and swerving, and I was caught between worrying that I might either be kissing someone's license plate or that I was about to become a human hood ornament for the car behind me.

I turned my bike around as fast as I could and accelerated out of there like a wounded deer from a hunter's rifle. I found a sunny spot about a mile down the road and parked. I had been put through the wash and soak cycles in less than twenty seconds. I kicked back, pulled one of my stogies, and puffed on that baby until things dried out a bit. I then put on all my bulky rain gear for the first time since Washington and realized how spoiled I had been the past month with the incredible weather I had experienced.

Now that the Michelin Man had been resurrected, I was off, prepared for a hurricane if needed. Of course, God, in his infinite sense of humor, decided to abstain from drenching me any further. Now I was bulky, dry, and very hot and uncomfortable.

I arrived in Milwaukee that evening and called Phyllis, my cousin Kevin's wife's aunt, whose name they had given me just two days earlier. Hey, I'll sponge off anybody who has a roof over their head. She told me to come by in about an hour, so I found a local restaurant and had a bite to eat, telling the guys next to me about my ride and making small talk.

Phyllis was probably in her fifties, with short gray hair and medium build. The house was not fancy by any means, but it was certainly more than adequate for my needs. She was babysitting her granddaughter Adrianna, who was just over four years old and was evidently the product of a mixed marriage. I must say, she was probably one of the cutest kids I've ever seen, both physically and behaviorally. Even though Phyllis had not known me from Adam, she went out of her way to make me feel at home.

People like Phyllis were constantly impressing me during this trip—the type of people who would show kindness to a stranger and make the stranger feel as if they had known him his entire life. These were the teachers of the land, the lessons of giving and of caring with no hope of reward or return. These lessons were strong ones. "Do unto others as you would have them do unto you" had never meant as much to me as it did on this sojourn. I saw actions, not words.

To date, I had traveled 6,700 miles and was averaging a bit under $35 a day for everything. Not bad. The free lodging and camping had certainly helped my average, and I knew as time would move on that there most certainly would be emergencies that would require extra capital. Conserving costs early on seemed to be working.

The next day, I rode my trusty partner to the Harley-Davidson plant, where the company had begun in 1903 and where my bike's transmission and engine had been originally built. I must say that I felt very proud that I had made it to this place under my own Harley's power, and knowing that my bike and I had probably traveled further than anyone else on that tour made this event very personal to me. As I slowly walked past the bins of pistons and gears, I wondered if any of those parts would open the world up to another rider as mine was doing for me. In a way, I suppose my bike was "experiencing" the same goal I had only a week earlier…we had both come back to where it had all begun.

My final destination for the day was South Bend, Indiana, the home of Notre Dame and Glenn, whom I had met at Mickie's house in Sturgis. To make my commitment, I would need to ride the interstate once again and, even worse, ride it through Chicago, but it would easily cut off several hours, and even with that, I would barely make it by sunset. I would soon find that I needed those spare hours.

It was a beautiful day, with blue skies and temperatures in the seventies. I rode the perimeter of Lake Michigan, staying off the main interstate as long as I could, but as the Chicago city skyline appeared in the distance, it was inevitable that I would have to forego the roads I had come to love and use an on-ramp. I had found that my dislike for a city of any size was growing daily.

Before I knew it, I was entering downtown Chicago. The traffic was moving quickly, but all four lanes were at full capacity. I made the decision to take the expressway, which is designed to separate those cars that did not need to exit any time soon and to therefore keep the traffic moving. The single lane was a tight one, with the center divider to the left and a concrete barrier to the right, and there was absolutely no shoulder whatsoever. It definitely required a commitment, but I figured this would be the quickest way to get through the dreaded city. Besides, what could go wrong?

Unfortunately, almost the moment I made the irreversible decision to take this path, I began feeling my rear brakes drag as they had when Cindy had been on the back in Lincoln. My heart sank. "No, not now, not now," I kept saying to myself. Directly behind me was a row of cars almost pushing me to go faster than the seventy I was currently experiencing. I looked ahead, knowing there were no exits and nowhere to pull over. I was absolutely helpless.

I winced as I felt the bike continue to drag as I kept the speed constant. I found myself having to turn the throttle a little more to compensate for the additional drag of the brake, confirming my fears that the problem was worsening. After several miles, I reluctantly looked back and saw smoke pouring from the rear brake. I was in agony. About five miles later, the first exit mercifully appeared, and I immediately pulled out of the express lane and onto the shoulder to survey the damage. The once flat and shiny silver brake disk had been transformed to a dark bluish color that looked more like a crescent moon from the side as the intense heat had completely changed its form. Then, the misery not yet complete, it began to rain heavily. I was having a very difficult time seeing the positive side of life at this moment.

It was late afternoon, and I was in East Chicago, which is a very long way from Lincoln, Illinois. Let's just say that I was *very* noticeable there. I limped off the expressway, found a McDonald's, and parked my ailing bike in the parking lot to let her cool down further. I ran inside to avoid getting any wetter than I already was and must admit, I was more than a little nervous. I ordered a Diet Coke and selected a seat near the window so I could watch all my belongings getting sufficiently soaked and contemplate what my next move should be.

As I sat there, a wiry black man in his sixties startled me out of my trance. "That your bike?" he said, a little louder than I would have liked.

"What's left of it," I said and quickly explained the little predicament I was in. We talked for a few minutes. I couldn't tell if he was just being friendly or if he was one cylinder short of a big twin. I certainly wasn't in the mood to chitchat, and, not knowing his intentions I was feeling a bit defensive. He never sat down as he began to share his own stories about his bike experiences.

"Yep, once in a while, I'd ride my cycle to the park and take a little nap on the grass, but I always had my thirty-eight caliber under my motorcycle jacket," he said. "Nobody knew I had it but me. Let me tell ya somethin'…more than once, I pulled that baby out when some dude be tryin' to take my ride. Ain't nobody takin' my ride. You know what I mean?" The volume of his voice began to rise a bit as he told me several more stories of life in the city and he became oblivious to the ice cream cone he was holding, the ice cream melting through the bottom and dripping off his hand.

"So I come out of the drug store," he says, "and there's this dude trying to push my motorcycle away. Now the key to surviving out here is, you gotta have a big belt buckle. You can do a lot with a big belt buckle." As he said this, I instinctively looked down and noticed the oversized belt buckle he was wearing. "I slowly took my belt off, snuck behind that dude, and flung the buckle over his shoulder. Cut that sucker wide open. There was blood everywhere. He won't be trying that again, I'll tell ya. Some people tell me I overreacted, but that's the way you gotta be out here." Just then, his gaze flew past my eyes and out the window in the direction of my bike. I looked around and saw a couple of twelve-year-old kids slowly walking in front of my bike and staring at it. "You gotta be careful of those kind," he said. "They'll break out your mirrors and kick your bike over for no reason at all. Ain't no sense in it." Yep, I was definitely ready to leave the big city.

With that, my new streetwise friend said his good-byes as his ice cream cone had almost completely melted, and I leaned back, exhaling loudly, and once again wondered what I was going to do. About a half hour had passed since I'd taken my first sip, and I made the decision that I would try to limp in to South Bend and try to find repairs there. At least I would have Glenn's house as a central location. It would be dark in another three hours, and seeing that it was after four o'clock, I figured I better get moving.

Practically the entire time I had been inside the golden arches, I had noticed a man sitting in the driver's seat of an old Impala, parked right next to my Harley. He hadn't moved in all that time, and I couldn't help but wonder if he was waiting for the Harley's owner to return for some reason. Why would he just be sitting there that long by himself? He was a black man, probably in his late twenties, sporting a goatee and a dark beanie pulled just above his eyes. Suffice it to say, he would have looked a lot tougher on my Harley than I did. I made the executive decision that to protect my possessions, I would strip off the nice-guy approach and put on the best bad-to-the-bones look I could muster. I strutted to my bike with lips pursed tight, a bit of a squint, and made it a point to look directly at him all the way. We made eye contact for at least five seconds. He didn't blink, and neither did I.

Now, after hearing my ice-cream-cone friend's account of his life in East Chicago, I was becoming more than a little concerned. I mean, this man was *not* blinking or looking away. I quickly made another executive decision and decided to abandon the tough-guy script post haste. Once I came within five feet of his open driver's window, I looked straight at him and turned the Clint Eastwood scowl into a Bozo the Clown smile and asked, "How are you doing, man?"

His own scowl immediately departed and was replaced with a toothy white grin, minus a few teeth. "Doin' real good. How about yourself?" he replied.

"Had a rough day," I told him.

Immediately, the world was at peace again. We made friendly small talk for a few minutes, and as I was backing my bike out of its parking spot, he yelled out, "You all be careful out there now!"

"Will do!" I yelled back as I shifted her into first and rode out toward the freeway on-ramp.

Wow, what a lesson. I thought of how many times I had pre-judged other people by the way they looked or the way they looked at me. I have often found that if my first impression is a negative one, it is often wrong. Making judgments on people without knowing them is completely unfair and irresponsible and can do wonders in destroying potentially great relationships before they even start. How many times could a smile or a kind word have stopped an act of violence or saved a life? I was determined to make this a rule for the rest of my trip and hopefully my life.

It was becoming clear that I was not going to make it to my intended destination. After being on the freeway for only a few miles, the brake was barely holding up. Luckily, I saw a sign off the freeway that pointed the way to a local Harley dealer, and after following its direction, I went inside and explained my predicament. It was late, only an hour before they closed, and normally they wouldn't have entertained taking me in that same day. I was relieved when they told me they usually gave preferential help to those on the road. They had me out of there by 6:00 p.m., $200 lighter.

Darkness had fallen nearly two hours before I pulled into Glenn's driveway. His wife, Joan, came out to meet me and, to my surprise, was a fairly large woman, probably outweighing Glenn by a good 150 pounds. She was as friendly as could be, and they quickly offered me food and shower, both of which I accepted immediately.

We sat around and talked about nothing particularly important in their quaint little living room. After such a long day, it was good to relax in a nice cool house. I had not unpacked my tent in two weeks, and I knew that Glenn and Joan's would possibly be my last stay in a house until I reached Nova Scotia, at least two weeks from now.

The next morning brought tentative skies, and, as always is the case in this situation, I needed to make the decision, rain gear or no rain gear. I took a chance and forewent the water-repelling suit. It paid off, as God, in his infinite mercy, decided to spare me the soaking I had received so many other times when I had made the wrong decision. The riding transitioned from the flat, crop-filled plains of the Midwest to the lush green carpeted farms of Ohio. Although this was still fairly flat riding, the country homes and tree-laden fields made the viewing more enjoyable than it had been in the past few days. I was also entering Amish country and took great delight when seeing the old-fashioned horse buggies parked along the road or in front of local stores. Occasionally, I would catch up to an Amish family rolling down the road in their horse-drawn carriage and would instinctively lay off the throttle as I passed them, making sure I didn't spook the horses. I wondered what they thought of my two-wheeled camper as I cruised by. They probably didn't envy me.

Living in Southern California and working in the technology field, I had certainly been caught up in the fast-paced lifestyle of business and activities, running through airports, making deadlines, preparing for meetings, and sitting in traffic. Suddenly, the gentle clopping of hooves on the pavement surface seemed a welcome change from the bustling world I was used to.

As I was passing through a tiny Ohio town, I noticed an extremely skinny guy who couldn't have weighed more than 125 pound, with long scraggly hair and a number of tattoos that littered the white skin exposed by his dirty black tank top. He was riding an old, fully chopped 1956 bright yellow panhead Harley that stuck out with its gorgeous custom paint job. As I rode by him, he quickly turned right onto the same road I was traveling and within a few minutes had pulled up next to me. As I glanced over, I saw him quickly motion for me to pull over.

After sharing my story, he informed me that his bike had been featured in the popular Harley magazine *Easy Rider* in 1972. This bike was considered a hardtail model, which meant that it had no rear suspension whatsoever. This was the same type of bike that was featured in the movie *Easy Rider*. I asked him how far he had traveled at one time on this rigid frame, and he said four hundred miles. I couldn't imagine. I silently awarded him the iron-butt award and snapped a few pictures, along with a few of me sitting on the classic ride.

I was nearing Ann Arbor, Michigan, around two that afternoon and had two possible contacts with whom to stay, neither of whom I had ever met. They had been provided to me through a good friend, but after calling both several times, I found that nobody was home. I knew I should have called a few days back. It really wasn't that late, but for some reason, I had an intense desire to quit riding for the day and see a movie. I'm not sure why I had this sudden desire, but when you're on vacation, you get to do whatever you want to do. So I found a theater in Ann Arbor and decided to watch *Apollo 13*. It took all the sales ability I had to talk the manager into letting me park the Harley on the sidewalk, in front of the fancy theater, to help guarantee its safety and the chance that all my stuff would still be there when I came out. I think he did get a little nervous when he saw me putting cardboard under the bike to keep the oil from permanently marking my spot at his establishment, but by then it was too late, he had already committed.

I tried to find a free camping spot that night, but there were just too many homes throughout the rural area outside the city. I think my camp-locating talents were getting a little rusty from lack of use. After about an hour of dead ends, I finally settled for a campground near a local lake. Unfortunately, the campground was very crowded, and I started to realize how much I had enjoyed my alone time when facing the elements. This feeling was further endorsed when I found myself constantly harassed by a little seven-year-old boy who wanted me to give him all my leather goods. At first it was sort of cute, but that didn't last long. He refused to leave me alone and followed me around while asking over and over again, "Can I have your gloves? Can I have your gloves? Can I have your gloves? Can I have your gloves? Why not? Why not? Why not?" I made the mistake of telling him that even if he asked me fifty times, I wouldn't give him my gloves.

He then proceeded to repeat, "Can I have your gloves?" all fifty times. "Why can't I have them? Why? Please? Please?" Then he followed it up with fake crying. Suddenly, the single life didn't seem so bad.

The boy's mother was nowhere in sight, but his mother's female friend made her way over, not to shut the kid up but to talk my ear off and not so subtly hint how badly she would like a ride on a Harley again. She *definitely* was not my type. I tried to ignore her repeated suggestions and tried to keep busy setting up the tent, but between her and the little annoying one, I was ready to run into the lake fully clothed, screaming, "You can't have my gloves and you can't have a ride!" and then drown myself.

The next morning, I found a very cool back road that took me through the Detroit area, which consisted of both pavement and dirt. It took much longer this way, but it was worth the detour as I rode by extremely expensive homes deep in the country woods. I had no desire to spend time in Detroit, so my stay there was purposely limited to just passing through. My goal for the day would be Niagara Falls, and I decided that my path would be through our neighbor to the north, even though it meant strapping the old helmet back on my dome. Once across the river that connects Lake Huron with Lake Erie, I was again motoring eastward down Canada's Highway 3.

Not an hour in, while riding through one of the nameless small towns I would pass through that day, something made me look into my rearview mirror. Reflecting back at me were those dreaded flashing red lights of a Canadian Mountie. This was the first time I'd been pulled over, and here I was in another country. The officer slowly stepped out of his patrol car and strolled my way…and then proceeded to ask me about my ride. He just wanted to chat. Small towns!

This turned out to be one of the longest days of the trip, more in time than in miles. By the time I entered the city limits of Niagara Falls, I had spent a total of nine hours in the saddle, covering 370 miles. It was early evening, and after such a long and tiresome day, this magnificent location seemed anticlimactic. Tourists were everywhere, traffic was thick, and parking was nearly impossible. I spent only about an hour there, took a few pictures, and was ready to find a camp spot and rest my weary body.

As I was getting ready to leave, I met Bob from Boston, who was on his first solo Harley ride ever. Now if you saw Bob, you would have sworn he had been born on a Harley. There was not a follicle of hair on his head, and his earring and long, dark goatee only accentuated the required look. He wasn't very tall, maybe 5'9" or so, but his frame was a stocky and muscular one that would make you think twice about mixing it up with him. Once I started to talk to him, however, I discovered that his tough-looking exterior did not seem to match his lighthearted personality.

As it turned out, Bob was fairly new at riding anything with fewer than four wheels, and it was clear he was having the time of his life. He shared a story of something that had happened to him a few days earlier that had me rolling with laughter. He had been crossing a fairly long bridge in Massachusetts where the pavement was replaced by a metal grating. People who don't ride bikes would not understand that when you ride over this type of surface, the front tire wobbles excessively because of the metal ridges. This really is not a big deal, but Bob apparently had not been ready for this new sensation. He told me, his voice rising, that, about 100 yards across the bridge, he had started to panic and had yelled to himself, "I can't do this!" He had then pulled over next to some constructions workers, shakily pulled out a cigarette, and told them he couldn't cross. Unfortunately for him, the lane was one way and separated by a divider from the traffic going the other direction. He was stuck. Here's the funniest part: The construction guys actually stopped traffic on the one-way side of the bridge so he could ride back to the side he had come from. I couldn't imagine the embarrassment of such an act, but hearing this "tough guy" tell it made it just that much better.

Darkness was not far off, and I had no idea where I would stay that night. Now that I was entering upstate New York, the road began to once again provide me the curves I had longed for since leaving the Black Hills. Now that I was entering mountains, I knew that great riding would be my companion for many weeks. I was beginning to get a little desperate for a place to bed down and found a KOA just outside of Niagara that would rent me a plot of grass for a mere $22. No way would I pay that much again. I found an information booth in the hopes of finding somewhere to sleep before darkness fell.

I was told there was a state park "just" outside of town for $11. I figured the shower alone was worth the money and I jotted down the surprisingly complicated directions and headed down the road. I knew I was low on gas, but because it was "just" out of town, I figured I would be okay. Two miles out of town, the engine sputtered and coughed. I turned the gas switch to reserve, and the motor quickly responded. "How far is this place?" I asked myself a bit nervously as my eyes constantly scanned turnoffs and road signs. Ten miles later, darkness had fully engulfed me as well as my mood. My only companion through the dark forest was the constant hum of my engine and the nagging feeling that I had missed a turn somewhere. Maximum reserve capacity was about twenty miles, and I was nearing that mark fast.

After spending more than nine hours on the bike already, the thought of hitchhiking or walking to a gas station was not high on my list.. *I should have paid the $22*, I thought. *I'd be in a hot shower right now.* Eight miles later, I finally saw a sign that wasn't there to tell me the speed limit. There was a town two miles off the road. If there was no gas there, I would be in trouble, because many of these little towns were not open late. I felt I had no choice and leaned the bike to the left and moved down the small two-lane road. The first two stations were closed, but the third was open. It was just closing, and I was its last customer.

I did finally find the state park and tried to figure out how "just outside of town" could have possibly meant twenty-three miles. I set up camp in the darkness and enjoyed an incredible hot shower. For some reason, this was the first night I REALLY felt I was far from home. New York. Those two words meant the other side of the country to me. I had ridden my motorcycle to New York!

The next day, I decided to take things a little easier on myself and make the next few days shorter ones. It felt wonderful to be leaning into corners at 60 mph again, first left, then right, taking in the mountainous scenery before me as my eyes stared intently into the next turn. I rode for about five hours that day and decided to spoil myself with a motel in Rochester, New York. I took inventory of my supplies and mailed back those items I had not been using. When all was said and done, I lightened my load by fourteen pounds, including one entire bag.

Walking out of the post office, I looked down and noticed that my 501 jeans were beginning to unravel at the leg bottoms and small holes were beginning to emerge all over the denim leg coverings, most probably from the constant wind resistance. I also noticed that the oil leak I had been monitoring was getting worse. That wasn't good. It was Friday night, and although I felt like going out and meeting people, my money reserve was a bit low, so I decided to be antisocial and go out the next night, wherever that might be.

That night, I perused my map and decided to spend the next night in Rome, New York. I figured this would be a good move for two reasons: one, Rome had a Harley dealership and I could further check out my leak, and two, I had always wanted to go to Rome. Well, not quite the same, but now I could truthfully say that I had been to Rome. Well, it seemed like a good idea at the time.

What I didn't realize was that I had chosen Honor America Day to visit this small town. Honor America Day is an annual patriotic festival that features floats, clowns, drum corps, marching bands, antique cars, you name it. Does that sound like a parade? Yes, it does. Does a large parade in a small town pretty much take over the entire area? Yes, it does. So when I motored into Rome, everything was closed, including the Harley dealership, and as I kept trying to venture across town, I was consistently cut off by the endless parade. People, floats, cars, and, yes, clowns were everywhere. I was getting very frustrated. So, to do my part in celebrating this great holiday, I found an apartment complex and washed my clothes there.

Rome is nestled in the Adirondack Mountains, so I had assumed that finding a place to sleep would be an easy task. Wrong. People were everywhere because of the celebration. I was beginning to hate Honor America Day. I must have ridden fifteen miles out of town, bordering the Delta Lake, but could find nothing. I pulled into the driveway of a small general store and asked the owner if I could pay to sleep in the large yard behind his place. I felt pretty awkward even asking, like I was a vagrant or something, but I figured what the heck, the worst that could happen is he would say no. "No," he said.

"Why not?" I asked, surprised that I had not been afforded the same kindness I had become accustomed to.

"Insurance reasons," he replied.

"Okay, thanks anyway," I said, walking out the door, thinking he could have come up with a better excuse than that.

For the first time on my ride, I was beginning to feel some bouts of depression and loneliness. Ever since I had entered New York, the intensity of my ride just didn't feel the same as before. The people didn't seem as friendly, and events weren't going as smoothly as they had up to my arrival in New York. I was feeling a little pitiful. I ended up spending two hours sitting in the local Pizza Hut because I couldn't find any place else that was open.

I soon found myself in a very small town called Westernville, about fifteen miles outside of Rome. It was a Mayberry-like town, and I discovered a library located in the town center that sat diagonally on the block corner. Because of this unique position, it would adequately hide me from the street, and the high hedge in back would sufficiently conceal my presence from the houses to the north. The back door was located about three steps up from the large backyard and was fairly shielded from public view. I figured I could bed down on the small landing below the light and hopefully not be discovered before morning. I was running out of choices.

I decided to ride back to Rome, as I assumed there had to be some event going because of the holiday. I figured that talking to people would probably be what the doctor ordered to get me out of this funk I was in. Sure enough, the giant park in the middle of the city, complete with old restored fort, was prime for a big night of orchestra music and fireworks. All the families were heading there with their blankets and coolers in tow. I walked through the park, careful not to step on carefully laid blankets or little children, and found a small patch of green not yet settled. I slowly sat down as I flashed a smile at those around me. After about forty-five minutes, no one had said a word to me. Not one person introduced themselves or asked me about the motorcycle apparel I was wearing...not even a hello. Then I thought, *"Why should they?* This was not their responsibility. If I always waited for the other person to make the first move, I would be waiting the rest of my life. I always seemed to do that. I decided to take action and scoped out three women, probably in their fifties and sixties, who were sitting near me.

"So what's this all about, anyway?" I asked the lady closest to me. They filled me in on some of the history of the event. I was successful in jump-starting the small talk. They then asked me where I was from, and there it was, an honest-to-goodness conversation. They turned out to be very friendly, offered me something to drink, and introduced me around to some other people in the area, who then proceeded to feed me. I was soon known as California John, and for a short time, I felt my loneliness subside a little.

Speaking to these women taught me another lesson: A person is usually alone until choosing not to be. How often had I let opportunities pass me by because I had been too shy, too embarrassed, or too unsure of myself? Yet, looking back at the times when I had started a conversation or decided to break the ice, I realized I had seldom been disappointed in the rich conversation that followed. People want to interact with each other, and unless someone takes the initiative, a positive experience can easily be lost forever. The sad part is that the moment lost could have been a life-changing experience.

The orchestra did an outstanding job, and the fireworks were...well, they were fireworks. It was getting late, and I was getting ready to get some sleep. I was hoping that somehow, my perennial and often over-exaggerated whining about my lack of night accommodations would weigh heavily on my new companions and they would take pity on me. I gave them the best puppy-dog look I could muster, but to no avail. When I told them I was going to head down the road and try to find a place to sleep, they said, "Okay, it was very nice meeting you." Yeah, like sixty-year-old women are going to invite a strange biker over for the night. Well, it was worth a shot.

I pulled into Westernville around midnight and coasted onto the library's lawn as quietly as possible. No cars, that was good. I parked my bike close to the library wall and gently set my sleeping bag on the porch. No tent tonight.

As I was doing this, I saw some things I hadn't noticed earlier—spiders. There were spiders all over the place. The porch was outlined with a wooden white railing, and there must have been twenty spiders making their home there, busily working on their web designs. Now, I don't necessarily have arachnophobia, but I am more a lover of pets with four legs or fewer. I tried not to let this bother me because they seemed to be quite content to remain on their personalized webs, which hung from the wooden porch railings.

As I crawled into my bag, I looked up and quickly witnessed a spider the size of a half dollar rappelling from the ceiling of the porch in the general direction of my face. He was making pretty good speed, too. I don't know if some spiders are good-looking and others are ugly, but at this moment, this was a very ugly-looking insect. It didn't take me long to realize that the thought of spiders dancing on my face all night would definitely affect my quality of sleep.

I, along with my sleeping bag, quickly made a move. I scanned the area for alternative sleeping locations and noticed a picnic table near a grove of trees not far from the building and near the high wall. That would have to do. I transported my sleeping bag to the top of the table and slid in, remembering Glenn's stories of doing the exact same thing on some of his rides. The weather was still very hot and humid, so curling up inside the bag was not an option. This was very unfortunate, because this weather was perfect if you were a mosquito. The moment I would stick my head inside my bag in an attempt at temporary reclusion, I would create my own personal sauna. Combine this with the two dogs in the park who were quite hot for each other all night, and that equaled about four hours of sleep for this novice library camper. A true no-win situation. Now I was lonely, depressed, grumpy, *and* tired.

I woke up the next morning around 5:30 and found myself drenched in the morning dew. The hot, wet weather had transformed into cold, wet weather, and I was shivering almost uncontrollably as I found myself only half-covered by the bag. The moment I began to move, my back quickly informed me that it did not appreciate the replacement of my air mattress for a hard wooden picnic table. Not one of my better camping experiences. As much as I dreaded exiting the warmth my sleeping bag offered, I knew that Westernville would soon be waking up, and I was not ready to be the center of attention or to be taken to the local jail for trespassing, especially on a Sunday. I forced myself out of "bed," packed up the scooter, and hit the road once again, hoping the day would renew my spirits.

The low overcast turned into a bright and sunny day, and I relished any chance I could to absorb the warm rays, even though it was still early. As I wound through the forested turns, I dreaded the shady spots created by the tall trees, as the temperature would dip at least fifteen degrees, sending chills through my leather-jacketed body. As rough as the night had been, it felt good to be up and riding so early for a change. The beauty of the Adirondack Mountains and the lush green hills that greeted me through the misty morning made me forget my loneliness for a while, and I looked forward to a promising new day.

I arrived in Lake Placid at high noon and pulled off to the side of the road to catch glimpses of the Olympic structures used during the 1980 winter Olympics. I remember, as a nineteen-year-old kid, sitting in the living room of my home near Lodi, watching the US hockey team and the "miracle on ice." I'm not a hockey fan, but for some reason, I had watched every game of the series, completely oblivious that I was experiencing one of the greatest sporting achievements in the history of the Olympics. And now I was riding through that city fifteen years later.

A few hours past Lake Placid, I exited another glorious mountainous turn, when Lake Champlain suddenly appeared in the distance. I soon neared the long line of cars waiting their turn to be transported by ferry across the sky-blue lake. Being on two wheels once again afforded me the advantage of moving toward the front of the line, and I did so, feeling no guilt whatsoever. I parked, dismounted, and waited for the ferry that was barely visible on the horizon, coming our way. After I had spent not more than a few minutes standing and stretching, a man in his twenties pulled up next to me on his Honda sport bike, wearing a full-face helmet and riding leathers.

A sport bike is more like a road-racing bike, and the rider must lean forward to ride as he hides behind a small aerodynamic faring. These bikes are made for speed, and his leathers were not the black leather I modeled but a blue-and-red full-body suit with thick padding in strategic areas. These two classes of motorcycles and riders are on opposite ends of the spectrum, with speed on one side and cruising on the other. I remember one race shop had a tee shirt with two Harleys on a mountain road with a sport bike behind them, obviously impatient to pass but with no room. The caption said, "If you want to sit on a sofa...stay at home."

He turned his bike off, took off his color-coordinated red-blue helmet, and, after seeing where I was from, immediately began asking questions. I found myself bragging incessantly about my faithful riding companion and just how reliable my Harley had been. "Really?" he replied skeptically more than once, because Harley, until recently, had not been regarded as the most reliable of bikes. There had been years when the bikes actually leaked oil on the showroom floor! I shrugged off his cynicism and continued the boasting about the dependability of the newer models and threw in a few wild hand gestures for emphasis. His constant nodding told me I had made my point and that not only had I convinced him but he was sure to run out to the nearest dealership and buy his own.

The ferry's horn sounded loudly, telling us it was coming into port. The incoming cars drove off the ferry's heavy metal ramp, and the sound of cars starting their engines behind me was my cue to lead them onto the vessel. My converted friend had replaced the helmet on his head, and I simply dangled mine from the handlebars by the chin strap. I reached for the start button, as I had done hundreds of times before. Although I couldn't see them, I knew that many eyes were fixed upon me, waiting for me to start her up and hear what she sounded like. I figured I would dazzle them with a loud rev of the engine once she jumped to life, just to share with them what a real motorcycle sounded like. I always love this part. I'm sure it is a male thing.

With a cocky grin on my face, I pushed the starter button and heard the awesome sound...of silence. My lower lip immediately dropped below my foot pegs. I looked over at my Honda friend, and he at me. He, mercifully, did not break out in laughter right there in front of me but simply smiled and said, "Bummer," as he rode up the ramp onto the boat. I felt many a silent laugh behind me as I pushed my bike aboard, tempted to make loud Harley noises with my mouth but deciding against it.

I knew it had to be the stupid battery cable again and could not believe my bike had picked this very moment to make a fool of me. Pride goeth before the fall. That was when I had realized that the only difference between the words "cool" and "fool" is one letter. I also knew I would have to push the bike off the ferry on an uphill ramp and wondered how I would manage to do that in front of all these people. Fortunately, a gentleman who had walked onto the ferry took pity on my situation and offered to help me push the bike when we landed. I don't think he realized how much I appreciated that.

My new best friend in the entire world and me, pushed the bike up the off-ramp and off to the side of the road, and I made certain I did not make any eye contact with the departing vehicles. My friend on the Honda waved and yelled something to me. I would like to think he said, "Nice bike, wish I had one!" but I kind of doubt it. Within thirty minutes, the battery-cable problem was fixed and I was on my way to Burlington, Vermont.

Once there, I tried to call a good friend, whom I had recently heard lived there, but he was not at home. The feeling of loneliness had not left and, in fact, was stronger than ever. I really wanted some companionship, but it just wasn't coming together. Because Burlington was a college town, I cruised down to the central area and located an outdoor pub. I hung around for a while, making small talk with the bartender, sipping a beer, but nothing really clicked with anyone. It was a sunny summer Sunday, and everyone seemed quite involved in personal discussions. Feeling a little dejected, I decided to head out of town and find a place to camp for the night. My lonesomeness was getting worse, and I was growing more and more disgusted with myself for feeling like this.

Dusk was approaching, and I needed to find a place to sleep. I felt that the two-lane road I was using to take me to Montpelier would surely surrender to me a fitting mountain stay for the night, and I was right. I followed my instincts when I noticed a sign pointing to a ski resort and decided to take a little detour. Not more than five miles in, I noticed a dirt road to the left. I looked around to make sure nobody saw me, and I slowly turned onto the dirt, where, moments later, I was sitting on top of a plateau that overlooked the valley. This was one of the best locations I had found in some time, and certainly, was a wonderful change from the library picnic-table experience the night before. I really needed to meet some new people, and I quickly fell asleep, determined to do just that.

As I cruised toward Montpelier, Vermont, for breakfast the next morning, I had a strange feeling that something was going to take place, but I wasn't sure what it might be. That hope picked me up a little as I entered the city limits of Montpelier. I had been to this beautiful New England town once before on business, when I was only twenty-four years old. It had been my very first computer trade show, and I remember being inexperienced. I do remember that it was Columbus Day weekend and the changing colors of the leaves had been indescribably beautiful that time of year. White buildings with the traditional New England black shutters dotted the landscape and you could count on seeing at least five or six church steeples in the distance. All this nestled against rolling forested hills. This would be a good place to eat breakfast.

I inquired of a couple walking down the street where I might find a good restaurant, and they excitedly told me of the "best place in town." I was soon disappointed when I found it was closed on Mondays. I would soon be glad that it was. I cruised down the quaint main street complete with outdoor cafes, gift shops, and various assortments of local businesses. As I glanced to my left, across the street, I noticed a nice-looking place with outdoor seating. The weather was near perfection, and I'm sure if I had eaten inside, I would have been ticketed for failing to enjoy the Vermont outdoors.

Soon after I had settled into my patio chair, my waitress appeared, asking if I wanted coffee. My quick response of yes must have added urgency to the matter, as she was back with a hot steaming cup in a matter of seconds. She was very cute, with brunette bangs that hung down toward her eyes and fell around her head just above the shoulders. Her slender figure was more athletic than shapely, and I could tell she was an outdoors type of girl. What really got my attention was her intelligence. Her wit was endless, and as she asked me about my ride, we traded sharp one-liners back and forth, cracking each other up. It quickly became clear she was a very deep thinker. Her name was Kelly. A few moments later, two ladies in their fifties seated themselves at a table next to mine, and before long, we were all engaged in active conversation with an emphasis on one-liner jokes. Exactly what the doctor had ordered.

When I opened the miniature notebook that should have contained my bill, I found it had been replaced by a note, which read, "On the house, have a great trip." A large smile came to my face as I set the bill down and took another sip of coffee. She sheepishly appeared through the door, coffee pot in hand, and I thanked her several times for her generous gift. After another hot refill, I propped my boots up on a chair and drank in the Vermont sunshine. It had been a good morning and a fitting way to end the month of July and to mark my journey's 8,000th mile.

Moments later, Kelly returned with a determined look on her face, stared me right in the eyes, and said, "I have a proposition for you. If I can get the rest of the day off work, how would you like to go horseback riding with me in the beautiful hills of Vermont?"

The two ladies next to me started howling with laughter while chanting, "Go girl, go girl."

I grinned and said, "Gee, let me think....Yes."

"Be right back," Kelly said with a huge smile as she quickly turned and disappeared through the kitchen doors. Somehow, the sunshine on my face seemed to feel warmer now. My loneliness had lifted, and I thought about how critically important it is that we share ourselves with people. We are wired that way. It is the way God made us.

Kelly returned about five minutes later and said, "Let's go!" I followed her yellow Volkswagon Jetta through the tight mountainous turns that took us up and away from the capital of Vermont. Following each turn signal, the roads seemed to get a little narrower, until finally, the asphalt gave way to dirt. We passed through a little one-horse mountain town called Calais, and not soon after, the yellow car found home and turned left into the driveway of a modest single-story home. To the right was a small corral where two horses were nervously pacing back and forth. Kelly was staying with her parents over the summer so she could save a little money while completing her education and teaching degree.

I parked my luggage-laden bike in the driveway. Before moving toward the corral, Kelly and I just hung around the driveway and took some time to get to know each other a little bit. It was soon evident that my suspicions that Kelly was a deep thinker had been right on the money. Her sentences consisted of carefully chosen words and phrases that forced the listener to concentrate on what she was saying so as not to miss the messages behind the words. There was passion in her voice, and she often used my name in her discussions, pulling me in even further. She held very strong opinions about many issues, and I knew we would be in for some lively discussions as we became more familiar with each other, but what struck me the most about Kelly was that although she maintained a somewhat opinionated and strong personality, it was balanced by an almost childlike innocence and a humility that bordered on insecurity. She seemed to be living as a dichotomy, as if she were confident in her opinion yet needed reinforcement. It was an interesting mixture, but one that was very magnetic and likable. I wanted to get to know her more.

I teased her a little about picking up strange men, and she emphatically claimed she had never done "this kind of thing" before but that something had made her take the chance. She had made a decision that highlighted what my journey was all about, and it was paying off. I asked, "So, would you have asked a guy to go riding who had not been riding a Harley?"

She paused and, with a wisp of a smile, said, "John, I don't think so." Is it any wonder I love my bike so much? "Let's go riding!" she said, and we headed over to the corral.

"Have you ridden before?" she asked as we opened the gate and headed to the shed where the saddles were kept.

"Oh sure, a few times," I replied, stretching the truth as much as I could. Actually, the last time I had really taken a horse for a ride was at church camp when I was all of thirteen years old. It hadn't been a pretty sight, and this particular camp occurrence would not exactly go down in the annals of great equestrian achievements.

I had been attempting to show off to a girl who had not given me the time of day to that point. She had been at the corral and I had been determined that I was going to make an impression on her. When asked which horse I wanted to take for a ride, I had quickly chosen the largest horse I could find. The girl in charge had objected to this choice because of its size and because it did not have a saddle. "Don't need one!" I had immediately responded. "I've ridden bareback before," I lied.

"Okay," she had relented, and, with the aid of the fence, I had hoisted myself up onto the horse's huge back. Nothing I could do or say had made him move, and with the pretty girl watching, I had felt that my control over this situation was beginning to wane quickly. So, being the thoughtful corral girl she was, she had smacked him hard in the butt with a switch. I'm not sure if horses can actually "lay rubber," but this one had taken off like the glue factory representative was after him. He had hugged the perimeter of the corral fence at full run, twice jumping the ditch in the middle. I'd never jumped a horse in my life. I was pulling on his mane until the hair was nearly coming out in clumps, while yelling, "Whoa" at the top of my lungs. Nothing had mattered then except getting back in one piece.

My horse was heading, full speed, directly for the twenty or so other horses grouped together at the point where my wild ride had begun. Then, as quickly as it had begun, it ended. The horse had buried his hooves in the ground, probably breaking the Guinness World Record for horse stopping, and, as physics dictates, I had continued onward, flying over his head and hitting several horses' backsides on my way down, coming dangerously close to becoming a human horse enema. I had then slid along the ground in a quasi upside-down position, ridding all of my upper shoulders of my smooth, tan skin. Needless to say, I hadn't gotten the girl.

As this scene played in my mind, I wondered if I was wise in hiding my challenging horse experiences. I guess you never outgrow trying to impress a girl. "Nice horsey," I whispered into the horse's ear as its large dark eye stared through me and its head moved up and down nervously. Kelly brought the saddle over, and I let her do all the cinching and fitting, because it was obvious she knew what she was doing. "She's pretty gentle," she said as I placed my right foot into the stirrup and slung my left leg around the horse's back, settling nicely into the saddle. The creaking of the leather as it moved around the horse's back brought a smile to my face. I was riding a horse in Vermont.

I followed Kelly through tight wooded trails, which opened up into green grassy meadows. "Wanna race?" she yelled as we come upon yet another open pasture area.

I dug my heels in, stood up in the saddle, and gave it my best hyah! Hey, I didn't do badly, but I was scared to death. When the trails forced us to a walk, we talked about religion, society, and relationships, and although there were many issues we did not agree on, we each held a deep respect for the other's opinions.

At one point, we came upon a grouping of maple trees connected by long plastic tubes and a valve where the tasty sweet sap could be set free from its wooden jail. I instinctively knew this was all part of the maple-syrup process, but this was all very new to me and I inquired as to how the process worked. She explained how the spigots are opened and the thin liquid is collected through the tubes. When it is heated up, you get syrup. I asked if we could go over and suck on a tree to give it a taste. She stopped her horse, turned around, and looked at me like I had three heads. With a glare that balanced on the edge of sarcastic disgust, she said, "Are you serious?"

"Yeah," I dumbly replied, not getting the hint that I probably should pass my question off as a joke at this point.

"Sap can only be collected in the spring," she said, rolling her eyes.

I looked at her, and in an attempt to set her straight, replied, "I'm from Southern California, where our four seasons consist of earthquakes, floods, riots, and fires, and you think that I was born with the knowledge that maple tree sap can only be sucked in the spring?" With that, she rolled with laughter and almost fell off her horse. This would become an ongoing joke. In fact, during the next Christmas season, I would receive a beautifully gift-wrapped maple syrup set. The attached note would explain that the syrup had just been sucked out of the tree that morning by her sister.

After riding through small towns and touring an old New England church in a field, we decided to head back. When we exited the woods, the corral and driveway were in sight, and behind my bike was parked a sedan. "Dad's home," she said. I was suddenly a little nervous. I am sure his curiosity had been more than a bit aroused when he had pulled up to find a Harley with a California license plate and his daughter and horses both missing. Once we met, Kelly's father and I hit it off quite well, and I ended up spending the night at their house.

I took Kelly out to dinner that night and promised her a ride on the bike. She had never ridden a Harley before, and I felt that I was providing her with a first-time experience just as she had provided one for me. She got on the back, and we headed into town, where we once again found ourselves discussing many serious issues while devouring scrumptious Italian food. It seemed we did not lack for anything to talk about, and the conversation eventually turned toward past and current relationships.

As it turned out, I was able to give her some fairly sound advice regarding some relationship issues in her own life, because she seemed to be going through much of the same doubts I had experienced in my previous situation. In my life, however, I had chosen to ignore them and the results had been disastrous. I could tell that my words carried much more weight with her because they were saturated with experience. It was freeing to me that I could see positive results bloom from an ugly event in my life and that with each person I could potentially help, my past would become less painful. This morning, Kelly and I had been strangers, but tonight, we were sharing deep, life-changing words of encouragement. What a difference twelve hours can make.

On the way home, as we were cruising over one of the dirt roads toward home, something hit me in the hand and bounced off my chest. It felt like plastic and probably weighed no more than two pounds. I was very lucky I was not hit in the face, because I was wearing no eye or helmet protection. I turned around in search of the flying debris and found a very irate bat lying on the ground with a bloody wing broken. He hissed at me, and I was amazed at the number of sharp teeth crammed into his small mouth. That was a first.

Kelly called in late to work the next morning so we could chitchat a bit longer, knowing we would not have the opportunity to do this again for some time, if ever. She told me that I had made her summer, and I let her know how important and timely her offer had been to me. Her willingness to take a chance in life and approach this stranger had broken the feelings of loneliness and self-pity I had been experiencing over the past few days. This one simple act had positively affected two people's lives and created lifelong memories.

We had a great breakfast that morning, and I knew it was time to continue on. Kelly had been an oasis in a desert of loneliness for me, and it was very hard to say good-bye. Our twenty-four hours together had flown by. We gave each other a huge hug and we knew we would always stay in touch. It was a good way to begin the first day of August.

Later that day, I crossed the state line into Maine. I was absolutely dumbfounded that I was actually in this state. Maine was one of those states that had just seemed incredibly far away, like another country. I had actually ridden my motorcycle to Maine! By now, I had been on the road for just under two months. I silently thanked the Lord for the safety he had shown me, the people I had met, and the lessons I had learned thus far.

Unexpectedly, Maine turned out to be one of my favorite states for riding. It is a beautiful place in the summer, and I thoroughly enjoyed my ride that day. I rode to a town called Naples and had a very hard time finding a place to camp...too many homes tucked away in the woods. Finally, I found an area behind a boat-repair warehouse where I could hide myself in a thick brushy area. I ventured off to a local tavern to relax a bit and listen to a little music. An older gentleman, sitting to my right, engaged me in a little conversation, and it turned out he was also a bike rider. The time passed quickly as we shared stories.

Mother Nature called, and I excused myself and headed off toward the bathroom, leaving my things in front of the bar stool. When I returned, a very rough-looking younger man who had obviously been drinking long before he

got there was sitting in my chair. It turned out that he was a serious local trou-
blemaker and lived with one of the notorious bike-gang leaders in the area.

I tapped him on the shoulder and politely said, "Hey, man, that's my chair."
He turned around and just stared at me. The older guy I had been speaking
with echoed my claim, but it didn't seem to matter. About this time, my chair
stealer's equally drunk friend began to take notice and fixed a glare upon me
as well. Now, sometimes I can let this kind of thing go and sometimes I can't.
I don't know why, but this time, I couldn't. I felt the anger begin to rise, and
I said in an even tone, "That's my stuff, and I want my chair."

There was silence for about fifteen seconds, and then he half laughed, half
smirked, and said, "Take your chair, man," and sat on the stool next to me.
After about a minute, he turned to me and said, "So you want to tell me what
you're doing in these parts?"

Without turning to look at him, I blankly replied, "Not really." With this,
I seemed to gain his respect, for what that was worth. He apologized for the
chair incident and stuck his hand out. I took it and made unwanted small
talk. He later invited me over to his place for the night, and I quickly refused.
I believe in taking chances, but well-calculated ones. Sometimes, you just
know not to get involved.

I decided to call it an early evening, and on my way out, I met Shawn, a big,
burly, dark-haired, bearded man who was one of the bartenders. He looked to
be in his late twenties, but I am guessing he looked older than he really was.
We talked a little outside, and I soon found out that his passion in life was
playing snare drums. He looked more like a bouncer than a snare drum
player, not that I know what a snare drum player should look like. He had
competed professionally and was ranked eighth in the world. I hadn't even
known there were snare drum competitions. He was a very nice guy, but an
hour of snare drum talk was about my limit. It was great, however, to talk to
someone who was so excited and passionate about something in his life. I
headed back to camp, and although there were still people working at the boat
repair shop, they didn't seem to care that I passed by their establishment and
disappeared behind the brush. It was a good night's sleep.

Another gorgeous day greeted me as I rode nothing but beautiful country
roads. I decided to put my map away and simply take back roads that pointed
in the general direction of northern Maine without knowing where exactly I
was or what roads I would be taking. I felt like I was on a magic carpet as the
two-lane roads, void of traffic, transported me up and down rolling hills and
gradual curves. My soul felt like the billowy white clouds that hung overhead,

alone and free. There was not one other place in the world I wanted to be at that moment. If the trip would have ended this day, it would have been worth it. Everyone should experience this kind of freedom.

Maine's backdrop was a landscape painter's dream, with green rolling hills for as far as the eye could see, sporadically intermingled with groupings of pine trees representing individual forested neighborhoods. Scattered throughout this picturesque panorama were long, white barns and houses connected as single large structures. I assumed that the heavy snows of winter required safe and warm passage between the two buildings.

By late afternoon, the combination of forest and farmland had changed to all forest, and extremely dense forest at that. I had been cruising north on Route 11 for about an hour and kept a constant watch for deer and moose as I had been warned to do by those familiar with the area. My mind reverted back to that first day as I had swerved my bike through the thick Southern California traffic. *No car-pool lanes to worry about here*, I thought as a huge smile came to my face. My destination for the day was a small town called Millinocket, Maine, about two-thirds of the way up the state.

As I crested a small hill and rounded one of its many turns, a vista opened up along with a rest area for anyone who wanted to relax and snap a few pictures. I needed to stretch the old legs so decided to do just that. A few minutes later, I heard and then witnessed another Harley pass by me with the rider's ponytail suspended horizontally by the wind. About five minutes later, the same sound seemed to be returning, as the same Harley had apparently turned around and was pulling into the rest area where I currently was relaxing. When "he" pulled in, it didn't take me long to realize that he was actually a she. As it turned out, Karlynn was taking two weeks off work to ride a quick loop around Maine and then back to her Connecticut home. Now there was a cool girl. We rode into Millinocket together, and she bought me dinner before continuing on. Had I known she was buying, I would have ordered something a little more expensive than a chicken salad on whole wheat for $1.50.

Karlynn was a somewhat attractive lady, but in a tough kind of way. She was feminine but also had a tomboyish quality about her. Maybe it was just all the leather. I very much enjoyed talking with her, and I do remember she had one of those great smiles that automatically puts the recipient in a good mood. She was tempted to stay in town that night but decided it would be better to move on and get some more miles under her belt. We traded phone numbers, and we promised to stay in touch.

Finding a campsite would not be a problem tonight. Locations were plentiful because of the expanse of deep woods and the surplus of snowmobile trails that cut perfect paths through the timber. I found a nice trail just outside of town among the thick trees, marshy ground, and numerous insects. My temporary forest abode was extremely secluded, and the solitude was welcome.

For the most part, I enjoyed the ritual of setting up my nightly camp spots, except for one element of the ceremony, which was blowing up my air mattress. I came to dread this chore so much that I invented a contest with myself to see how many breaths it would take to blow the stupid thing up. I figured that harnessing my competitive spirit might make this task a little more bearable. I believe my personal world record was fifty blows. Only a man could invent a contest with himself and be completely excited at besting his last effort.

At other times, I would try to rush the process by blowing my brains out and pumping the mattress up in world-record time. As soon as I would regain consciousness, I would start over again because the air had leaked out during my temporary sleep. Well, I might be exaggerating a little. Every evening, I chastised myself for not paying the extra money for the self-inflatable brand.

After hiking the woods of Maine for a while, I decided to go into town. I worked out at a local gym, grabbed a shower, and inquired of the attractive manager where the nightlife might be. She told me of a place downtown called the Blue Ox. That sounded like a good place to me. What I didn't know was that after I left the gym, she called her mother and a few other friends to inform them of the new stranger in town. Like I said before, small towns are a real ego booster.

I arrived at the Blue Ox that evening and planted myself at the bar with the full intention of just relaxing and basking in the reality that I was in northern Maine. I dialogued with the bartender for quite some time and called my brother from the pay phone to let him know how far I had come. During the time I was there, I noticed a long table that was slowly beginning to fill up with locals, all women, whose ages ranged from the mid-twenties to late forties. After a time, the oldest of the crew sauntered over a bit awkwardly and said, "There's an awful fun table over here, and I think you should join us." Far be it from me to deny such a friendly request and not be sociable.

We talked most of the night, and my ego was enjoying the fact that I was the center of attention. This sure never happened at home. They caught themselves up on the local gossip, using names I did not know, but I nodded like I did. Theresa was the older woman who had invited me over to their table; she had lost her husband in a plane crash a few years back. I could tell that she was still suffering from the loss but was trying to forget the pain any way she could. She'd had a few drinks by this time and was eyeing me like I might be the main course for the night. She seemed like a very nice lady, but definitely lonely. One of the girls whom I did get to know better was Patty. She had short brunette hair, was in her late twenties, and had a great smile, and I loved her cutting and sharp personality. She was divorced with two children, but she had a classy quality about her that I really liked.

The tavern closed about 1:00 a.m., and Patty and I decided to go for a ride to a nearby lake. It was getting fairly cold, and I needed to make a detour to my campsite so I could retrieve my jacket. Patty rode on the back as I made the left turn off the paved road and into the dark forest. She put her lips to my ear and kiddingly asked that if I decided to kill her and cut her up in the woods, to leave a note for her family. It was a pretty morbid joke, but until she said that, I did not realize the trust she had put in me, a stranger from out of town.

Riding down the narrow dirt road to camp, I managed to hit at least three good-sized rocks in the dark, one of which dented the bottom side of my exhaust pipe and nearly put us on our backsides. I stroked my bike's tank and apologized for my insensitivity but secretly felt I had now paid her back for the little prank she had pulled on me at the Lake Champlain ferry.

I am sure Patty was relieved when, after I showed her my tent setup, we began riding out toward the road again. We cruised out to the lake and talked beneath the stars. She reinforced much of what I had seen to this point—that many people in small towns feel they are stuck and unable to get out. They have children at a young age, many are divorced in their twenties and are barely getting by, much less have money to pack up and start over. Patty was in this exact position. She conveyed a type of hopelessness about her situation, and I couldn't do much more than listen. I felt sorry for her and anyone else who felt trapped in life with no way out.

I returned her home around 3:00 a.m. and gave her a kiss goodnight. It seemed every guy in the bar that night, married or not, had been on the hunt for a one-night stand from anyone who would be willing. Patty had been especially bothered by one married local who would have given anything for a little tumble that night with her. Society would tell me that was what I should be doing to be cool or a man's man. It's just not my value system. That night, I wanted Patty to know that there are guys out there who actually look to women for more than one-night stands. It may not have been much, but there's one girl in a small town who knows she was respected that night.

As I headed up to Edmunston, Canada, the following day, I knew I would once again be leaving the States for some time. My goal had changed somewhat, during the trip, and I was now intent on reaching the northern tip of Newfoundland. My goals just seemed to get me further away from home.

When I reached the signs informing me I was reaching the Canadian border, I was looking a little rougher than usual with my skullcap, beard, and longer hair. The immigration people were nice enough, but as I came out of the office, they informed me that they were going to have their weapons- and pot-sniffing dog smell around the bike a bit. I didn't even know a dog could smell weapons. The border agent looked at me intensely and said, "Anything you want to tell us before we start?"

I confidently responded, "Sniff away."

The group of men seemed to take a liking to me, and one man in particular offered the garage area as a storage facility for my bike while I walked around town, as Edmundston was located literally on the border. I told him I would take him up on his offer that evening and asked if he knew of any local campgrounds. He told me of one just about five kilometers out of town. It definitely wasn't the cleanest or prettiest campground in the world, but it only cost me $3 American. That made it a lot prettier and cleaner.

Later that evening, I headed back into Edmundston and stored my bike in the immigration garage. I walked around town, visited a few stores, grabbed a bite to eat, and mingled with a few people listening to music from an outdoor band. Communication was difficult, as I discovered that no one in Edmundston ever chose to speak English to me, although I was told most people there could. It was French all the way. Now, I have been to Mexico many times and my Spanish is fairly nonexistent, but I knew enough to put words together and never felt uncomfortable in not knowing the language. Here, I felt very uneasy for some reason, like a real outsider. I continued to work through the city's street and noticed a very large old church located in the center of town that was brightly lit up with giant flood lights.

I also noticed something very bizarre. There were spiders everywhere! There were literally thousands of them all around me...on the ground, on the buildings, in the trees, and in the streetlights. Edmundston was absolutely full of large ugly brown spiders. This place was dropping on my favorite places-to-visit list very quickly.

Feelings of isolation and loneliness began to creep back into my soul, and I wished I had someone to talk to in English. I went back for my bike, talked to the immigration guys some more, and turned in around midnight. It had been a somewhat hollow evening and had been a huge letdown compared to the previous four nights.

I was awakened by the sound of raindrops pelting the tent. As I rolled over onto my back and opened my eyes, the sun perfectly silhouetted about fifteen large spiders that were perched on the outside of my tent. Rain and spiders...perfect. Suddenly, my desire to roll out of my nice warm sleeping bag took a major turn for the worse. I was reminded of my tent's inability to be completely waterproof as I sat up and discovered that a pile of my possessions was soaked. I dreaded the task of packing up in the rain. It rained hard the entire day, and I managed to cover only 150 miles through the New Brunswick roads. I found a motel to dry everything out and worked at trying to improve my attitude. The rain did not let up all night.

The rain had stopped by morning, but the weather was still dark and drizzly. I rode through the rest of New Brunswick, briefly touched upon the eastern coast, and then headed inland to Nova Scotia, where I was due to stay with a family I had met through another friend during a wedding in Northern California. I called Greg McLean once I reached the small town of Stellarton, and the voice on the other end was so friendly, you would have thought we had been friends for years. I told him the location of the pay phone I was calling from, and Greg and his oldest son, Chris, came by in their family van to show me the way to their home. Greg was as friendly in person as he was on the phone. His wife, Mary, was the sister of the man who had married one of my good friends in California. Like I said earlier, nobody was safe from my visits.

Their hospitality was overwhelming. Jared, the youngest of the three kids, was temporarily booted out of his room so I would have a comfortable place to stay, and Greg continually "forced" beers and good food upon me. Just what the doctor had ordered.

Greg and his brothers owned one of the largest carpet stores in Nova Scotia, and as I had sold carpet when I was in my early twenties, we could discuss the business a bit. After talking to Greg regarding the Canadian tax system, I was almost grateful for the tax system that we had in the States. Between the provincial and the goods and services taxes, Greg had to pay a 20% tax on his $25,000 van. With this, coupled with the declining quality of health care and social services and lack of tax write-offs such as mortgage interest, I could see why he was very upset during the discussion. If I ever wanted to get Greg riled up, all I had to do is bring up the tax issue. It was like watching Pavlov's dogs salivate.

That first night, we all went out with some of Greg's friends, and although I had every intention of paying for my meal, Greg insisted it was on him, emphatically repeating to me, "You don't worry about the price, get what you want." We then went to a country dance club, and I soon found that people in this part of the world had absolutely no idea how to dance to Country and Western music. As we stood up at the second-floor railing, I noticed two very attractive women sitting together, and Greg all but dared me to go over and talk with them. A man may have many weaknesses, but never dare him. I went over and started to talk to Kathleen. She was a little wary at first but warmed up a bit as soon as I turned on the charm and wit (translation: she knew I wouldn't leave and there was nobody else a whole lot better anyway). Greg came over after seeing my success, called me a dog, and stated that he and the others had to get going. I asked Kathleen if she could take me home (–to Greg's home) later, and she agreed. Kathleen's friend, Darlene, also joined us, and we had a good time hanging around that night.

Around three in the morning, Kathleen drove Darlene and me to her house so Darlene could take home her own car, which had been parked there. Kathleen and I went inside for a while and started talking. We soon found ourselves delving into fairly personal events in our past, and I found out that she had been married and divorced with one small child. From what she told me, she'd had a pretty tough relationship. She asked me if I had ever been married, and I unconsciously glanced at my watch and looked at the date before answering. I looked up at her with a twisted grin and said, "Well, as a matter of fact, I was married a year ago today." *Nice timing,* I thought. How often does a single guy say that?

I couldn't help but think how my life had changed in only one year. My expectations and goals had been completely different then. I'd had a steady, well-paying job, I had been about to be married for the first time and had assumed we would be talking about children about this point in my life. Instead, I was out on the road, completely alone, in search of adventure, talking to a girl in Nova Scotia at three in the morning.

Although that year had been a difficult one, both materially and relationally, it had also been a time of intense growth. The truth is, we never seem to truly know how strong we are until we are tested. As I look back on my life and compare the good times and the bad times, there is no doubt that the times when I have grown the most have been times of struggle and pain. If we can make it a habit to recognize the benefits, we are much more able to deal with the pain. You play with the cards you are dealt.

So here I was, definitely not being miserable, and talking to Kathleen when there was a knock on the door. She slowly walked over, opened it, and said in a very startled voice, "What are *you* doing here?" First of all, a knock on the door at 3:00 a.m. is not a good sign. Her response was the second bad sign.

The knocker turned out to be her *very* drunk on-again, off-again boyfriend. Big surprise. I had no real intentions of doing much more than getting to know this girl, but I was sure he wasn't going to believe that. *This is something I definitely do not need*, I thought as I tried to make conversation with the slurring and weaving man. After a few minutes, I could tell he wasn't going to try anything, probably because he wasn't sure which of my five heads to swing at anyway. I suggested I head back to Greg's, and Kathleen was all too eager to drive me over. Well, that was fun.

A few days later, it was time to continue my journey to Newfoundland. I had absolutely no idea what this island would be like or what I would be getting myself into, but the thought of reaching an island that far north and that far from home definitely was an adrenaline rush. I arrived in North Sydney, Nova Scotia, around noon, and waited for the ferry that would take me to this mysterious place that had recently become my new destination. The ferry finally arrived, and my excitement grew as it slowly floated closer to port. The enormity of the ferry surprised me. It had a little of everything, including restaurants and a movie theater.

The weather was ideal, and the pants and tanktop I was wearing were more than sufficient in keeping me comfortable and warm. The motorcycles were the first to board, and I pulled in next to an older man who was securing his Honda Gold Wing using tie straps connected to the boat. He seemed very gruff at first, and his face reflected age beyond his actual years. I asked him for advice as to how I should anchor my motorcycle down, and he, somewhat reluctantly, showed me the ropes in preparing my bike for the seven-hour ferry ride ahead.

My first impression of this man did not hold long. After I had talked with him for a short time, the gruffness began to melt a bit and he appeared to enjoy the bloke from California who had taken an interest in him. He lived in Corner Brook, Newfoundland, and was returning home after a solo motorcycle trip through Nova Scotia. His name was Reuben, and it didn't take him long to let me know he was dealing with some major personal problems in his life, with marital woes heading the list. As he opened himself up to me more and more, it was evident that he had lived a turbulent life. I was fairly certain, however, that his marital problems were not exactly one sided and that his wife had had her hands full in dealing with his past. I think, deep down, he knew this to be true as well.

What really stuck out were his stories of severe alcoholism that had robbed him of much of his life. His large bulbous and pitted nose was a testament to that lifestyle. He literally had not been sober for twenty years! I asked how this was possible, and he told me his routine. He would have a number of beers in the morning, take five or six beers and some whiskey to work, and continue the ritual at night. Reuben said, "You could always tell who the alcoholics were at work by the size of their lunch boxes. On weekends, I would drink a flat (24) of beer by myself *before* going out. It gave me confidence." Most everyone in Corner Brook had known of him because he had been the "town drunk," he told me. After meeting some locals in Corner Brook over the next few days, I would find this to be true.

Reuben had been sober for eighteen years now, but it was difficult for me to comprehend a life that had been lived that way. He had been drunk when he had gotten married and through much of his married life. Now they were struggling, and although I did not delve into the details, it seemed to me as though his wife wanted to leave him and he didn't know how to change so she would stay. I detected a sadness in his eyes, of years lost forever that could no longer be retrieved, and now of a possible future spent in self-inflicted loneliness. My heart went out to him, and I was content to play the part of the avid listener. We talked off and on for most of the ride, and the time passed quickly. It was obvious that he appreciated my willingness to lend an ear and ask questions. I am sure very few people had taken the time to care enough, and I must admit, I found myself honestly caring for the man.

The announcement over the loudspeaker confirmed that we were about to arrive in Port aux Basques, Newfoundland. It was close to 8:00 p.m. I again reset my watch because in Newfoundland, it was four and a half hours later than it was at home in California. It was starting to get dark, and a feeling of loneliness once again began creeping up on me. Reuben was heading to Corner Brook that night, but I chose to forego the night ride so as not to miss out on any beautiful scenery along the way. I decided to camp somewhere near the port town. Reuben gave me his phone number, and I told him I would definitely call him.

The announcement was made to man the vehicles, and I went below to put on my gear and prepare my bike for departure. As with all ferries, the motorcycles had been parked in the front of the ferry and would be the first to exit, with mine in the front. I would be leading hundreds of cars and trucks off the ramp in my own personal parade. Very cool. The huge metal door began to lower with loud creaks and moans as the springs and hinges rubbed together without the benefit of lube. Automobile and truck engines began to roar to life, and I firmly pressed the starter button to add to the roar. The engine turned over at normal speed but refused to start. I couldn't believe it! What was it with my bike and ferries!?

As the motor continued to turn over, sucking precious energy from my battery, I prayed for the miracle of ignition, and after about a minute, she let out a backfire that sounded like a cannon blast. To make matters worse, the sound reverberated off the thick metal ferry walls, making it sound much louder than it really was. I sheepishly looked behind me and saw an older lady sitting in the passenger side of a pickup directly behind the blasting noise I had just made. Her eyes and mouth could not have opened up much wider, and that is probably the closest she has ever been to having a full-fledged heart attack. We briefly made eye contact; if looks could kill, this book never would have been written. The bike finally and mercifully choked to life, and I could not figure out why my trusty friend was suddenly feeling so sick.

Once I exited the ferry, I not only felt very alone but was also unsure of my bike's ability to get me around the island. Would it start in the morning? Could my battery handle the long cranking it might take to start? Would it suddenly die in the middle of nowhere? I didn't even know what language they spoke here.

I found a campground a slight distance from Port aux Basques but discovered that showers were not available. I figured it wasn't worth paying for if I couldn't wash the grime away and decided to find my own place to sleep. I found an old dirt road a ways down the highway that led me to an open area in the brush, and I set up camp there.

I ventured into town, hoping to catch a little night action and to perhaps meet a few people to lift my spirits. The bike had started, but not without some cranking. This was not good. Port aux Basques was a fairly small town, and after touring the entire place, I noticed that one bar had two chopped Harleys parked out front, probably the same bikes that I had seen on the ferry. *Good enough*, I thought and pulled into the parking lot.

Inside were about three locals, a lady bartender and the two Harley dudes I had indeed seen on the ferry. Nester and Dan were friendly chaps, and it was obvious that Dan had been drinking a long time before he had set foot in this bar. He welcomed me with open arms and, after pleasantries, stated in a very loud voice that I needed to be "screeched."

The process of being screeched is a Newfoundland tradition. To do it right, the following steps must take place, as I understand it. The host pours a shot of some nasty local dark rum into a glass, and the new person must repeat a quite lengthy verse or song native to Newfoundland. If the new person messes it up in any way, he must take a shot of the rum and then start over. This ritual is repeated until the verse is done perfectly. Once, or if, the stranger gets to the end of the song correctly, he must kiss a cod fish that is usually sitting there staring. They let me forego the song, but I did take the shot and kiss the fish. I was now screeched.

As it turned out, these two Harley men were from British Columbia, living out a dream they had shared for many years. They were to be gone for about a month, and they were shoving everything they possibly could into those precious thirty days. One thing was obvious: They were absolutely thrilled that they were actually doing it, and they commented on it often.

I found that English was spoken in Newfoundland but the accents could be so heavy that a stranger had no idea what was being said. One of the locals looked at me and, with a heavy accent, asked if I wanted a draw. I said, "Huh?" He asked again if I wanted a draw

The bartender looked at me, laughing, and said, "A toke." I declined the invitation to partake of his special cigarette, but Dan jumped at the opportunity, and they went out and did it up.

Nester was nearly falling asleep and not feeling well, and I was getting ready to head back. Dan returned from his draw, had two more beers, and inquired as to where I was staying for the night. Apparently, they had not set up their tent yet. He asked if they could stay with me, and I explained that I had no problem with neighbors but wasn't looking for roommates. He assured me they would erect their own tent.

I was a little wary of riding with drunk bikers, so I stayed very alert and cautious. As it turned out, it was a good thing. I was leading the crew, and just as I was about to turn left off the straight road, I took one quick look behind me, and there Dan was, passing me on the left, doing about eighty. That would have been one nasty wreck.

They followed me down the half mile of dirt road, and I arrived there just ahead of the two sloshed party animals. I parked my bike and watched as

Dan, the drunker of the two, pulled his bike near to where I was and proceeded to fall down, bike and all. I held my laughter within and waited for him to get up and pick himself, but he just laid there like a turtle on its back, rocking back and forth. I lost it. I walked over to him, laughing uncontrollably, and picked his Harley up for him. He loudly complained that he had twisted his knee, whereby Nester unsympathetically berated his friend by slurring, "Sherves you right, you big ash ole."

Listening to these two guys put up their tent just made me laugh harder. Every other word was a four-letter one and usually referred to many impossible physical acts that I won't expand on here. I'm sure they included the other's mother from time to time, and it seemed that no subject was safe as long as it degraded the other guy in some way. I'm not sure how they did it, but they managed to get their tent up. Their snoring was so loud that I am fairly certain many a moose came by looking for its long-lost love.

Not surprisingly, I was a bit more on the chipper side than my buddies were the next morning. Once again, the weather was flawless, with not one cloud in the sky. As I had feared, my bike was very stubborn in its starting routine. I thought perhaps that the salt in the air from the open ferry may have had some effect on the engine, but that didn't make a whole lot of sense. It was really bothering me. Once started, she ran like a trooper, and we headed toward Corner Brook.

Newfoundland is a beautiful island consisting primarily of rolling hills, forest, and thick brush. The occasional lakes and streams, interspersed here and there, made me feel more like I was in the Rockies than on an island. Once in the town of Corner Brook, I found a group of volunteers washing vehicles as a fundraiser for adult disabilities. This was exactly what I was looking for because I wanted to get the salt off the bike before the salt had a chance to work its rusting talents.

While the bikes were being washed, two local kids, around thirteen years old, boldly approached me on their bicycles and told me that they had just been looking at some magazines about Harleys. I could tell they had seen few bikes in person and had never really been near a Harley in their lives. They reminded me of me at that age. I asked Dan and Nester to give the boys a ride, as my seat was full of luggage. I have no doubt in my mind that by the look on these boys' faces, that ride made their year. I took their picture on the bikes and promised that I would send them a copy, with the negative, so their friends would truly believe they had been given a ride by "real bikers."

Nester and Dan went on to the city of St. John's, on the eastern side of the island, to continue their partying ways, and I bid them farewell. I gave

Reuben a call, and his wife picked up the phone. She sounded very nice. Reuben had told her of our meeting. Reuben had left a message that he would meet me at a certain place by the mall. I went back to the mall area, and my two young friends on their bicycles found me again. I asked them to check around the back for Reuben, and they excitedly got on their bicycles to help me out. I smiled to myself at their youthful enthusiasm to hang out with me.

Reuben and I finally got together. I could tell that he was very touched that I had followed through with my promise to call him. He showed me around the area as I followed behind his Gold Wing. He apologized for not being able to put me up, but with his marital problems, he figured it would not be a real good idea. I understood and had not expected an invitation.

Reuben showed me where I could find the YMCA, and I decided to go there, work out, and grab a shower. While I was pumping some iron, I began talking to a young, well-built kid named Paul. Through our conversation, he seemed absolutely enthralled by what I was doing. He left the workout room for a few minutes, and when he returned asked me if I would like to come to his folks' house for some good home cooking. It took me all of one nanosecond to reply in the affirmative, and suddenly, my evening meal was secured.

The dinner was delicious, and after telling Paul's avid moose-hunting father a few moose-hunting jokes, I was in. After my second piece of homemade blueberry pie, Paul and I left and checked out a few nightspots in Corner Brook, but there wasn't a whole lot to see. I still didn't have a place to stay that night but was relieved when Paul offered his couch. My second night in Newfoundland was an easy one, and I had made a few friends in the process. My loneliness had all but vanished.

As the alarm went off in the morning, I arose with excitement. This would be the day that I would reach the pinnacle of my trip, the northern tip of Newfoundland. It would be a good five-hour ride, and I planned to make camp somewhere in the woods that night. My goal would be a place called L'Anse aux Meadows, which is famous for being the oldest known settlement in North America, settled by the Vikings.

The road I would take would twist and turn through beautiful Gros Morne National Park and then parallel the western coast for about two hours. I would then cut inland through a very desolate stretch of land where, finally, the road would turn northward once again toward my final destination. The ride through the Gros Morne National Park was incredibly scenic, and I gracefully cruised through the winding two-lane road through mountains, lakes, and valleys until I was forced to turn right at the ocean's edge. The highway heading up the coast was much more desolate than I had imagined and was virtually void of people, but this desolation made the ride even more beautiful in a way.

About three hours into the ride, I noticed two older ladies standing by their disabled car as I passed them. I turned around and asked if they needed help. Their exasperated reply was, "We have no idea what we are doing." The flat tire was a simple problem to fix, and within fifteen minutes, the new tire was in place. Through our brief discussion, I discovered that the car owner's sister lived fifteen miles from my home in Southern California. It's a funny world sometimes.

An hour later, I stopped for a little cigar break, at a point where I could actually see the Labrador coast, hardly believing where I really was. The bike was starting a little better, but the desolation of this place made me nervous. A local man appeared out of nowhere on a little four-wheel ATV, with glasses as thick as Coke bottles, and spoke to me in the weirdest accent I have ever heard in my entire life. Many people warned me that the accent here could be tough to understand, but so far, I had not had much of a problem. With this guy, all I did was nod a lot and agree to a lot of things I couldn't understand. Not being sure what I was actually agreeing to, I thought it wise to continue on before I unknowingly traded my Harley for his quad.

As I cut inland toward the end of my trek, the landscape became very barren and exposed. Strong winds whipped in from the south, and I rode at a steep angle just to keep the bike moving in a straight line. I thought, *Don't let me down now, good buddy, not here.* Not thirty seconds after I had made this silent request, my bike sputtered for approximately five seconds and then kept running as if it was playing with my head. My heart was beating a mile a minute at this point, and I don't think I took a breath until I was once again in the shelter of the woods, twenty minutes later.

I reached my final objective a few hours before darkness set in. I found the visitors' center, which was perched on top of a hill overlooking the site of North America's first settlement, parked my bike in the lot, and slowly walked toward the edge. Gazing toward the horizon, I could see three or four icebergs floating by in the far distance. Now that was wild! I stood there in awe as I tried to comprehend what was taking place within me. I was actually gazing at icebergs in the middle of August and had accomplished this feat on only two wheels.

I had to call Eric and share this time with him. "You won't believe it," I said, "but I'm sitting here looking at icebergs." Eric had taken his map to work, and as we were talking, he told me he had found the place from where I was calling. That simple act meant a lot to me. It meant he was really interested in what I was doing, and in a way, I felt as if we had arrived together. Mark would have been proud, and I wished he could have been there to share this moment with me as well. Then again, I think he was. Three brothers, together again, sharing a victory together.

Words cannot possibly be written that would adequately describe my feelings over the next hour. I guess that's when you know you have a lifetime memory. As I think back to that time, a never-failing peace seems to wrap itself around my very self and I experience those sensations all over again, no matter where I am. My insides start to flutter and my heart starts to race as if I'm going out on my first date. This journey had cost me tens of thousands of dollars in expenses and lost wages, and in looking back, I would not take ten times that amount to give up what I experienced in that one hour. Did I feel successful? You bet I did. I sat and stared at the horizon for more than thirty minutes, never wanting to leave, never wanting to lose the emotions I was experiencing.

Although I had reached the zenith of my excitement, I also tried to prepare myself for the depression that would surely befall me as soon as I turned my bike away from this site and headed back south. I knew that although there would be much more adventure ahead, it would be slowly taking me back to California and ending this incredible dream. I was tempted to stay here a few days but decided against it. I felt like I should keep moving, but I will never forget that time.

After an hour or so, I hesitantly and sorrowfully turned my back to the water. I walked back to my motorized companion, which seemed to be radiating as much pride in her accomplishment as I was in mine. I just stared at her for a few moments as select memories of the past two months replayed in my mind. I rode down to the road where it made a final turn to the north and ended at the icy water's edge. I placed my front tire into the sea that separated the Atlantic Ocean and the Strait of Belle Isle and realized I could go no further than this. I had truly made it.

As I was about to make my final turn back, the emotions came again. I took a picture at the genuine end of the road and stared out to the horizon with tears in my eyes. I had traveled 9,700 miles to be here, and every mile had been a gift. I reluctantly turned my bike around and started back, looking over my shoulder as often as I could. It would be hard to believe that any future experience could top this.

I found a great camp spot about twenty miles out of town in some deep woods and shrubs. I had been constantly warned to be on the lookout for moose because these 1,500-pound animals have killed many a biker on the road, but so far, I had seen only a dead one lying on the shoulder. The moose here were more than plentiful because there were no real predators on the island except for the two-legged variety.

The moose here were also very large. I heard stories of cars hitting them and flipping the moose on top of the car. In its zealousness to get free, the moose would flatten the vehicle like a pancake, usually killing all inside. Although large animals, they could easily and quickly make their way through the thickest of brush, making quite a racket in the process.

I was awakened the next morning by what I thought had to be a moose making his way near my camp, but by the time I was out of my tent, he was gone. My camp spot overlooked a beautiful lake with a small, tree-covered island in the center and was surrounded by a carpet of trees. The sun was just beginning to rise, and the reflections off the lake's surface gave it an eerie and beautiful presence. At that moment, it was hard to conceive that heaven could be more beautiful than this place. I just stared and drank in the majesty of the treasure before me.

I packed my things up and began my journey back to Corner Brook. The morning was fairly cold, and I had put my thermals on for the first time. I was dreading the desolate stretch of highway that would cut over to the coast, as it had been so windy the first time. My concerns turned out to be valid. As I reached this section of the highway, the winds were almost half again as strong as they had been the day before and my bike was leaning over at an even greater angle than it had yesterday. It didn't help that this wind happened to be icy cold.

As if this wasn't bad enough, as soon as the wind hit, my engine began to cut out and to sputter badly. My heart sank to my boots. "Not now, please, not now!" I pleaded. I was talking to her, rubbing her gas tank, coaxing her forward. At times, she would almost completely quit and then suddenly start again. She was constantly backfiring and sputtering, and my doubts increased whether or not I would make it back. A half an hour later, I finally made it to the last turn when woods once again sheltered me from much of the wind.

I glanced back and, to my despair, noticed that my sleeping bag had been completely blown off of my pack! It almost seemed fitting that the morning of the first day since I had turned back from my goal and its euphoria would begin like this. I just sat there thinking of all my options. I finally turned back into the wind and, after twenty minutes of searching, finally found my sleeping bag lying off to the side of the road.

My bike continued to run horribly as I began to ride along the coast. I had made several visual inspections of the engine, but nothing seemed obviously wrong. There were now threatening clouds all around, and rain was now a very real possibility. I was fighting a fierce headwind, and between that and my bike's poor performance, I couldn't accelerate over forty miles per hour. The constant sputtering and backfiring were slowly eating away at me. I knew that the small fishing villages would be of no help and that the only Harley dealer anywhere nearby was located in St. John's, more than 600 miles away! If this bike's heart quit pumping, I would be in big trouble.

Hours later, I limped into Gros Morne National Park, happy to have made it that far. According to my odometer, I still had plenty of gas, but I did not realize the tremendous negative effect the wind had inflicted on my gas mileage. As soon as I entered the park, I ran out of gas. I switched the lever to reserve but knew there were no gas stations within the park itself. All I could do was coddle my injured bike through the hills the best I could and get as far as possible before I ran completely out.

About twenty miles later, I was literally on gas fumes when I rounded a corner and saw a small gas station and store I had not seen the day before. I couldn't believe it. The temperature had climbed to the high nineties, and, with my long johns still hugging my body, I felt like I was about to melt.

I again looked over my bike for any hint at what the problem might be and decided to remove one of the spark plugs to check its condition. Then I saw it. A loose spark plug connection to the coil. That had been my whole problem since the ferry! I was ecstatic that my perceived major predicament had now become so trivial. I tightened the connection, and my best friend of the whole trip fired up loud and strong as if to say, "It's about time!" Without a doubt, I was in a great mood now.

It was Saturday, and I decided to check out the night life in good old Corner Brook. When asked where the "hot spot" was, everyone gave me the same answer: Gary's. I still needed a place to spend the night and discovered a spot outside of town, under some power lines within the protection of sparse woods. I set up camp there.

Apparently, nobody goes out very early in the evenings in Corner Brook, especially when it is warm during the day. I would assume the brutally cold winters will make anyone a sun worshipper when it makes its appearance. I arrived at Gary's around 7:30 p.m. and, for the most part, sat by myself for two and a half hours, nursing a few beers and waiting for someone…anyone…to come through the door. If anything will make you feel like a loser, this will.

Mercifully, around 10:00 p.m., people finally started showing up. Notice I said "people." Namely, men started showing up. After the first twenty-five guys or so had entered this establishment, I was starting to question the type of bar I was in. I thought, *Great, I'm in a gay bar and I'm wearing black leather.* Fortunately, women finally started arriving, which made me feel a bit more comfortable.

Sitting at the bar, I met a local man named Wade. He was a handsome man in his early thirties, and his mannerisms and looks reminded me of a good friend back home. His 5'9" build was athletic, and he had short dark hair with a matching moustache. We bugged out early because the unusual warm weather had kept many people home that night, and we decided to have lunch the next day. I went back to my camp spot, sat back, and gazed at the stars for a while. I still could not get over the fact that I was looking at these stars from Newfoundland ground.

Wade had offered to buy me lunch, and I made it a strict policy to never turn down free food. While I was waiting for him at the restaurant, I called my friend in California to find out if the Baja 1000 racing team he was trying to put together would be a reality or not. The four-and-one-half–hour time difference definitely woke him up earlier than he wanted to be on a Sunday morning. He gave me the bad news that he could not get the team together because of financial reasons. I was disappointed.

I had really wanted the Baja 1000 race to be the final leg of my sabbatical. The memories of my first Baja 1000 race were nearly as intense as my L'Anse aux Meadows experience, and I had figured it would be the perfect way to end this particular adventure. I had also recently talked to my brother on the phone and found that some race friends of mine in Southern California had contacted him to race the Baja 1000 this year as well. It would be his first.

As Eric and I talked about whether he should or could enter this race, he was giving me the same dream-killing excuses I have heard others repeat time and time again, like, "Yeah, I want to, but I just can't afford it right now" or "I'm not sure I have the time." I was quick to respond that I knew how important this would be to him and that he would never forget it. I also reminded him of just how successful my trip had been so far. My advice was simple. I told him to do whatever it took to fulfill this dream and that I would support him any way I could. He sounded hesitant, and I was a bit disappointed, thinking that he might pass up this stellar chance to fulfill a wish of a lifetime.

Fortunately, later in my trip, Eric told me that he would indeed make it happen. It proved to be an experience that he would cherish the rest of his life, and he now has absolutely no regrets about the decision. Was it expensive?

Yes, it was. Was it hard to find the time away from his business? Sure it was. So what? He did it anyway, and he wouldn't change anything.

I was still concerned about my ability to find a team, so I called another friend who had expressed an interest in me riding with his team. He also did not sound too awake as I described my situation, and he promised he would keep me in mind. At least there was a chance.

After Wade treated me to lunch, we went to his parents' place to hang out a bit. He turned out to be a decent guitar player and singer, and I relaxed while listening to him hammer out some classic rock songs. I also met his friend Peter, who stopped by to see the stranger in town. Peter was building himself a thirty-seven–foot schooner in his backyard. I told him I had to see this, and we picked up and made the trek to Peter's place.

This boat was huge! Peter was building it completely by hand and had been working on it for over two years. Images of Noah flashed through my mind as the monstrous craft sat, half-built, on dry land. He claimed he had never attempted anything like this before and had just decided to do it. I was again amazed at some people's ability to attempt that which seems impossible.

I asked him what he hoped to do with it, and Peter immediately replied, "Sail around the world". Wade looked up and asked him how he could possibly afford to do such a thing. Peter's answer was truly motivational and genuine as he replied, "I don't know. I'm not going to worry about that yet. If I let the fact that I never built a boat before get in the way, I never would have started building the bloody thing in the first place."

Peter unknowingly summed up, in that one phrase, one of my major hang-ups in life. How many times, I thought to myself, had I looked too far ahead and talked myself right out of doing something I really wanted to do? How many times had I overanalyzed the situation and allowed my negativity or the negativity of others to dictate what I did? How many times had I let the fear of failure stop me from trying? Peter reinforced my newfound philosophy of focusing not on the result but rather on the process: Just do it and let the results take care of themselves. Peter was a tribute to this reasoned doctrine, and I found myself physically standing, about fifteen feet in the air, on his dream…a dream he was fulfilling slowly, day by day.

I would be heading to the ferry the following day and sadly leaving this island. I had arrived knowing no one but had made some very good friends. Wade and Peter mentioned an outdoor festival near the town of Stephenville that was taking place that night, and I agreed that I would join them.

Wade did not smoke heavily, probably three packs a week or so, but I had commented that his money could probably be better spent on his true passions of life instead of smoke. He told me he was thinking about quitting but never had the motivation. I knew Wade loved sailing, and I gave him an idea. I said, "Get a picture of a sailboat that you would love to own. Cut it out, and pin it up over a can. Every time you get the urge to smoke, put the smoke money in the can. Every month, put it in the bank and don't touch it. Someday, you'll have your boat." He loved the idea, and I witnessed, that day, his last "official" cigarette...as far as I know.

We attended the outdoor festival, and naturally, because it was an *outdoor* festival, it began to rain. I soon found myself in a motor home with Wade playing guitar and singing songs with four very drunk women folk. He played and we sang until 5:00 a.m., after which we headed back to our motel room. Watching drunk people sing while I am sober is definitely an experience that I do not wish to repeat any time soon.

Wade, Peter, and I ate breakfast the next morning, and I once again felt sadness in saying good-bye. This trip had become difficult in that way. Striking up friendships and then having to leave them was getting to be emotionally strenuous. Wade and Peter had demonstrated true friendship to the stranger from California, and I would miss them. It was a short two-hour ride to the ferry, and I decided to stay more to myself on the ferry ride back, simply reflecting and relaxing. The ferry would land in Nova Scotia around 9:00 p.m. in darkness.

I remained inside the ferry the entire seven hours, and when the call to "enter our vehicles" came over the loudspeaker, I headed down to my bike. There were about six other motorcycles on the ferry, mine being the only Harley. I pulled my black leather garb on and then asked around if they knew what the weather was like outside the giant metal doors. One of the other bikers said it had been raining "a little" but that they thought it was pretty dry on the mainland. I was relieved. I definitely did not feel like battling the elements at night while trying to find a place to camp.

My bike was facing the huge metal door that swung downward and that would also serve as our exit ramp from the ferry. The sudden lack of motion told us we had docked. My loud engine came alive as soon as I hit the start button, and I was relieved that I had finally broken the "ferry curse."

The engine was crisp and loud in the enclosed compartment, which immediately drew the attention from those around me, and I was secretly relishing the stares I knew I was receiving. The large steel door started to slowly fall, and, to my dismay, heavy sheets of rain were pouring down from the sky.

Unlike the other bikers, whose bikes were equipped with large fairings and who had put their rain gear on earlier, I was not prepared. I was the first bike off, and in a matter of seconds, I could feel the cold water running down the inside of my jacket. I found an overpass and spent the next twenty minutes finding and then putting on my rain gear. The ritual of finding a free camp spot is hard enough, but trying to find one in the dark and in the rain is a challenge I would not want to repeat. It took me an hour to find someplace that would give me some shelter from the constant precipitation as well as some concealment from the outside world.

Fortunately, it stopped raining just long enough for me to get unpacked and place my items inside the tent. The minute I zipped the door shut, the rain began again. "Thanks for the break, God," I silently prayed. I felt very comfortable and dry in my little shelter from the storm and fell asleep quickly to the rhythmic sound of rain pelting the roof.

Cindy in Lincoln, IL.

Phyllis & Adrienna (Milwaukee)

My temporary buddy and his '56 Panhead Hardtail

Lake Champlain ferry - Just before my bike would not start

Horseback riding with Kelly

John vs bat (Bat lost)

Kelly & parents

Ahhh...Maine backroads

Campsite outside Millinocket, Maine

Ferry to NewFoundland

Nester & Dan (Morning after kissing the cod)

Camping with Nester & Dan

Lance 'Aux Meadows & Oldest colony in N. America

Northern tip of NewFoundland

Campsite Lance Aux Meadows

Paul from Cornerbrook NewFoundland

Peter standing on his dream

Wade playing a little guitar

CHAPTER 7

Places of the Past—Heroes of Today

Although the ground was soaking wet, the weather was staying fairly dry. I decided to take a little detour and cruised around the famous Cabot Trail, which runs the perimeter of one of the peninsulas in Nova Scotia. After visiting the Alexander Graham Bell Museum, I headed out on this scenic loop, which was definitely out of the way, but then again, who cared?

The first one-third of the trip was fine, but as the elevation increased, so did my discomfort. I was suddenly plunged into fog, rain, and icy-cold conditions. Because I had chosen to only wear my leathers, it didn't take long for my body to begin emulating the freezing conditions around me. This ordeal lasted approximately two hours, and by the time I was back on the main road, I was very tempted to get a motel. I toughened up though (the motels were too expensive), and I made it back to Greg and Mary's house in Stellarton, where I made myself at home for a couple of days.

These two days were productive ones because I was able to take care of a number of maintenance items that needed attending to on the bike. The tread on my rear tire bore a close resemblance to Michael Jordon's head and was a definite safety hazard. All told, I spent about $245 on needed parts and fixed some minor problems in the comfort of Greg's driveway. The last day at Greg's, I took the opportunity to give the whole family a ride on the bike, one at a time, of course. I made the same trip around the same set of city blocks about five times, and the people working out in their yards were getting a little annoyed at the noisy bike every fifteen minutes. Greg captured it on video, and I am sure this footage will live on in the McLean family history archives for years to come.

When time came to say good-bye, it was, once again, very difficult. They had been so friendly and hospitable, it was almost beyond imagination. Greg had told me that when they had traveled to California for his brother-in-law's wedding, people treated him so great that he had sworn if he ever had the chance to return the favor to someone else, he would. Luckily, I had turned out to be that first person.

The weather was overcast and threatening but stayed dry. The day of riding was fairly uneventful, but it felt good to be moving, and I felt much safer with a new rear tire under me. I camped in the forest outside of Saint John, New Brunswick, started a comforting fire, and reflected on the past week. I pressed the power button to the "on" position of my portable radio, and the song "Taking Care of Business" exited the tiny speaker. I thought, "*It's been a while since I've had to take care of business.*

The next day, I left Canada for good. The weather had returned to sunny and warm, and I was in one of my favorite riding states, Maine. I located the local Harley dealership and replaced all of the bike's fluids. It was then that I noticed a problem that I would need to keep an eye on for the rest of the trip. I discovered an internal leak where the engine's motor oil was continuously leaking into the clutch primary unit. I would have to make sure I did not run low on oil while also draining the oil out of the primary so it would not get too full. The dealership recommended I fix it there, but the cost to fix this at a shop would have been prohibitive, so I chanced it and moved on.

While working in Massachusetts in 1985, a friend of mine and I had taken a trip to Bar Harbor, Maine, and I had eaten a stuffed lobster that had not been bested to this day. I had never forgotten that place, and before this trip was started, I had vowed that I would find it once again. This probably would not seem like an important thing to most people, but it was just something I wanted to do.

After working out and showering at the YMCA in Ellsworth, Maine, I continued on to Bar Harbor in search of this restaurant of ten years before. As I entered the city limits, I had forgotten how large the town was and was beginning to doubt whether my memory could direct me to the right place. Dusk was approaching quickly, and I knew finding a camping area in such a touristy location would be tougher than usual, so I decided to find a place to lay my head before continuing my search. Finally, I found a somewhat suitable area outside of town, just off a hiking trail. Not exactly a legal area, but I felt I was nicely concealed and was hoping I would not be awakened by a police officer.

I returned to town and, after some memory jogging, finally did find the restaurant. I called my friend, Brenda, from the place we had been together in ten years earlier, and we reminisced about old times for a while over the phone. It felt great, talking to her from this spot, and she was absolutely floored that it was me on the phone. That phone call perfectly rounded out the whole experience. I splurged for the first time on my journey and ordered the stuffed lobster dinner. It was as good as I had remembered it. Check off another goal.

I was awakened the next morning by hikers, who, I am sure, were not real thrilled to see a Harley parked off to the side of their favorite foot trail. I figured it was time to get the heck out of there before some mad hiker took after me with a walking stick. I knew I had the incredible Maine back roads ahead of me, so it didn't take much effort to get myself going that morning.

It was now Saturday, and my day's destination was Portland, Maine. As I was cruising along a nice secluded back road through the forest, I suddenly felt something crawling on my hairy chin. Before I could react, a pain shot through my jaw and straight up into my head. I quickly reached up and flung the thing from my beard. I was too late, as the bee's stinger had already done its damage. I located the stinger, pulled it out, and continued on with a very sore jaw, opening and shutting my mouth like a guppy out of water for the best part of an hour. The downside of not wearing a full-face helmet.

Nearing Portland, I began noticing several things about some of my likes and dislikes. First, I wasn't enjoying my rides along the ocean nearly as much as on the inland country roads and mountains. Second, I had found that the less people that were around me, the better I liked it. Even medium-sized cities were beginning to annoy me. I seemed to have been pulling into myself more the past few days and I didn't have the desire to strike up conversations and meet people as I had throughout most of my ride. The past few weeks had been both very emotionally fulfilling and emotionally draining. I had worked hard at developing new relationships and had experienced incredible highs followed by expected lows. I was saying good-bye to a lot of people I had come to care for in a short period of time. I began to realize that I needed some time to myself, time to process my emotions.

During this time, I was also doing some heavy reflecting into myself and who I really was—not what others saw, but who I knew I really was. When one takes the time to do this in a no-nonsense way, the conclusions are often not pleasurable. The reality is that to change one's habits often requires the confession of weaknesses that must be dealt with. These internal back roads had revealed many weaknesses to me, especially when witnessing so many other people's successes. I had to come face to face with those traits in my life that were obstacles to my growth, things that I knew I had to change if growth were to continue. Perhaps for the first time in my life, I felt I had the strength to change.

As my bike and I neared Portland after about eight hours on the road, the number of cars began to dramatically increase around me, as did the number of homes. It was becoming evident that there would be no free camping tonight, and before I knew it, I was riding along the ocean's coast, trying to find a cheap motel or campground. Unfortunately, the words "cheap" and "motel" are mutually exclusive when near the ocean. Night was approaching fast, and I was finding myself becoming very grumpy.

Getting desperate, I pulled into a campground to ask their rates. An older woman came out, saying they didn't take motorcycles because of insurance reasons. Gee, where had I heard that before? I knew insurance had nothing to do with her reason for rejection, much like in the rejection from my friend near Rome, New York. I was not in the mood for this attitude, and I was trying to keep my temper in check when she suggested another campground and handed me the phone. The voice on the other end asked me what I was driving, and I told him a motorcycle. He asked, "What kind?" I could feel my blood start to boil as I told him. He said that Harleys were too loud and would not be accepted. We traded a few comments back and forth, and I slammed the phone down. Well, I certainly was in a better mood now.

Darkness was almost upon me, and I was no longer in the mood for people of any size, weight, or disposition. I hopped on the bike and headed inland. Because I was still somewhat near Portland, the density of homes was still pretty heavy, and I simply could not find a place to spend the night. Finally, I saw a clearing through the woods that was full of cutoff stumps and shrubs located between two houses. The houses were blocked from view by a thick stretch of trees, and I figured this was probably my best bet. I off-roaded my bike over the stumps, dirt, and shrubs as far back as I could, then immediately killed the engine, hoping no one would investigate the strange rumbling sound.

The ground was covered with large green ferns, which I quickly pulled up and "expertly" placed all over my motorcycle. I walked back to the road and saw that my camouflage idea had worked. My beautiful maroon Super Glide had been converted to a giant fern. I set up the tent and was fairly certain I would not be spotted from the road. I fell asleep, thankful I had managed to find a place to lay my weary body for the night.

The next few days would be spent with several friends outside the historic city of Boston. I chose to ride the coastline through New Hampshire, and although it was a beautiful ride, there were just too many people and cars everywhere. I felt like I was back in California. Maybe I was becoming a hermit.

I stayed at the house of one of my good friends' sister just outside of Boston. Patty and Steve were more than hospitable. They had two small children named Misha and Connor, and I must say that Misha's name will forever be burned into my memory. She was three years old, extremely cute, and the most active kid I have ever seen. The reason I will never forget this particular name is because I heard it 1,522 times during my brief stay.

A typical conversation with Patty would go something like this: "So Patty, do you like living here?" "You know John, it is really great. I love the—Misha! Misha! Stop that, Misha.—I really love the area and—Misha, get down from there. Don't make me come over there, Misha.—Anyway, the area is a little cold, but—Misha, don't put leaves down John's back. I mean it. Misha! That's it, Misha!" I was worn out just listening.

I took advantage of the comfortable climate the day after I arrived at Patty and Steve's and walked the famous Freedom Trail in Boston. I love history, especially the colonial period. The year I had lived in New Bedford, Massachusetts, I had tried to absorb as much history as I could because very little in California dates back much further than the 1840s.

Boston would be my first stop in what would be seven days of historical visits that would stand out on my trip, second only to the reacquainting of my extended family. My eyes would be opened in ways they had never been opened before, and my appreciation for this country's history would be elevated to new heights. Many new lessons were yet to be learned.

I also ended up staying one night with Barry and Nermin, the couple whose wedding I had attended in St. Lucia in May. It was great seeing them under these very different circumstances, and I was very happy that their matrimonial state had lasted longer than mine had, although using me as a benchmark isn't exactly shooting for the stars. We spent some time looking at the pictures that had been taken on the island and of the wedding itself. It was great to reminisce. Nermin also took the time to show me various sites around the area, including the schoolhouse where the song "Mary Had a Little Lamb" was written. Well THAT made the entire road trip worth it.

My stop the next day would be New Bedford, Massachusetts, my home away from home back in 1985. The home of Moby Dick. When I had first moved to New Bedford, I had been only twenty-four years old with absolutely no idea of what I wanted to do with my life. My roots were deep at home and I was dating someone who had become very important to me. The last thing I had wanted to do was leave all of my relationships and security behind.

I remember that I had just given my notice of resignation to my brother, whose computer company I had been working for at the time. I had known I didn't want to do what I had been doing but I had absolutely no hint of what

I wanted to do with my life. I earnestly prayed that God would provide me with an open door of some kind and if he could put a rush on it, I would appreciate it. I can't explain it, but after doing this, I felt a peace about my future and that things would be okay—not easy, but okay. Not two weeks later, a door had opened up, all right, but not a door I was expecting.

Eric's company was merging with another company in Massachusetts, and they wanted me to come work for them for a few months. This had come completely out of left field. Although I did not want to leave my hometown, I had known that if I didn't follow this road, I would be missing out on something, perhaps something big. After all, why pray for something and then ignore the answer? Those few months turned into a year and created invaluable experiences I never could have dreamed of from home. This time set the course for the rest of my life, and I never returned to Lodi again.

At the time, I was nothing less than petrified. I knew absolutely no one back east, I had very little money, and I didn't own a credit card. I would be staying with strangers for a while but then would be on my own with very little money to buy furniture or any real essentials. I remember buying my first black-and-white TV at a secondhand store. The TV had a giant black bar at the bottom that scrunched the picture up about two inches. I'll never forget watching the U.S. Open Tennis Tournament and watching these men with full bodies and one-inch legs running around the court, hitting the ball. Hey, what did I expect for fifteen bucks?

I think everyone remembers their first real independent time away from home and the fear that usually accompanies the move. I was not only afraid of being away from friends and family but was also very fearful about the job position I was taking on because, frankly, I had no idea what I was doing. I was being thrown into something that was totally over my head and I had no one whom I could lean on or ask for advice. I experienced so many fears and emotions during that time that I felt completely overwhelmed. Those types of feelings stick with you for a lifetime, much like a smell takes you to a time from your past. Now, for the first time in ten years, I was about to revisit those places.

As soon as I neared the town of New Bedford, sure enough, memories started to flood my mind. It felt good to be here under such different circumstances. Somehow, I found the house I had stayed at, tucked deep inside South Dartmouth, right next to New Bedford. It had been so long that I really could not remember how to get there, but I had just let my senses take over and happened to make all the right turns. I saw the old office building down in the historical district where so much of my fear had been centered, the old

YMCA where I worked out every day and the pub next door to the office, where I would eat fish and chips by myself while wondering what the heck I was doing so far from home.

I was able to get in touch with the girlfriend I'd had when I'd lived here, and we were able to meet briefly for lunch. She hadn't changed much at all, and the all-encompassing smile that had drawn me to her in the first place had lost none of its luster. She wasn't married yet but was serious with someone, and I was happy for her. I could have talked to her all night, but it was time to move on. This place offered nothing more for me than memories, mostly good and some not so good. I would be leaving the place where I felt I had become a man.

I rode through Newport, Rhode Island, and Jamestown Island, where I had lived the first few weeks of my stay those ten years ago. More memories. I once again turned my bike away from a place that felt somewhat familiar and continued on toward the unfamiliar. I stopped for dinner a few hours later, and as I started my bike, the sickening sound of a failing battery met my ears once again. I was afraid the little "fix" I had made back in Missouri suddenly wasn't holding up anymore. I was fairly certain my battery was no longer being charged. A bike can usually run for quite some time with a dying battery, but once the battery gets to a certain point of discharge, it's walking time. I hate walking.

I knew that the constant illumination of my motorcycle's headlight would be a constant drain on my battery's limited storage of energy, and I contemplated disconnecting the light but was afraid to take any more time than necessary. I had friends in Connecticut, and I decided that I would try to make it to their place before my bike gave up the ghost. After about ninety minutes of riding, I could feel the engine losing a little power, and I knew the end was near. I had to get off the freeway and fast.

Fortunately, I was near the West Haven, Connecticut, exit and quickly veered off the freeway onto the exit ramp. As soon as I did, my bike lost its pulse and I coasted to a stop by a Mobile station. The good news was, I made it to civilization. The bad news was, it was after 5:00 p.m. and everything was closing up.

After an hour of pleading my case on the phone to anyone who would listen, I finally found a Honda shop that agreed to store the bike overnight. They claimed they would have a Harley mechanic on duty the next day and that they would take a look at it in the morning. It took me another half hour to find a towing company that would agree to tow a Harley.

After dropping my bike off at the shop, the tow-truck driver agreed to drive me to a nearby motel. My budget was really going to get gouged. As it turned out, I stayed at the motel for two nights, and the cost of the repair lightened my wallet by more than $300. "It could have been much worse," I consoled myself as I thought about the many isolated locations I had been in the past two months.

Once the bike was ready to go, I headed out of town around 3:00 p.m., hoping to find a nice camping spot in New York. Forty-five minutes later, I realized that I had left my helmet back at the shop. It just wasn't my week. I thought about every option short of going back to where I had come from and couldn't come up with a better solution. Trying to take my own advice, I didn't let myself get too upset over this little glitch and returned to the shop, where the mechanics had taken bets on how far I would get before I realized my mistake. Nothing feeds your ego more than men taking bets on your stupidity. I thanked them for their sensitivity to my predicament and decided to call it a day. I called up some friends I had met in the Caribbean just four months earlier, hoping they would put me up for the night. Although they couldn't quite remember me, they told me to come on over just the same.

Jim and his brother John were extremely generous in their hospitality. Their girlfriends were also over, as well as a couple of friends, and we had a great time talking and laughing till our sides hurt. I had met Jim the last night I was on St. Lucia during a huge island block party. He would have had trouble recognizing his own mother that night, so I was not too upset when he could not connect a face to my name over the phone. We had a few good laughs over that one.

The next day, I crossed over into Pennsylvania and the Poconos and decided to camp near the town of Easton, Pennsylvania. It was Friday night, and I was in the mood to meet some people and, hopefully, have a little fun. Easton looked like a fairly large town on the map, and I noticed it was also a college town, so I figured the odds of finding some decent places to hang out that night were definitely in my favor.

I spent an hour trying to find a campsite within ten miles of town. Although there were adequate trees and forest, there were houses everywhere, and "No Trespassing" signs seemed more plentiful than trees to hang them on. After about an hour of searching, I found a steep dirt road that climbed a nearby hill a fair distance from any houses. The private-property sign was there, but I was desperate. After making sure no one was looking, I put her in first gear and headed up the steep grade.

For the first time in my life, I wished my Harley was a little quieter. It is not easy trying to sneak into a hiding place with the loud Harley rumble echoing throughout the mountains. The road was steeper than it had looked, and the rear bike tire was actually spinning as the traction and steepness of the hill combined to slow my progress.

As I crested the hill, I found myself at the perimeter of a large cornfield. I putted down the dirt road a ways and found a somewhat narrower road to my left that would provide me an excellent hiding place among the corn stalks. I quickly set up camp and, before heading into town, pinned a note to my tent begging for mercy if my temporary home should be discovered while I was away.

I ventured the twelve miles into Easton, worked out at the YMCA, and grabbed a needed shower. The nightlife in Easton was, shall we say, nonexistent that night. I found one establishment that had the only live band in town, but I argue the meaning of the word "live" in this case. Completely frustrated, I gave up around midnight and headed back to camp. As it turned out, the college students had left for the summer and the town pretty well packs it up during their absence. Nice timing on my part.

Around 3:00 a.m., I heard a noise that, at first, seemed to be part of an awful dream. As sleep slowly left me, however, I discovered that it was coming from outside of my tent. It was a low, growling noise that sounded like it came from deep within the throat of some kind of a beast. This noise would continue for about five seconds, followed by an immediate screaming, high-pitched bark that resembled the voice of the wicked witch in *The Wizard of Oz*. The bark ricocheted off the mountains and echoed loudly throughout the valley.

I bolted up out of my slumber and tried to look out the mesh lining but could see nothing but darkness. Whatever it was, it was only about ten feet away. Then I heard another cry at the opposite end of the tent. *Great, I'm surrounded*, I thought. Whatever they were, they did not seem happy that I was there. I could hear them rustling around in the corn, and the screams became more frequent and louder. I must admit, I was a bit scared.

After a half hour of this repetition, my fear began to turn to anger. I'm grumpy enough when I am awakened from a deep sleep, but to be kept awake puts me in a whole new realm of hostility. My flashlight was still on my bike, and as my temper overtook my fear, I ripped open the zippers to my tent, stormed out into the cold night in my underwear, grabbed my flashlight, and yelled, "Kill me or let me sleep! Come on! Come on!" The rustling of the animals intensified, and as much as I tried, I could not find the source of my late-night distraction.

I went back into the tent, somewhat proud that I had taken on the "unseen beast" in my underwear and that the beast had fled. I heard them screaming off in the distance, probably sharing with each other how incredibly hideous I looked in my BVDs. I was soon asleep once again, only to be awakened an hour later by the same routine. To this day, I do not know what kind of animal taunted me that night, but those sounds will be etched in my memory till I die.

When morning came, I looked for clues of what may have caused my sleepless night, but I found no evidence. I inconspicuously putted down the hill and continued my ride through the Poconos and along the Delaware River. I spent four hours at Washington's famous Delaware crossing and drank in the history of the place like a fine wine. Actually sitting in the room where Washington ate his last Christmas dinner before the crossing that night was an awesome feeling. I tried to picture the scene and wondered what had been going through this hero's mind as he had prepared for the surprise assault on Trenton.

His men had been discouraged and were cold. The revolutionaries had lost battle after battle, and morale was at an all-time low. The daring crossing of the Delaware River on that cold Christmas night literally turned the war around. What a decision that must have been, making a bold move like that during a period of so many recent failures.

So often, we fail to consider the troubles of those famed leaders we admire so much. More often than not, true greatness comes out of hardship and pain. This was driven home to me time and time again as I spent the next five days visiting various historical areas and truly attempting to understand the leaders of those times and the decisions they'd had to make. Many of these heroes had more than their share of failures, yet they had persevered. Many of these heroes had suffered horrific losses of lives under their command, losses of personal relationships, and numerous emotional trials, yet they had overcome.

My history lesson would continue at Valley Forge, which was my next stop after visiting the location of the Delaware crossing. Because I was due to meet some friends just outside of Philadelphia that evening, I did not have an opportunity to spend as much time as I would have liked at this historical place but knew I would be back again someday.

I met Clint and Andrea that evening, a couple I had also met on the island of St. Lucia. They barely knew me, yet they treated me like royalty and went out of their way to make me feel at home. Their openness to this acquaintance reinforced my faith that there are many good people out there and continue to set an example for me whenever I may find myself on the receiving end of a traveler who is looking for a place to stay.

The next day, we decided to be Philadelphia tourists. Although Clint and Andrea had lived there many years, they themselves had not taken the time to fully experience this side of Philadelphia, and they seemed as excited as I was to finally investigate their "own backyard."

We visited Freedom Hall, the Liberty Bell, the Benjamin Franklin Museum, and much more. I stood in amazement as I gazed at the original head chair and ink well used to sign the Declaration of Independence and the Constitution. If they could only talk. It was a fantastic day of learning and experiencing the history of the City of Brotherly Love and of this great country.

Not all facts were as educational, but they were fun. For example, taverns in the eighteenth century would serve their drinks in the volumes of pints and quarts, and it was not unusual for a patron to have a bit too much of the devil water and lose count at the amount of swill he was consuming. In this case, the bartender could be just a little off in his bar tab, always to the bar's advantage, of course, and the unknowing consumer would be paying more than his fair share. The rule was, you better keep track of your pints and quarts. Thus the phrase "Mind your Ps and Qs."

The next day, I bid farewell to Clint and Andrea and headed off to York, Pennsylvania, where I toured the local Harley plant. The plant I had visited in Milwaukee primarily specialized in building the engines and transmissions, whereas this plant assembled the entire motorcycle. I have never seen so many brand-new Harleys in one place in all of my life. I truly was in Hog heaven. My bike again sat proudly in the parking lot, gazing at the place where she had truly been born. When I returned from the tour, I found a small puddle of oil under her, but I don't think it was a leak; I think she was just getting emotional.

Moving onward toward Gettysburg, Pennsylvania, provided additional historical infusion. The huge battlefield and war museum were incredible. I highly recommend this place to anyone interested in American history and of course, the Civil War. I only had a few hours that day and knew I could not possibly begin to soak up all that was there in this short amount of time. I made the decision to find a camping spot that night and to continue the expansion of my historical research the next day.

It seemed as though every day around 4:00 p.m., the same feelings of anxiety would swell within me: *Where am I going to sleep?* It was an uneasiness I seemed to have no control over. The same feeling hit me here as I was struggling to find a place to lay my head. The town was surrounded by the famous battlefield, and I could have taken my chances to camp on it, but if I were caught, who knew what would happen? I decided to take Highway 30 up into the hills and, hopefully, find a place not more than ten miles out of town.

As I hit the ten-mile mark, I began to get frustrated. Nearly every dirt road led to or near a house or cabin. Then I saw what looked to be an old dirt road that was blocked off by cement pylons. Well, blocked off for cars, anyway. I slipped my bike through the cement blockades and found myself deep in the thick woods near Gettysburg. It was an unbelievable find! At the end of the road was a very old house that barely resembled anything of a structure now. I guessed it had been built sometime in the 1800s or earlier. I looked up and noticed two deer prancing by me as if to welcome me to the neighborhood.

I set up camp and began writing in my journal. It was sobering to think that more than 130 years before, boys far younger than myself had been roaming the woods where I was now camping. Boys with weapons in hand, shooting at each other...at Americans. What a senseless time.

That evening, I went to a local tavern a few miles outside of Gettysburg to get a bite to eat. A couple had noticed my bike and began to actively inquire about my ride. As it turned out, the man had just purchased a motorcycle and was looking forward to taking a long-distance trip of his own but seemed hesitant. After telling him of my experiences and my philosophy of not waiting until it might be too late, he seemed to be quite motivated. I'm not sure his girlfriend was as excited to hear my advice as he was, but one thing was for sure, I had told it to him straight.

As I returned to camp and turned my bike off for the evening, the sounds of the night were deafening. The insects were partying hard that night, and I needed to use my ear plugs to keep out the loud mountain noises. I could almost feel the ghosts of slain soldiers walking the woods and knew I was camping in a place where death and suffering had been all around. As I lay there that night, there was absolutely no other place I wanted to be at that moment in time. My journey just seemed to be getting better and better. Many times when we choose to fulfill a desire, the reality of that desire actually becomes greater than our expectations. So it had become with this.

I spent four more hours the following day at Gettysburg and continued to absorb more and more facts about the bloodiest three days of war in this nation's history. I continued to ride on through Pennsylvania, stopping briefly at Harper's Ferry, finally arriving at my final destination for the day, a former coworker's apartment. Beth and her husband, Nole, were very courteous but not so sure they were excited to have me there. I didn't know Beth that well, and I thought that I may have been a little presumptuous in asking to stay there. Regardless, they offered me the couch, and it was a welcome change from blowing up the infamous air mattress.

I was very excited about my next day's adventure because I would be spending it in our nation's capital, Washington, DC. I had only been there once, and the visit had been brief. This would be my last "official" history stop before riding west and then down toward the southern states.

The day was a full one. I toured the Capitol, the Library of Congress, Ford's Theater, the Lincoln Memorial, the Korean Memorial, and the Smithsonian Air and Space Museum My feet were screaming by the end of this day, and I was more than ready to head back to Beth and Nole's for a little rest and to resume my investigation of this great city the next day. That morning, I had decided to take an extra day and sheepishly asked Beth and Nole if I could crash one more night. It was one of those moments when they hadn't answered right away, had shot stares back and forth, and had then stuttered, "Sure…that would be fine." I'm so bad.

I was worn out from the previous day's activities but desired to see so much more. I visited the Smithsonian's National Museum of American History, where I gazed at General Washington's original uniform, Archie Bunker's chair, the original star-spangled banner, and the original red shoes used in *The Wizard of Oz*, to name just a few. So much to see. I was truly overloaded with information by this time, and although there was much more to view, I realized my limitations and left the rest for future visits.

I had purposely left the Vietnam Memorial for last, as this would be a special place for me. I wanted to end the day by visiting my brother Mark for a while. I had been to this wall once before, but it had nowhere near as meaningful as it was now. This time, it was going to be just him and me, and knowing I had made it here on my own, in the way that I had, would make it even more exceptional.

After some searching, I finally found the engraving that spelled his name, and I just crouched in front of the panel of lost lives. I wondered what it would have been like had he been given the opportunity to marry his fiancée and start a family like he had always planned. It was, after all, because of him that I was riding a motorcycle in the first place. Tears filled my eyes as I thought of the many possibilities that could have been. I bowed my head, and a man's gentle voice from behind asked if I needed help in finding someone.

He was a volunteer, and I told him about my brother and of the trek I was on. He was very interested, and we talked for a few minutes. He took a few pictures of me pointing to my brother's name, pictures I will treasure always. At that moment, I could feel Mark smiling down upon me as if to say, "I wish I could be with you on this trip, bro." The truth was, I knew he had been with me all the way. I had been only seven when he was killed, but I missed him terribly at that moment.

That morning, I had purposely worn a special tee shirt that I had purchased at a Harley dealer's shop in New Hampshire. The words "NEVER FORGET" graced the top of the shirt in large bold letters, and below was a picture of the Vietnam Wall, with a long-haired Harley dude standing next to his bike. He was looking into the wall as he held a set of dog tags. Staring back out at him from the wall was a combat soldier dressed in his fatigues and ready for war. It was a pretty moving shirt. I received a lot of positive comments on it that day, and each time, I told the person why I was wearing it. I felt extremely proud of my brother who had given his life for this country, no matter what the circumstances had been. Of all of the heroes I had learned about over the past week, he was still the greatest of all. This was a fitting end to an eventful day of discovery. I had crammed my head full of facts and images and was mentally exhausted after the ten hours of constant exploration I had put myself through that day.

As I was riding toward the Blue Ridge Mountains, I reflected upon my past week of historical discoveries. I felt a tremendous amount of pride and patriotism for my country, and for the first time in my life, I really felt I understood where this nation had come from. It brought home how this country's rugged past had shaped its present and how my past had shaped me. I felt proud of our heritage. I felt extremely honored to be an American.

Cabot Trail, Novia Scotia - Wet and very cold

McLean family in Novia Scotia

Camouflaged bike in NY

Bike problems in Connecticut

Cornfield campsite in Pennsylvania

Cliff & Andrea

Lincoln Memorial - My #2 Hero

John at the Vietnam Wall - My #1 Hero

CHAPTER 8

Just Down-Home Folks

I was looking forward to a quiet camp spot in the forest that night as I turned onto Skyline Drive, which runs along the top of the Blue Ridge Mountains. It seemed as if it had been an eternity since I had enjoyed the solitude of camping by myself. Dusk was close at hand, and the many fire roads that ventured into the forest were more than adequately blocked by locked gates. After searching for fifteen minutes or so, I finally found a road that was gated but looked as if I could possibly squeeze by. My poor Harley once again played the role of a dirt bike as I rode through knee-high grass and squeezed between the gate and the nearest tree. Just made it.

I putted along the dirt path for about a half mile when suddenly, five deer leapt across the road directly in front of me. I set up camp at the deer crossing, and as I finished unrolling my sleeping bag in the tent, I heard the sound of sticks breaking behind me a short distance away. As I turned to look, I saw a black bear slowly meandering through the woods not fifty yards behind me. Now for all I know, black bears are not a big deal to the local folk, but you don't see many of these guys in Southern California. I wasn't sure whether to be scared or to go take a picture, so I compromised and tried to get a picture of him while being very scared. My attempt was futile, as I lost sight of him in the deep woods. How cool was that?

I returned to camp, lit up a cigar, and walked around my "front yard," feeling darn good about things. I had been noticing that as I traveled along the back roads, through the woods of the east, many of the trees' branches were covered thickly with giant, puffy plumes of silk. I was not sure what little creatures made these silk monstrosities but had assumed they were by giant spiders of some kind. I had always wanted to get a closer look.

I noticed one of these "silk branches" about two feet over my head and gazed up at it from below. I realized that these silk homes were not created by spiders but from some type of silk worm and that this particular branch was thick with them. I also noticed that among the many worms sat a huge, ugly, and, I would assume, unwelcome spider who was content on munching away at the convenient smorgasbord of worms before him.

Now, I don't love spiders by any means, but they don't bother me all that much, either. In fact, I had become fairly used to them, because they seemed to be everywhere out here in the east. Although my spider tolerance was fairly high, I still could not get used to the big ugly ones, and the one I was looking at was huge, and he was big-time ugly.

I don't know why I did it, but I have found that I do a lot of stupid things in life, so I guess nothing really surprises me. Without really thinking, I drew a deep breath of cigar smoke and blew it up into the silk monstrosity to see what kind of reaction I would get from its inhabitants. I got a reaction, all right. The spider dropped like a rock, stopping short by a silk thread, about two inches from my face! Luckily, no one noticed the ritualistic dance and yell I performed immediately after this event. It was definitely not a "cool" show of emotion. It was then I discovered that spiders do not like smoke.

As daylight slowly melted away, the incredibly loud sounds of the forest again grew louder and louder as if someone had control of the volume knob and was slowly turning it up to ten. The creatures of the forest knew night was almost upon them and were, once again, preparing to party all night long. Without my earplugs in place, I would have found it impossible to sleep.

A problem that was beginning to have an effect on me was the continuing shortness of the days. I was being surrounded by complete darkness by 8:30 p.m. I consider myself to be a notorious night person, and trying to fall asleep by 9:00 p.m. was a chore, to say the least. These were the times when I could have used some good conversation to pass the time, but I figured it was a small price to pay for the many benefits the solitude of riding alone had provided me.

That night, as I lay on my back in my tent, I awakened from a half-sleeping state and gazed upward toward the dome of my tent. My heart began to race as I saw one of those infamous huge, ugly brown spiders hanging on a web inside the dome area right above my face!

I closed my eyes, holding my fear inside as best I could as I frantically searched the floor for my flashlight with my left hand. I kept telling myself, "Don't shake the tent, don't shake the tent," as I imagined this gross eight-legged, smoke-hating insect falling on my face. After about a minute of searching for my illumination device, my cerebral matter began to kick in a bit and I began to wonder if I could have dreamt this nasty situation. I was praying for the best.

The flashlight soon confirmed my deepest hopes, and I found the spider to be only a figment of my dream state. I sighed deeply, and after my heart rate dropped to normal, I dozed off.

Once again, I woke up, as I felt something crawling over my bare chest. In my near-dream state again, I grabbed whatever it was and threw it off. When I came to my senses, I realized that something actually had been on my chest and that it would probably be a good idea to know what that thing was. Once again, I grabbed the flashlight and looked around. It was one of the harmless long-legged spiders that I usually found on the outside of my tent in the early morning hours. I was in spider hell!

The weather was beautiful as I hit the road around midmorning. A few hours later, I stopped at a small restaurant for lunch and noticed a man mounting his road bike for a bit of afternoon touring. I wanted to ask him if he knew of some great roads for riding in this area and found that I still had to force myself to make initial contact.

People who know me would never believe that, in many instances, I struggle to initiate conversations with strangers, even though most times it proves to be a very positive experience. This trip was slowly confirming my beliefs that meeting and experiencing other people was a powerful way to get more out of life, but it was still not coming naturally. Maybe it never would, but the important thing was, I was overcoming these feelings and stepping out. I was doing what I knew was right, not what felt comfortable.

I finally went up to him and asked if he had any advice as to where I might go for some incredible riding. Once again, my philosophy of being open to people paid off. The friendly rider gave me invaluable advice on a route through Virginia, into West Virginia, then back again toward the Smoky Mountains.

Thanks to him and to my willingness to ask, the riding over the next few days was unbelievable! Tight and twisty roads that cut up and down ridge after ridge of thick forested mountains were my reward for stepping out of my comfort zone. If I had been in spider hell the night before, I was now rewarded by experiencing biker heaven. While my buddy was sharing his wise travel counsel, he had made it a point to tell me about Warm Springs, Virginia, a small town near the border of Virginia and West Virginia that included two natural mineral baths dating back to the 1700s. I needed a bath anyway and decided to include this stop in my travel plans that day.

Later that morning and after more than one wrong turn, I finally found two fairly large white octagonal-type buildings that looked to be what I was searching for. I pulled into the driveway that led to the building on the right, where I was soon met by a very large black woman who stared at me with suspicious eyes. With her hands on her hips and showing no hint of a smile, she asked me if I was looking for the men's bath, to which I nodded in the affirmative. She pointed to the opposite building and stated in a firm tone, "Right over there." I glanced toward the direction of her finger and then back to her again and smugly suggested that I had changed my mind and that it might be more interesting if I use the women's bath this time. Without blinking an eye, she replied, "That's just fine, but you gotta get through me first." I figured I would choose the path of least resistance and headed off to the men's hut.

I cautiously opened the old white wooden door and slowly peered in. The first thing to greet my eyes was a cadaver-like man in his nineties or so who couldn't have weighed more than 120 pounds. He was just floating there, on his back, with his eyes closed. I thought for sure he was dead, but I had always thought that, if dead, you floated face down. I looked around the circular room and saw another older man who was enjoying the water toward the shallow end of the pool and I shared with him my initial observation. "Naw, he ain't dead," he said, "he's just a good floater."

I quickly undressed and slipped into the wonderful ninety-eight–degree water. Oh yeah, just what the doctor ordered. Legend has it that Thomas Jefferson had architected these buildings at the age of fourteen, but the locals weren't sure if it was true. I spoke with several men in the huge bath, and they seemed genuinely interested in my journey's stories up to this point. One gentleman in particular took a special interest in the stories I had been telling and was convinced I should write a book. In fact, he was so insistent that I do this that he gave me his address and asked when he could expect the first copy. I told him I had no immediate plans to do such a thing but that if I did, he would receive the first one off the press. This was the first point in my life when the idea of actually writing a book was even a consideration, although I never really believed I would do it.

I must say, it was an exhilarating feeling to know that I was sitting in the same spot where many of this nation's past heroes had soaked their weary bodies. Many former presidents and Civil War heroes had visited this location, and it had become a common stopping place for the Civil War troops. The wood structure consisted of its original wood, with the exception of a few slats that had been replaced here and there. I left refreshed and invigorated and very proud of myself that I had once again taken the time to "smell the roses" instead of trying to "make time." Later that evening, I found an ideal camping location in the woods, and although it rained for the first time in weeks, my slumber was complete and uninterrupted.

As morning came, the clouds disappeared. The deep blue of the sky conveyed to me that incredible riding lay ahead. This day would be spent traveling through old West Virginia mining towns, many of which were victims of a very depressed economy. These people were very poor, and it made me thankful for those things I daily took for granted. One thing that had become very noticeable was that the people were extremely friendly to me as I passed through their small towns. I was kept just as busy waving as I was riding, and the broad smiles on their faces gave me renewed energy as I exited each town's border. "Why couldn't all the towns in America be like this?" I wondered.

I later entered a small town called Richwood, West Virginia, and decided it was time to change the spark plugs on my bike. Richwood was nestled against tree-covered mountains on three sides and couldn't have been home to more than a few thousand people. As I turned left onto the small town's main street, I immediately noticed a fellow sitting on a park bench, staring me up one side and down the other. His head was large and square and seemed to sit directly on his shoulders, with no apparent need for a neck. The shoulders topped off a very round torso, which was loosely fitted with a giant Tweety Bird tee shirt. He squinted at me with an open mouth, more than one tooth missing, unsure what to make of the outsider who had infiltrated his hometown. My first impression of this fellow was that the elevator probably did not quite reach the top floor and he probably just sat on that bench most of the day. As with my experience in East Chicago, my first impressions are usually wrong.

I had parked my bike in front of the auto parts store and begun to search for the appropriate tools out of my tool bag when I heard a loud voice behind me getting closer and closer. It was my park-bench friend coming toward me at full speed. He yelled at me in a heavy West Virginia drawl, exclaiming, "Dayim, I thought there was an earthquake comin' into town, but it was just yore Harley!"

I thought, *Oh no.*

He talked to me relentlessly, hardly pausing for a breath. He talked to me as I finished taking the plugs out. He talked to me as I walked into the parts store. He talked to me as I walked out of the parts store, and he continued to talk to me as I finished putting the spark plugs into the bike. In the middle of one of his sentences, he noticed an older lady walking across the street and yelled, "Hayyy Bayybeeee, whooooooooo!" He then looked down at me and in his best Gomer Pyle impersonation and said, "That's mah wahf." I smiled at that one and had to admit, this guy was growing on me just a bit. His name was Paul and I noticed that although he talked a lot, he was not just rambling on about aliens or weird topics but was actually making sense. Perhaps I had underestimated him.

After he noticed that I was prepared to hit the road again, he asked, "What's your plans? You headin' on out? I was hopin' we could get ourselves a pop and jaw a little bit." Thoughts raced through my head, and my first inclination was to politely decline and say that I needed to get on the road. What excuse would I use? After all, this would be the easy way out, right? What if it would be a waste of time? What if he really turned out to be a fruit loop? Suddenly, my thoughts reverted back to the oath I had made to myself before leaving on this trip, the oath that I would take the time to meet and learn about people. That whole comfort-zone thing. The question was, would I regret this decision to leave without getting to know the Tweety Bird man?

I remember a time when I had been attending a business meeting in San Francisco at the Marriott Hotel near the airport. I happened to be there the corresponding day that the survivors of the infamous Bataan Death March were having a reunion and had found myself in an elevator with five gentlemen engaged in active discussion with one another. I had recently watched a television special on the Bataan Death March and remembered my admiration for these men and their uncommon willingness to keep themselves alive through unmentionable hellish conditions. They had chosen life even though their bodies had become no more than skin covering bones. There I was, looking into the faces of the men who had experienced this historical nightmare. Everything in my soul wanted to interview them, to ask them if I could join them for the evening or if they could just give me fifteen minutes of eyewitness accounts of one of the greatest survival stories in this world's history. I had longed to know their feelings, their trials, and how they had overcome them. I had yearned to pull strength from their experiences.

For whatever nonsensical reason, I did not open my mouth in the elevator that day. I fought an internal struggle and lost. My comfort zone had robbed me of an invaluable encounter. The elevator door had opened and they had walked away from me. As the elevator door closed tightly behind them, I had felt like the weakest man alive. I couldn't even say hi. What a golden opportunity had been lost! A huge regret had been born, to forever be remembered.

Although I could not turn the clock back on that particular event, it made me realize a very basic philosophy of life: Regrets seem to last a lifetime. So here I was, with my Richwood friend looking at me for an answer. Do I stay or do I go? "Well," I said, "I haven't eaten yet."

"There's a cafe right up the road, meechya thar," he replied excitedly. He was gone up the road before I had a chance to reply.

"Well, this should be interesting," I said to myself as I motored my bike up the hill and into a parking lot across from the restaurant. As I was walking toward my bike ready to motor up the hill, Paul kept looking back over his shoulder as if wondering whether I would really go through with what I had promised. Perhaps people had done that to him before, I don't know. What I did know was that I had no intention of backing out now.

The place I was meeting Paul was a small downtown café, and the only table available was one near the front door. The place was packed with locals who, I am sure, were very familiar with Paul and his ways. Many curious stares were directed toward our table by people wondering who the stranger was and why he was sitting with the local guy. Paul didn't lack for anything to say, as he talked a mile a minute about life in Richwood. He looked much older than his twenty-nine years, and he shared with me how he'd had a pace-maker implanted in his chest since his early twenties. He had recently married Margaret, who was older by some fifteen or so years, and he promised that she would join us later. Paul and Margaret were being financially assisted by the state, but supplemented their income as much as possible through working with leather goods or digging up onions in the hills above the town. They lived in a mobile home and, from what I could tell, were barely making it. One thing was for sure, though: he seemed genuinely excited to be talking with me and he seemed like a very happy man.

Every once in a while, Paul would stop in the middle of a sentence, lean out the cafe door, and yell to one of his buddies out on the street. His loud voice would echo within the cafe walls, and people would shoot him semi-irritated looks. One time, he excused himself and went to talk to another local boy out on the sidewalk. He came back with a big grin on his face and proudly stated, "I just talked to my friend over there by that pickup truck and told him I made mahself a friend from Caleefornia." This guy was truly beginning to melt my heart.

His wife, Margaret, soon joined us, and if she sported any teeth, I didn't see them. I did notice she was modeling the same line of Tweety Bird apparel that Paul was wearing, and as I looked at them sitting together, I saw they made a somewhat unusual pair. One thing seemed quite obvious, though: they really seemed to love each other.

After the waitress delivered the bill, I told them that it was time for me to be moving on. Paul looked over at me with wide-open eyes and said, "Your money ain't no good at this place." Not catching on, I asked him what he meant, and he repeated the same line.

"No, no," I protested, "you are not buying me lunch."

Before I could make a move, Margaret grabbed the bill, looked at me with determined eyes, and firmly stated, "Ah got the check. What are you gonna do about it?"

I laughed in obvious defeat and said, "I guess you got me."

Just before leaving, I took their picture next to my bike and promised to send them a copy, which I did. Paul wanted to make me a leather key chain for my Harley, and I thanked him in advance for the offer. I had made two very good friends in Richwood, West Virginia. As I rode away, I thought about these two people who were struggling to make it on their own and in spite of this had seen fit to buy lunch for a stranger from California. Suddenly, the Bataan Death March regret was not as great, because I had learned from it. It had allowed me to meet these two special people from Richwood, and my life was better because of them. To this day, my eyes moisten up a bit when I think of the unconditional friendship these two showed me. I will never forget it. The back roads had taught me another invaluable lesson.

I continued down Highway 20, reveling in my recent Richwood memory as well as in the beautiful scenery around me. Around three in the afternoon, I decided to stop for gas, although I could have definitely gone farther on the gas that remained in my tank. I can't explain it, but for some reason, I felt a need to stop at this place. I went inside to pay for the petrol I had pumped, and while waiting in line, an older gentleman began asking me about my bike. He was probably in his late forties or early fifties, with long, straight, salt-and-pepper hair pulled back into a stringy ponytail and with a raggedy mustache hanging over his upper lip. His name was Larry, and he was certainly a friendly sort of guy.

During our conversation, Larry mentioned pulling a small sailboat from Mexico to his West Virginia summer home using a Honda 250 Rebel motorcycle, which is a very small towing vehicle for such a task. I told him that I had a hard time believing it and would have given anything to get a picture of that setup. He invited me up to his summer place, located about twenty minutes away, and told me he could hook it up in a flash if I wanted to take the time.

Now I may be a little thick in the head, but the truth about living life to its fullest was finally starting to get through. I readily agreed, this time with no hesitation, as I realized that each time I had taken time out for an opportunity such as this, it had always paid off.

As usual, this decision turned out to be a good one. Larry lived life on the edge, and although he didn't have a lot of money, he seemed to squeeze all he could out of the life he had. If Larry didn't know how to do something, he would just fiddle around with it until he could get by and have fun. He dabbled in flying; sailing; playing guitar, accordion, banjo, harmonica, and well, you get the idea. In the summers, he lived in an old motor home parked in a residential-type area far back in the woods that was designed for summer living only. I don't remember what kind of car he had, but it was definitely a heap, and he let me use it to run down to the showers. This guy was willing to give me the shirt off his back.

I had no intention of spending the night, but the homeowner's association was having a full-blown potluck lunch down at the recreation center, and Larry invited me to join him. Now, there may have been things I've had to learn the hard way over my lifetime, but turning down free food, especially in large quantities, has never been one of them. I greedily accepted the gracious invitation, and I found myself surrounded by glorious home cooking.

It was getting late, and Larry suggested I camp the night in the grassy area near his motor home. I agreed to this plan because I didn't have much daylight left anyway and had no place to stay that night. It was Saturday evening, and he mentioned that he would be heading down to a small town around seven to "jam" with some locals. He invited me to join him, and I quickly accepted.

We headed out in Larry's "ratty Toyota" and drove the thirty or so miles to a little grocery store in the next town. Attached to the side of the store was a cage-like room where about seven men were "pickin' and grinnin'" with their various instruments. It was *Hee Haw* all over again, with the exception of the buxom beauties, which I greatly missed. One gentleman was especially good on the banjo, and the group had everything from steel guitars to harmonicas. These guys played for about three or four hours and I had a great time just sitting back and listening to the bluegrass music entering my ears. The store lady provided me with free coffee, and I wished to God I knew how to play a guitar so I could join in. What a great night.

Larry and I had breakfast the next morning, and I was once again glad that I had taken the time to get to know yet another stranger. Larry promised to stop by my place in Southern California someday or to perhaps sail to a nearby beach and give me a call. I wouldn't put it past him. He had taken a stranger into his confidence and made him feel at home. That kind of hospitality forms a lifelong bond of sorts that will always be there and will be returned to if the chance ever arises.

The rest of the day was uneventful but was saturated with wonderful riding through the Blue Ridge Mountains. The Virginias will always remain a very special and beautiful place in my memory, for the scenery, its riding and, most importantly, its people.

I arrived in Marion, Virginia, on the Sunday night of the Labor Day weekend. I had made the decision to continue on to Kingsport, Tennessee, or some town of decent size because I was in the mood to meet some more people. My experiences with the locals had been so favorable over the past few days, I didn't want the momentum to end. Although Marion was a decent-sized town, I was looking for something a little larger, someplace that would offer me a selection of places to hang out. As I began to exit Marion, my bike began to make those sounds that can send a biker's heart straight down to his foot pegs. It was the sound of sputtering.

I was not happy. I kept driving out of town, hoping it would clear out, but it was getting worse. After a few minutes of me coddling the throttle, she quit all together and I coasted into the parking lot of a warehouse. Well, at least the weather was nice. A couple immediately pulled in next to me and asked if I was okay, because they had heard the distressing engine noises. I told them I would need to work on it and did not know what the problem was. I was hoping they would volunteer their home for the night and offer me a ten-course meal, but my answer seemed to satisfy their curiosity, and they left. Well, you can't hit a home run every time.

I began the monotonous routine of taking off the luggage, checking battery connections, and looking for anything semi-obvious. Nothing. After considerable testing of this and that, I finally discovered the problem to be a broken wire behind the ignition coil. I jury-rigged a special connector, and to my relief, my little buddy fired right up, ready to move on.

By this time, it was too late to make my intended destination before nightfall, so I figured I would suck it up, stay in Marion, and meet some nice people there. After all, it was a decent-sized town and it was a Sunday night on a three-day weekend. The opportunities seemed hopeful. I found a small grassy area behind the warehouse and figured that would be as good a place as any to camp for the night. The somewhat secluded location kept me well hidden from the road, and it being a holiday weekend, I figured no one would be coming to work the next morning.

After washing my soiled clothing at the local laundromat, I was ready to hit the town. Look out Marion, here comes John. I had been meeting people left and right lately; I was on a roll. It was time to make some contacts, meet some new people, and maybe even introduce myself to an attractive woman or two. Wrong! I soon discovered that Marion was a dry town on Sundays. I came to the conclusion that I would probably not meet anyone that night, but I could still entertain myself. I would go see a movie. Wrong! Marion didn't have a movie theater. After the third person laughed at me when asked what I could do in this town, I figured that was probably a sign. I had picked one of the most unexciting locations in America in which to break down. I figured I could either head back to my warehouse campsite or sit at the Kentucky Fried Chicken and watch them fry up a batch of wings.

As I began to get ready for my unexpectedly early slumber, I noticed several things about my camp's surroundings that had escaped me before. First, there was a bright halogen light that would remain on all night long directly above my tent. This would not be really conducive to sleep. Second, I was all of one-half mile from the interstate freeway, which, for some reason, I had not noticed until this very instant. Strike two for a good night's rest. Third, someone was now working in the warehouse on a Sunday night on Labor Day weekend. Now I had to worry about being turned in to the authorities for trespassing if I was discovered. The evening was capped off when, after unpacking my toiletries, I found that my toothpaste tube had conveniently busted, covering all of my other items in the bag in the tartar-control, cavity-preventing substance. Well, if things didn't go wrong occasionally, we'd never appreciate the good things.

The trucks on the interstate lulled me to sleep, all right…around 2:00 a.m., and I arose in the morning a bit on the grumpy side. I had actually gotten to the point—around midnight, I believe it was—when I was hoping the ware-house worker would turn me in to the local cops so I would have a quiet jail cell in which to sleep. As I sleepily walked out of my tent, I was immediately greeted by a worker who had supposedly decided he needed the overtime and showed up to work that morning despite the Labor Day holiday. I sheepishly waved in his direction, and he looked at me more than a bit strangely. I guess it's not every day they have someone camping at work.

I was tired, but I was also ready to hit the road before the entire workforce decided to show up. The goal for the day was the Smoky Mountains. I was in the mood for some serious back-road riding and once again found roads that were not displayed on my map. Certainly not the fastest way, but definitely the most memorable. Once I arrived at the entrance to the Smokies, the weather turned extremely hot and humid. To top it off, I was surrounded by thousands of tourists and realized that I had once again taken my solitude for granted.

I rode the main highway through the Smokies, and although the ride was beautiful, it was anticlimactic compared to the scenery I had witnessed over the past two months. As I crested the final ridge, I looked over North Carolina and could see nothing but hills and trees. *Perfect*, I thought, *finding my next camping spot will not be a problem tonight.*

As I crossed briefly into North Carolina, I grabbed some dinner and then ventured to find a home for the evening. I had begun the process of looking later than normal because I figured my selection of campsites would be plentiful. The problem was that any dirt road that had been cut through the trees led me to a home or a development area. After about forty-five frustrating minutes of searching, I was starting to wonder if I would find a place at all.

I was now on a paved road that did not appear on my map, with a river located far down the hill to my right. As I leaned my bike into a sharp left turn, my eye picked up what looked to be a dirt road off to the right. I turned around. Luckily, my eyes had not failed me. It was a dirt road, but a bulldozer had pushed up a sizable amount of dirt to block any would-be four-wheel drivers from entering. Upon further investigation, I discovered a back way in that was still blocked by a wall of dirt, but to a lesser degree.

I was getting desperate. I eyed the dirt mound and figured with my vast dirt-bike experience, I could make it over. I looked around, and when I was sure no one was coming, I got a slight run at the dirt wall, hit it doing about ten miles per hour, and completely high-centered the bike on top of the mound, stopping me in my tracks and lifting my butt off the seat into a miniature headstand on the tank. Nice.

I guess 900 pounds of motorcycle, rider, and gear tends to limit one's clearance ability. I tugged and tugged to back the bike off the mound, and once I finally did, the bike's rear tire was flush against the three-inch edge of the highway. There was no going backward unless I stopped someone in traffic who would help me lift the back tire back onto the roadway. I was, shall we say, committed to the project at hand.

I took another run at it. Same result, but I cleared a little more dirt. The looks I received were priceless as people passed by and saw a fully packed Harley sitting at a forty-five–degree angle on a mound of dirt with the Harley's owner desperately tugging on the handlebars to bring it back to level ground. I was desperate to get over this hump of dirt before someone called the police or wanted to have a little "fun" with the California boy. For some reason, the song from the movie *Deliverance* started to play in my head. With that, I quickly dismounted the bike and began scraping as much dirt off the mound with my hands as I could and took another run at it. Still stuck, but making progress.

It took me a total of seven attempts before I finally crested the top. I was breathing so hard at this point, I nearly sucked the Harley patch off my vest. I began riding a web of dirt roads until I was as far back as I could go. I then managed, once again, to get the bike stuck in the mud. "This will work," I said to myself. I would worry about getting unstuck in the morning.

I set up camp and had a half hour before darkness would overtake me. I noticed that my hair was in dire need of a good washing, and after further assessment, I figured I should also probably do the miniature-bath thing because I was definitely a bit on the ripe side. The slope down to the river was very steep and somewhat dirty and muddy, and the trees were fairly thick. I grabbed a towel, clean socks, and my newly washed tennis shoes and gingerly headed through the trees and down the precarious slope.

When I would venture through the woods, I had learned to make it a habit of waving a long stick in front of me like a mad fencer to rid my path of any unseen spiders. More than once, I had become entangled in a giant spider web, and there is no way to remain cool as you are madly clawing at your face while screaming in the process. The stick worked much better for me.

Once down to the riverbank, I carefully washed up a bit and did the sponge-bath routine as I precariously balanced on a rock protruding from the water. I spent a great deal of time carefully wiping one foot, placing a dry sock upon it, and finally tying my shoe so that nothing new and clean became wet or muddy. I was proud of myself for getting my shoes and socks on without so much as a dirt smear when I realized I had forgotten to put my pants on.

If I had brains, I'd be dangerous, I thought. I squinted my eyes, looked up, and figured I could probably succeed in climbing the hill in my underwear without getting too scratched up in the process. I grabbed my pants and towel and hoisted my right foot up on the bank, then grabbed a nice thick root that protruded out of the ground. I then learned that you cannot always judge a root's strength by its thickness. As I heaved my body up the bank, the root decided to break at the apex of my most anti-gravitational position, and I flew backward into the river and found myself standing in water up to my chest. I felt like an idiot but couldn't help but start laughing at how stupid that must have looked.

I pulled my soaking body out of the river and climbed up the side of the hill, pretty much in the dark at this point, and looked down at my incredibly muddy shoes and socks. I laid things out to dry as best I could, lit up a cigar, and decided to reflect upon all the humiliation I had silently suffered this evening. I then decided to take a picture of my temporary residence before turning in, and as I tilted the camera down, the lit end of my cigar touched my hand and the camera went flying about ten feet, just missing two rocks.

There are times when you just know that you need to go to bed so you won't hurt yourself any more. After placing my earplugs in their rightful place, due to the insect noise, I slept like a baby. I guess degradation really tires a body out.

In the morning, I discovered that the cool night air does not bode well for drying clothes. "Good enough," I rationalized and slipped the damp clothes back on with a shudder. It took me a little time to get my bike unstuck, and I headed back toward the famous wall of dirt where I had entered the night before. I worked a little harder at smoothing out the exit with my hands, which paid off, as my bike easily scaled the wall the second time.

As I rode down the paved two-lane road, I was unsure of where I was actually going because the road I was traveling was not on the map. About a half hour later, the paved road suddenly turned to dirt. I hate getting lost without breakfast. Whenever I reached a fork in the road, I just stayed to the right. Even the word "fork" was making me hungry.

After riding dirt roads for about forty minutes, I rounded a corner. Suddenly, another Harley, also packed up with camping gear, passed me going the opposite direction! It was the only vehicle I had seen all morning! We looked at each other with strange looks of surprise on our faces as if to say "no way!" I yelled something incredibly intelligent like, "Yeahhhhh! All right!" and he just stared at me in that cool nonverbal way bikers do. I don't know why I didn't stop and get his story, and I'm not sure why he didn't stop and get mine. We just kept on going, not believing what we had just seen. *Two* crazy guys on a dirt road on Harleys with camping gear. What are the odds? About thirty minutes later, the dirt road finally turned to pavement, and thanks to the nearest road sign, I found my location on the map. Just like that, I had become "unlost."

My goal for the day was to reach a friend's house near Atlanta, Georgia, where my night's lodging had been secured a few nights earlier. I had come to discover that those days when my sleeping location was secured in advance seemed a bit more relaxed than those days when my slumber locations were unknown. Maybe I was getting soft, but the assurance of a nice bed coupled with a good warm shower just seemed to make the day that much more enjoyable and less stressful, perhaps the most important reason of all being that I did not have to blow up that devil air mattress.

My buddy Jim was a former coworker who had worked for the same company I had left in June. He had been laid off as part of a downsizing campaign that had taken place soon after my departure. Fortunately, he had already found himself a new job, and he was as hospitable as could be. That evening, he provided me with a welcome surprise by taking me to an Atlanta Braves baseball game, where I watched Greg Maddox pitch a 1-0 victory. I thought it interesting that twenty-four hours earlier, I had been deep in the North Carolina woods with a stuck motorcycle, soaking wet from falling in the river, and now here I was, watching a baseball game and munching on a hot dog. If this trip was anything, it was diversified.

I spent the next day completing all those little tasks that I needed to get done: developing pictures, performing preventative maintenance on the bike, fixing clothes, and doing those sorts of chores. Jim's house was graciously offered to me for as long as I needed, and I figured that this would be as good a time as any to do some relaxing before continuing on through the southern states. After Jim's house, I would have no contacts to stay with until Dallas.

Looking into the mirror, I had noticed that my hair was beginning to look like it was from the seventies disco era a bit too much and figured I'd better get it trimmed a bit. I visited the barber shop Jim frequented, and a very good-looking lady named Laura invited me to sit in her chair. I found out too late that the Georgian word for trim and the Californian word for trim must mean quite different things, because there now seemed to be much more hair on the floor than on my head. I was a little bummed that part of my biker look was being swept into a dust pan and discarded into the trash, but I guess it looked okay.

The owner of the barber shop happened to be an avid Harley rider and was the owner of a very sharp Heritage Softail, which sat out front. He let me know that he and a group of friends would be embarking on a short twenty-minute ride into Atlanta that evening to a place called Cabo Wabos and that I would be welcome to join them. I took him up on his offer and met them after work.

There were about eight bikes parked at the barber shop when I arrived, and I must say that I thoroughly liked every single person there. One of the women in the group was a thirty-eight–year-old white-collar professional who worked for Lockheed and was beginning to really question her position in life. She had come to hate her job, but the security of the handsome paycheck pretty much kept her there. She felt like chucking it all and doing something different but was very afraid to do so. In some respects, she had begun to crawl out of her complacency shell when she had bought her very own Harley and learned to ride. I told her that her comments sounded very familiar and told her what I had done. I don't know if it made a difference in her life, but you never know.

Another character who was part of this group was a guy named John. This guy was as big as a house and reminded me of the farm boy who could not only pick up haybales with one hand and throw them in the truck but could probably squeeze the milk out of the cow not using traditional methods. He was as nice as could be and taught me the number one southern phrase that works for all occasions: "Ah heard that."

I thought about this little reply and realized it truly is universal, not to mention kind of cute. "That girl sure is good-looking." "Ah heard that." "Boy, this car sure is slow." "Ah heard that." "Wow, that's the biggest zit I've ever seen." "Ah heard that." It is now part of my repertoire of phrases and works well when I don't exactly know what somebody said but am too lazy to ask them to repeat it.

I met the barber-shop girl for breakfast the next morning, and we had a good chat for a few hours. Laura was a single mom with a little boy named Dillon. She had the perfect southern accent and gorgeous long brunette hair…and I like long brunette hair. When we parted, she gave me an unexpected kiss good-bye and hinted she may come out and visit sometime. Ah heard that.

Because I would be staying one more night at Jim's, I decided to take a little day trip and headed out to Dawsonville, the hometown of NASCAR driver Bill Elliot. My brother is so into NASCAR racing that he actually tapes the races on the Sundays when he is not at home and watches them later. Because I was in the heart of NASCAR country, I decided to play the role of the unselfish brother and buy him a shirt. Hey, no expense is too great for my brother.

That evening, Jim and I went to the Cactus Club to get something to eat, have a few brews, and listen to a very good classic rock band. As we were leaving that night, the unthinkable happened. Something that every biker dreads and hopes never happens to them, especially in front of another person. I laid my bike down. Although most road bikes have a locking system as part of the ignition, my Harley did it a bit more simply. When the handlebars are turned to one side, two holes line up—one on the steering head and one on the triple clamps, where a padlock can then be installed through them. On occasion, it is possible that one forgets the padlock is in place and as one starts the engine and makes the initial attempt at straightening the handlebars, one soon realizes one's stupidity and takes the padlock off before continuing on.

As we were leaving the Cactus Club around one in the morning, I was actively engaged in conversation with another Harley owner while we both were readying ourselves and our bikes for the journey home. My bike was, of course, locked, and, unfortunately, was turned in the direction I immediately wanted to go. After bragging about my trusty companion to my Harley friend, I proudly mounted her like a prized stallion, started her up, and waved good-bye while taking off in an immediate turn. Traveling around ten miles per hour, I then attempted to straighten the bike out, but the padlock did not permit such a maneuver. Within two seconds, I was slammed on the ground.

I had always wondered if I would have any trouble picking up my 600-pound friend in case of such an event and soon found that, with the help of adrenaline and severe embarrassment, I had no problems accomplishing this feat. Amid my embarrassment, with skinned elbow and sore knee, I lifted the bike back to a standing position and surveyed the damage. The Harley dude asked if I was all right, and I sheepishly nodded my head while he rode away. I am sure he spent the next day calling every friend he had to share the story of the idiot from California. The damage was very minor, and I berated myself for being so stupid. Somewhere, I heard an inner voice reply, "Ah heard that."

Friday morning, I decided that I had sponged off my friend long enough and would set my sights for Alabama. I again refused to look at the map for hours on end and began to take back roads that would transport me in the basic direction I wanted to go...sort of west. I eventually realized that, unlike the Maine back roads, these roads tended to veer off in all kinds of directions and did not exactly follow a straight path, and I rode many miles in directions that were contrary to my goal. The amazing thing was, I didn't care that much. Four months earlier, this would have driven me crazy.

I was amazed at the number of abandoned homes that I would pass by, nestled in the woods just off the road. Although they were in dire need of repairs, they still maintained their basic structure, and the rooms and porches remained in tact. I stopped at a few of them; as best I could tell, they had been abandoned sometime during the late sixties. I sat in the old living rooms, strewn with newspapers and other trash, wondering who had lived there, where they were now, and what suffering had perhaps taken place there during such a turbulent time of America's life. I closed my eyes and almost heard conversations on the front-porch swing while someone was playing a blues song on an old guitar. I wish the walls could have spoken to me and unloaded their valuable information of years gone by.

I stopped at the post office in a small town that could not have contained more than 500 people and sent back another care package of items I had either bought or no longer needed. The postal worker was extremely friendly and engaged me in lengthy conversation about my trip and about life in Alabama. As I was ready to leave, she stopped me short of the door and gave me an apple for my trip. These random acts of kindness made me appreciate small towns so much more. The friendliness of the South had certainly been made evident through the many people I had met so far.

I entered the Talladega Forest, and because it was Friday, I decided to find a camp spot about ten miles outside the town of Talladega. It took a while, but I found an inconspicuous location in the forest and went through my home-building ritual once again. I went into town that night and for the first time on my journey had some good old Mexican food along with an icy margarita. Oh, that combination tasted good and immediately brought back memories of home and my many Mexico trips.

I found a club called Buffalo Bill's and listened to the band belt out one country music song after another. The place wasn't too full for a Friday night, and I figured it would be another quiet evening. Boy, when you're wrong, you're wrong. The waitress was a friendly gal named Wanda, and we got to chitchatting about different stuff over the course of the night. As 2:00 a.m. approached, I was getting ready to head back to camp when Wanda suggested I accompany her and three other ladies who worked at Buffalo Bill's to another club.

Apparently, there are private clubs that are open until five in the morning and are allowed to do so because of their private status. I asked the ladies how far this club was, and they claimed just a few minutes out of town. I continued to follow my "what the heck, might as well try it" philosophy and told Wanda I would be happy to go along. The club turned out to be a good half hour away instead of the "few minutes" I had been promised. We met the band's bass player there.

Because all the clubs in Southern California close at two, it felt somewhat strange being at this place at 4:00 a.m. The band was very good, and the girls I had accompanied were definitely feeling no pain. Because I wasn't drinking much, I'll give you three guesses who drove home. Now, I had never previously had the opportunity to be in a car with three very inebriated females

(Wanda was not in this category), but it is an experience I do not recommend for the faint hearted. Although it was fairly humorous at times, it made me wish for a video camera so they could view themselves the next day. Chances are, none of them would ever drink again if they saw such a thing.

After dropping everyone back off at Buffalo Bill's, I hopped on my scoot and began heading into the mountains back to camp. The fog hung low over the meadows, and I probably would have appreciated this exquisite scene more if it wasn't for the fact that it was six in the morning. I slipped into my tent at 6:30 and was asleep before my head ever hit my small air pillow.

At 10:00 a.m., I awoke in a deep sweat, as the sun had snuck over the trees and was pounding on my little shelter. There would be no more sleep this morning, and the three and a half hours of slumber I had enjoyed was not nearly enough for this rider. I slowly arose, wondering what I should do for the day. It was Saturday, and the decision to leave or not to leave was about the biggest one I had to make all day.

I decided that because it was Saturday, I would enjoy one more night in Talladega and check out the Talladega race car track and museum, which was about an hour or so away. I was not moving too quickly that morning, and I dragged myself into town for a nice all-you-can-eat brunch. I was much happier after that. That afternoon, a toothless but friendly tour guide drove me around the famous race track, and I was amazed at the steepness of the track at the turns. I was told that the race cars needed to travel a minimum of 80 mph just to stay at the top of the track. It was like racing on walls.

My body was in dire need of a shower, so I headed to the city of Anniston and found the civic center there. While I was in the locker room drying off, one of the guys who was helping set up for a production that night came in. He was very friendly, and I am talking way too friendly, if you know what I mean. I declined his continuous offers of staying at his house and soaking in his Jacuzzi, and if his eyes shot below my waist one more time, I was going to have to punch him.

I returned to camp, put on some new duds, and headed into town to visit Buffalo Bill's one last time and make it an early night. Yeah right. As I pulled into the parking lot around 9:00 p.m., there was not exactly an abundance of cars there. I did notice a nice-looking Harley sitting out by the front door. Standing next to it was the Buffalo Bill's bouncer, who was handling the cover charges for the night. He was probably in his mid forties, handsome sort, probably 6 foot tall, and reminded me of the actor Sam Elliott.

We started making small talk, and I found that the Harley out front was his. As we continued talking outside, people began showing up and heading in. Watching the majority of these people was a true education, as I witnessed just about every type of person imaginable come into this place. People were driving into the parking lot, already extremely drunk and going in for more. One guy showed up and was told that his wife *and* girlfriend were inside. He left. These two girls later got into a fight. One fully intoxicated guy in a Trans Am pulled in with his girlfriend, talked to me for about twenty minutes regarding the art of motorcycle riding, then went in for some "serious" drinking. About an hour later, he came out and wanted to drive home. We tried to stop him, but his significant other replied that he drove really well drunk. Only after he stuck his head out of the window and "fertilized the ground" while making moose mating calls in the process did she take notice enough to take the driver's role. I also witnessed a very drunk grandmother show up with her daughter and grandchild. She later had to be restrained by the police. I could go on and on about what I saw that night.

It wasn't as if I hadn't seen this type of behavior before, but for some reason, this night really opened my eyes, perhaps because I had been experiencing such natural highs over the past weeks and had become more focused in looking ahead in my life instead of only at the present. Trying to figure out what was real and of value versus what was temporary and unimportant. That night, I noticed a lack of fulfillment in many people's lives, and I felt that they were having a tough time seeing past Saturday night.

I also noticed there were many sad and lonely people there. People were crying, swearing, yelling, getting into fights, you name it. Nobody can tell me these people were "just having a good time." These people were hurting, and I genuinely hurt for them, even though I didn't know them personally. I remember talking to Jim, the bouncer, about this. He agreed and said he saw it every night he worked.

In a way, I felt very fortunate. I knew that without my Christian upbringing and personal relationship with Jesus Christ, I would be partying harder than any of the people I saw that night. It's just the way I know I am. I knew I would be very unhappy. This relationship has given me the contentment in my life that does not require a wild Saturday night to temporarily forget my problems. My highs are now natural ones based on solid truth, and these highs don't come with hangovers the next morning...an added bonus.

Around 11:00 p.m., my lack of sleep was starting to catch up with this old boy. Jim began talking about a place called the Red Horse, which was one of the largest redneck bars in the South. When I mentioned this place to several of the women whom I had chauffeured home the night before, their basic response was, "Are you crazy?" Oh, that made me feel real good. I repeatedly told Jim that I could never last that late anyway, because he did not get off until 2:00 a.m.

Well, somehow, I was still hanging around Buffalo Bill's at two o'clock. Jim had just finished dealing with an unruly guy who had a bad habit of packing a gun. The situation got pretty intense, and the cops were called in to smooth it out. We were inside Buffalo Bill's by this time, and I had every intention of heading back to my nice, comfortable air mattress for some much-needed shut-eye. The thought of sleep had never sounded so good in my life. I was proud of myself that I had held my ground and made my position clear and that I would not be riding the thirty minutes it took to reach the infamous Red Horse Club that night. I was in control.

Just then, Jim appeared, helmet and goggles in hand, looked at me, and said in a commanding tone, "Let's ride!" as he continued to walk past me. Now, those who do not ride these two-wheeled inventions would probably not appreciate this, but when these two words are spoken from one rider to another, ninety-nine times out of one hundred, the response will be, "Let's do it!" no matter what the feelings are at the time. It seems to be an involuntary response, much like blinking.

Everything in my body said no! My eyes, my brain, and my limbs—everything but my vocal chords had gotten the message hours before. Somehow, my voice box had not received the memo, and I was shocked at myself when I heard the words "let's do it" echoing from my mouth. I looked up and witnessed the surprised expression on everyone's faces. Who had said that?

I rode behind Jim's loud 1980 Super Glide and must admit I was feeling my second wind begin to take effect. It felt good to ride with another bike again. About a half hour later, I knew we were getting close, as I saw about seven guys, all wearing cowboy hats, pushing a giant Bigfoot-like truck off the road while yelling at the top of their lungs.

We turned left, and there was the Red Horse, packed with people and as lively as it gets. It didn't seem like 2:30 in the morning at all. Because Jim knew the bouncers, we pulled our Hogs up to the front door and parked them right there. Ours were the only bikes that I could see. The bouncers utilized metal detectors and patted down all newcomers as if all who were entering would soon be read their rights. Fortunately, I was able to skip this ritual because of my association with Jim. The place was fairly large inside and wasn't quite as bad as I had prepared myself for. I told Jim I needed to use the restroom and would find him a little later.

I stepped into the bathroom and was immediately greeted by a giant no-pest strip that looked to have been there a while, based on the number of victims it had managed to attract. As I was doing my business, a guy next to me looked over and started telling me the story of how his "old lady" had gotten smacked last night by a certain guy who'd had the nerve to show up again. He seemed to wanting my opinion as to what he should do.

I simply shrugged my shoulders and said, "Whatever, man." This seemed to satisfy his need for knowledge, and he left. I later rejoined Jim, who had just broken up a potential fight between two girls, and listened to the band. I've heard a lot of bands in my life, but this husband-and-wife team were definitely in the top three. From what I was told, they had been around when the super-group Alabama was around, and at that time, everyone went to see these two people instead of Alabama. I guess sometimes it's who you know that gets you to the top.

As I looked up, we saw that two of the girls from Buffalo Bill's had driven out to see us. They told us that if they had not seen our bikes, they were heading home because there was no way they were coming in by themselves. We all stayed until about five in the morning, and I actually had a really good time. My body was starting to shut down, and I suddenly realized how old I really felt. Jim and I mounted our bikes and made sure we loudly revved our engines in unison as we sped out of the driveway and down the frontage road.

We shook hands doing about 30 mph, and I waved good-bye. He had been a good friend that night, and even though it had been for a short time, I missed him a bit as I headed back to camp. This time, I got in an entire hour earlier than the night before and set my head down at 5:30 a.m. Once again, falling asleep was not a problem.

The next day was spent on the back roads of Alabama. The same abandoned shacks and small towns were scattered about as on the days before. By the time I entered Camden, Alabama, I was feeling wimpy and was considering a hotel, but I just couldn't rationalize the expense. It was getting dark around 7:30 now, and the pressure of finding a place to stay was starting to build. I then noticed that off to the right, although there were no roads, the trees of the forest were separated enough so that a bike could possibly fit through. I looked around, let some cars pass, and, when I was sure no one could see, pulled my bike off the road and began slowly threading my way through the trees cross country. It was getting difficult to see because the sun had nearly set, and I wanted to get as far off the road as possible for safety reasons. Every now and then, a spider web would grab my face and I would reach with my hand to rip it off, hoping there wasn't one of those large beauties somewhere on my head.

I finally found a spot that I felt would do the trick and quickly set up camp before it became too dark to see. I pulled my radio out, found a country station, and listened to its tunes as I was writing in my journal. Just then, I heard another sound and quickly turned the radio off. A car had pulled over just about fifty yards from where I was, and I could see about four large men outside the car. Heavy rap music filled the air, and I suddenly became cognizant of how truly weaponless I was. I was hoping they hadn't heard my radio…but why had they stopped here?

I looked around and grabbed the thickest stick I could find, then held my breath. They were huddled around the car. I could hear their foul language but couldn't make out what they were saying. I thought I could see them peering into the woods, but I couldn't be sure and wasn't certain if the faint darkness was sufficient to provide me adequate cover. After about ten minutes, I heard the car's engine start again, I breathed a sigh of relief as they began to drive away. The last thing I needed was to be attacked in the middle of the woods somewhere in Alabama. Once again, things turned out okay.

I had now covered more than 14,700 miles, and the end of the journey was beginning to become a reality in my mind. I found that the routine of setting up camp, breaking down camp, and packing the bike was becoming more and more tedious. In addition to this, the early-setting sun was forcing me to go to sleep much earlier than I liked, and usually, I would lie awake for hours before finally drifting off.

It had been my intention to travel to Key West, Florida, but constant hurricanes in that area had kept me from venturing any further south. I was disappointed yet somewhat relieved that I did not need to make the long trek southward, as this would have certainly added another week. The money I saved by arriving home a week early would help pay for the Baja 1000 race, if I could manage to find a ride. Although the rigors of camping and travel were beginning to take their toll, it did not seem to dampen my spirits in the mornings when I would first hear my motor roar to life and I would hit the road, loudly shifting from gear to gear.

Later the next morning, I crossed the state line into Mississippi and slowly worked my way southward. My goal was to make New Orleans the following day. I stopped in several small-town diners for a meal and enjoyed talking to the owners about life in the South and about my adventure. Just down-home folks with the best accents this country has to offer. It felt good to be in the South, a place I had never been yet had always wanted to visit. A place that now felt very comfortable.

I found a great camping spot outside of Gulfport, Mississippi, that was not too far off the highway but was so secluded, I would never know I was near a highway or large city. I smoked a few cigars, reveling in my lucky camping find, and then headed into town to find a gym, work out, and grab a shower and a meal.

When I had left for this trip, I'd had concerns about keeping myself in shape and staying clean while still maintaining prudent spending habits. The method I had used for the past two months had worked well. About every other day, I would find a local gym at the YMCA or civic center and use the workout room and shower. This process would usually cost me anywhere from three to five dollars and would easily kill two birds with one stone. It was the most inexpensive way to meet my needs, and I found it worked well.

After my workout that night, I ventured into an Applebee's restaurant, relaxed, and watched Monday Night Football. I laughed to myself at how different each night of my trip could be. The night before, I had been in fear of being attacked in the woods of Alabama and in bed by 8:00 p.m. and tonight, I was watching football in a nice comfortable pub at 11:00 p.m.

I felt a bit heavyhearted, having to leave my perfect camping spot the next morning, but New Orleans, a place I had always wanted to visit, was waiting. The weather was warm, even in the early morning, and that usually meant a hot and humid day ahead. I had an insatiable desire for waffles that morning, so when I saw the Waffle House just down the highway, I figured it had to be a direct answer from God. I devoured the holy wonders and hit the coast toward New Orleans.

The trip up the coast was beautiful and uneventful. Grandiose homes adorned the coast highway, and as the huge buildings of New Orleans loomed ahead, I wondered where I would find sleep that night. I was fairly certain I would be forced to stay in a campground if I wanted to be anywhere close to the city. I pulled into downtown New Orleans. Besides Milwaukee, this was the first large city where I had actually taken my bike downtown. I felt as if I was a visitor from another planet, as it had been such a long time since I had battled intense traffic and gazed upward at tall skyscrapers. I felt out of place and wanted to get out as soon as I could.

I asked for directions to the chamber of commerce and, after trying two places, finally found the information I was looking for. I picked a campground that was fairly close but still out of town a ways. It wasn't in the best part of town, but after checking it out, I felt that it would suffice. I was very concerned about the weather because this, without a doubt, was the most hot and humid day of my entire ride. It was stifling, and I wasn't sure how I would ever sleep at night or what I would even do for the next four hours. I had no shade, and the sun was bearing down hard.

On the way to the bathroom, I saw a man who had a small portable wire fence that created a miniature yard around the door to his motor home. Inside the temporary yard were five little yapper dogs, as I call them. We exchanged hellos and talked for a while. I explained what I was doing, and he sounded somewhat interested in my adventure. His name was Doug, and he invited me inside. The cold air within the motor home washed over my body like a refreshing dive into a mountain spring. The only thing that could have made this experience better would be sipping a nice cold margarita. Doug then offered me a nice cold margarita, chips, and homemade salsa. This was too good to be true.

Doug turned out to be a great guy from the Commonwealth of Virginia who was visiting New Orleans on his own. He was also in the computer industry, and we talked about absolutely everything. I asked if he would care to join me as I visited Bourbon Street that night, and he agreed that he would. There were not many strangers I would feel comfortable going out on the town with, but I felt very comfortable with Doug.

He then proceeded to offer his motor home to me for the night, which immediately solved my problem of how to sleep in this weather. I thanked him to no end and took him up on his offer. Doug had towed a car behind the motor home, which allowed me to leave my bike at the well-guarded campground, and I could now enjoy my evening in the city without worrying about my Harley being stolen. Doug was truly a godsend.

New Orleans was a very cool place. I love good, gnarly blues music, and we found several bars that provided this type of entertainment. To top it off, Doug was nice enough to buy me dinner that first night. Hey, it was the least he could do after forcing me to drink his margaritas, eat his chips and salsa, and use his motor home with air conditioning for the night.

The mixture of crawfish and Cajun food was unbelievably good, and I ate so much that I started talking with a Cajun accent. We happened to stumble upon a Christmas special presentation that was being filmed at the House of

Blues, complete with full gospel choir. It felt ironic to be listening to Christmas carols with the hot and humid weather outside. We ended up at a small bar where only two guys were playing some good down-home blues. The lead singer was a very different-looking fella. He was a white man in his thirties or forties, with long, stringy hair, thick glasses of which only one lens was in place, an old round rimmed hat, and only a few selected teeth in view. He was anything but good-looking, but he could play that guitar and harmonica to no end, and boy could he sing. I wondered what the story was behind this man and had a feeling it must be some tale. There are so many stories in that city.

We returned to Doug's motor home at 4:30 in the morning. The next day was pretty much spent relaxing in the air-conditioned motor home because it was another hot and humid day. We were contemplating taking the boats out into the swamp, but the stifling heat made us think twice. We ventured back to Bourbon Street that night, filled our stomachs once again with delicious Cajon food, and listened to bands play the blues. We made it an early evening and got in at 2:00 a.m.

I knew that later that day, I would "officially" be leaving the South. The southern states had made a very strong impression on me. They were full of friendly people always willing to help a stranger. The South was the home of people with the best accents in the entire world. It was small post offices that gave strangers apples for their journeys. The South provided me with incredible roads for riding and was a place where poor people will buy a stranger lunch, where you can watch the local musicians play bluegrass music in an outdoor room. It was a life-changing place, and I knew I would return someday.

Ah heard that!

Coccoon of worms and spiders in many of the trees - Creepy!

Bridge on the Appalachian Trail

Paul & Margaret - Richwood, West VA

Larry's Honda Rebel - Pulled this trailer from Mexico

Jammin' in 'The Cage'

More bike problems in Marion, Virginia

Scaling 'The Wall' for a campsite in the Smokies

Smokie campsite - Mud & all

Jim Griffin & family in Atlanta

'Biker' group in Atlanta

Somewhat small library in Alabama

Abandoned house in Alabama - One of many

Turn 2 - Talladega Raceway

Jim & John at Red Horse (3am with 2 Hrs Sleep)

Alabama campsite (Car with 4 men pulled over near me)

Doug & his dogs (New Orleans)

German couple in New Orleans campground

CHAPTER 9

Completing the Circle

Because of the lateness of the previous two night's excursions, Doug and I seized the opportunity to sleep in late on our day of departure—he heading east and me, west. It felt good to catch up on much-needed rest. We left the campground around noon and assured each other that we would continue to keep in touch. I couldn't thank him enough for all he had provided me during this very hot and humid time.

My next stop would be Dallas, and I figured it would take me a few days of hard riding to get there and visit the home of my friend of more than thirty years, John Fergason. As mentioned previously, John had accompanied me on my first Harley run to Canada, which I had reminisced about near Glacier National Park. I was looking forward to seeing him again. He had married only recently, and his matrimonial bliss had lasted a bit longer than my ten-day record. Not exactly a goal to set your sights upon.

After an hour of riding the interstate, I detoured toward a more westerly direction and began to experience some real Louisiana back roads. As one road turned into a slightly smaller version of itself, a few times over, I found myself not just in the boonies but in the boonies of the boonies. Much of the time, I had absolutely no idea where I was because most of the roads I was traveling were absent from my map. After a few hours, my western progress came to a stop as my unchartered road dead-ended into the Red River. I was forced to parallel the wide expanse of water northward via a narrow, pothole-filled country road that alternated between pavement and gravel every mile or so. It was wonderful riding, as the river served as my border to the west and large cotton fields, full of their white billowy crop served as my border to the east. After an hour of searching for a way across the water and experiencing more than one dead-end road, I finally found a small vehicle ferry that chugged my companion and me across the flowing ribbon of water.

Not long after the crossing, I was parallel to the Atchafalaya River, and once again, I was having problems in finding a ferry that would provide me a way across. After riding on a dirt road for more than twenty minutes, I was once again lost. I turned onto an old paved road and after a few minutes noticed that the number of deep potholes in the road was quickly increasing. Usually, I could maneuver around these obstacles quite well without slowing down, and I had become fairly cocky in my ability to do just that. Peering ahead, I thought I saw a fairly massive family of potholes coming my way, but, being confident in my ability to miss most of them, I refused to slow down. I then saw it. The giant pothole that would surely throw me and my bike to the pavement at 50 mph. It was about eighteen inches deep and two feet across, with an abrupt square edge on the opposite wall. This was not a good thing, and it was too late to slow down.

Fortunately, my dirt-bike–riding skills came through as I stood on the pegs and, with all my strength, pulled back on the handlebars to lighten the weight of the front wheel. Luckily, this worked and the front end skimmed over the top of the deep cavity, allowing the rear wheel to take the full brunt of the blow. This is an excellent maneuver on a dirt bike, as the rear shock is designed for big hits like this, but street-bike shocks are not designed to take this kind of abrupt blow. Unfortunately, I did not have much of a choice.

The loud smashing sound that greeted my ears as the back wheel hit the opposing edge sickened me, and my thoughts raced over the damage the impact must have caused. At least I was still on two wheels. I rode a while, listening carefully for any strange sounds that might be emanating from the rear of the bike and cursing my stupidity in not slowing down. After a short time, I began to hear some ominous sounds coming from the rear of the motorcycle, and I could only imagine that it was a flattened tire, bent rim, or worse. There was no one anywhere around me, and I wasn't even sure where I was. I had not seen a car in more than a half hour, and I was praying the noise would not lead to a serious problem.

I surveyed the damage and discovered that the only apparent injury was that the chrome belt guard had been ripped off its mounts. I was so relieved, I don't remember if I actually kissed my bike on the tank, but I know the thought crossed my mind. I pulled out my trusty fix-all bungee cords and supported the guard the best I could. I felt fortunate to be back on my way.

I finally found a bridge over the Atchafalaya River and soon wound up in a small town called Cottonport, Louisiana. Darkness was beginning to fall, and I needed a place to spend the night. I pulled over to the side of a Cottonport street and began to look at my map in an attempt to figure out what the next course of action might be. My current money supply was pretty anemic, and I needed an automated teller machine in a bad way. There were probably more ATMs in Southern California than there were cars, but I soon found these machines were as rare as hen's teeth in these parts.

As I was pondering my situation, a topless jeep pulled up next to me, and I heard a loud and confident voice ask, "Where ya come from and where ya going?" I looked over my shoulder and saw a man in his fifties who seemed to be full of energy and spunk. He maintained a boyish face highlighted with rosy cheeks and an all-encompassing smile. His gray hair seemed to be the only attribute to give away his age. He exuded confidence in his speech and actions, and I could immediately tell that he was probably a man of some importance. Next to him sat an older-looking lady, probably in her seventies, whom I assumed to be his mother.

I briefly explained my sojourn and that I was looking for a place to stay for the night. As fate would have it, this man, Max, had recently returned from his first cross-country motorcycle trip with several friends and had experienced the time of his life. Seeing me cruise through town with my fully packed Hog had brought back great memories for him, and he insisted I spend the night at his home. He didn't have to ask twice.

He had errands to attend to but directed me to a good local eating place. I inquired as to the location of an automatic teller machine, and instead of giving me directions, he peeled off a ten-dollar bill and promised to meet me at the restaurant later. I couldn't believe how well things had worked out for me that evening; once again, I had been the recipient of the kindness and generosity of a stranger.—a stranger who would in a short time become a friend.

Max's unselfish and generous example was one of many I had experienced during this journey. My beliefs in the goodness and the giving nature of the American people had been resurrected within me during this ride, and I had come to realize that the upstanding characteristics of the people of this great land are rarely found on the front pages of America's newspapers or during the six o'clock news. These publicized venues are normally reserved for stories of tragedy, dishonesty, and greed. No, I had found high-caliber people in places you wouldn't expect, in towns like Cottonport, Montpelier, South Bend, Richwood, and Sturgis. They are the unsung heroes of everyday life who are ready to hold out their hands to those who need them, and they have inspiring stories of their own to tell. If we find ourselves complaining about the lack of goodness within this country, it is only because we have not taken the time to look around. I know, because I experienced it.

I spent a wonderful evening at Max and Diane's house. Max had done well for himself over the years, and the house was exquisite. As I had expected, he was a doer. He owned his own road-construction business, loved flying planes, was an avid snow skier, and was currently involved in recycling tires. The accomplishments went on and on. Unfortunately, his body was also a little beat up because of the lifestyle he had enjoyed over the years, often taking things to the extreme, but I could tell he had no regrets and was always looking for new adventures.

Instead of the air mattress I had expected that night, I found myself lying on a plush, soft and comfortable bed. I drifted off quickly, knowing I would have a long day of riding ahead if I was to make Dallas by the next evening. This night had again proven that I never knew what to expect.

Max fixed me a nice little breakfast the next morning because he was usually up by 4:00 a.m. anyway. We started the day with good conversation, and I also had the opportunity to meet one of his sons. While preparing to leave, Max let me know, in no uncertain terms, that my impromptu visit had made his week. I let him know that the stories we had shared the night before had been encouraging for both parties, not just him. It made me feel good that a man who had accomplished as much as Max could still benefit from an average guy like me.

Max's brief comment taught me a powerful lesson. I have often minimized my ability to positively affect other people because I have made the mistake of often comparing myself to others, feeling that my input was insignificant because someone else was so much more successful than I. Comparing ourselves to others leads to one of two results: insecurity or pride. Neither is good. I have come to discover that anyone, no matter how successful, has much to offer another. I learned that the only person I should compare myself to is myself and that to truly affect anyone, I must be willing to share of myself honestly and sincerely. Max taught me that.

We said our good-byes on the driveway, and I thanked him for his hospitality. I felt good that I had made a small impact on his life this week. As I pulled out of the driveway, I shook my head and smiled at the good fortune I had enjoyed over the past twelve hours. I love this country!

I figured it would take me a good ten hours to make it to Dallas by nightfall, and I was right. After crossing over into the Lone Star State, I reluctantly succumbed to the dreaded interstate, realizing that I needed to make up some time. I pulled into John and Karen's place around 8:00 p.m. on a Friday night. It had been a long day, and my sore butt was a constant reminder of the many hours I had spent in the saddle. As I threw my leg off the bike and began to walk to the door, my soreness was immediately transferred to my gait, and I had more of a John Wayne approach than my normal suave stride.

John opened the door, and we gave each other a huge hug. John and Karen were fun as always, but she had been feeling a bit sick and would stay that way all weekend. I felt badly for her but was inwardly glad that at least she was the one who was sick instead of me. In fact, I had not been sick this entire ride. Never think thoughts like that. We looked over the pictures of their wedding, in which I had been a groomsman, from the previous February, and it brought back great memories of a time with good friends. It was a good way to spend a Friday night.

Saturday, John and I rode over to Biker's Dream, a supply store specializing in Harleys, and I replaced my broken belt guard. As we rode together, I glanced over at John's bike cruising next to mine, and my mind quickly journeyed to three years earlier, when we had shared our first lifetime ride together, to Canada.

Saturday night, John and I rode our scoots to the car races and just enjoyed each other's company after being apart for so long. It felt good to ride with him again, and many of the feelings from that first ride were revisited as we rode side by side.

The leak I had discovered in Maine was getting worse and was now leaking externally as well. Harleys do have a reputation for oil leakage, but we do not consider them as leaks, per se, but refer to the bikes as "marking their spot." Unfortunately, my bike was beginning to mark everything in sight. I had mixed emotions between taking the next day off and trying to fix the leak at John's but was afraid that the problem would not be an easy one to repair and that my limited mechanical ability would probably get me into more trouble than I was already in. I decided to move out the next morning as originally planned.

John arose early for work and woke me up, and we said our good-byes. At that hour, I didn't have quite the emotion I would have liked to share with John, but that's what he gets for getting me up at 6:00 a.m. A few hours later, I bid farewell to a very sick Karen and set out under cloudy skies. I had been very spoiled by the lack of rain for the past month and had a feeling that my luck was about to change…not for the better, but for the wetter. I was also beginning to feel quite sick, with a very bad head cold. I never should have made that comment about Karen earlier. A brutal head cold was definitely not something I wanted to deal with while heading into the cold and rain.

As I cruised into Oklahoma, I tried to hypothesize what the numerous thunderstorms around me were about to do and where they would strike next.

I had several directional options and chose to go west first, then north. It had been a long time since I'd had to decide the rain-gear issue, and as usual, I maintained the positive attitude that I would not need it.

I turned north at a small Oklahoma town and noticed a gas station with a nice overhanging canopy that would provide an excellent clothes-changing shelter. I debated whether to give in and put the gear on or to take my chances on the road, realizing that dressing myself up in the midst of a thunderstorm with no cover would not be pleasant. Stopping here obviously made the most sense, which was probably the main reason I decided to forego that decision and continue down the road, taking my chances. Nobody ever said you had to be smart to ride a motorcycle.

About five minutes after my mature, albeit lazy, decision, the rain began to pelt me heavily. I scolded myself for not doing the sensible thing and made a quick U-turn, heading back to the little town with the gas station like a little dog with his tail between his legs. The raindrops felt like miniature bowling balls when riding at seventy miles per hour, and I felt as if I were being stoned. By the time I reached the station, sheets of rain were pounding the ground all around, and the station attendants were having a good time laughing as I limped in like the wet dog I was. "Looks like it might rain!" I yelled sarcastically over the sounds of the pelting rain as I peeled off my wet leather. My throat felt like a piece of raw meat, and my sinuses were stuffed full of, well, stuff. This was probably the first time during my ride that I had wished I could be relaxing at home instead of being on the road.

Once I suited up, I hit the storms head on. My rain gear did its job well, but the rain never let up. I was forced to exercise serious caution, as many portions of the country roads had completely flooded in those places where the ditches could not keep up with the sudden downpour. Hitting one of these flooded areas at full speed would be a 100% guaranteed pavement kiss.

I finally reached Elk City, Oklahoma, and decided to get a cheap motel. I was wet and sick and had no problem in rationalizing the use of a brick-and-mortar shelter at this point. I had ridden 300 wet miles that day and was completely worn out. The warm room allowed my soaked possessions to dry, and it felt good to just relax and get as much rest as I could.

The next day was my 100th day on the road. I had traveled 16,500 miles to this point but was still 1,500 miles from home. Health-wise, I was feeling pretty miserable, and I knew that for the next few days, the terrain and riding would not provide me the kind of excitement I had experienced over the past

100 days. My motivation was ebbing, and my enthusiasm was definitely at a low point.

As I hit I-40, the crosswinds out of the south were blowing around thirty miles per hour, and I was on an endless stretch of straight asphalt that made the hours seem like days. That morning, I had decided to do the mature thing and start the day with my full rain armor snugly in place. Naturally, completing this maneuver all but guaranteed that no rain would fall. None did. Boy, it chafes my hide when that happens. After a few hours, I took the rain garb off and went back to my standard leather faire.

As I crossed into New Mexico, I turned northward onto one of the back roads that cut through the plains. It felt good to leave the boring interstate, although the flat and straight back roads weren't much better. Every time I would crest a small hill, I would continue to see miles and miles of straight black ribbon. I was a bit angry with myself for my feelings of discontentment, and I must admit that at this particular moment, I was not having that much fun. How different I now felt than I had with the straight roads of South Dakota.

Only two small events broke up this monotonous day at all. First, I found a tortoise "speeding" across the road and quickly pulled over, thankful for an excuse to stop, and positioned the confused animal on my bike seat for a special Kodak moment. He then kindly responded to all the sudden attention by urinating on the seat, and the urine then dripped down onto my chrome side plates. I later discovered that chrome and tortoise urine do not mix well, because tortoise urine apparently has a highly corrosive nature. I tend to imagine that other types of urine would have the same effect, but this is the only variety I have scientifically tested thus far.

A few miles later, I noticed a tarantula making his way along the road, and I once again disembarked from my seat and shot a close-up of this hairy beast. By this time, my spider tolerance was extremely high after experiencing the east coast woods, but I still couldn't get myself to pick him up. A head cold *and* a tarantula bite—oh yeah, that would have been a winning combination.

It was getting late, and I was in desperate need of another motel, but the towns I was passing through were just too small to support any. I had planned to stop hours earlier but was forced to forge ahead until I could find a place to sleep. My head felt like Mr. Potato Head, and after looking in the mirror, I noticed a definite resemblance. My cough was getting much worse, and all I could fantasize about was a warm bed with a television. I finally found a town around nightfall and managed to slip into a drug store just before closing time.

I loaded up with drugs and stopped at the first motel I found. I felt like I was wimping out, but the thought of camping when I felt this bad did not make any sense to me.

I made it to Farmington, New Mexico, the next day, and except for the bitter cold and windy conditions over the pass, the day was fairly unexciting. At least there had been altitude changes and actual curves in the road. My health situation continued to ruin my last few days, and I was afraid that the trip would end on a bad note. I also discovered that a severe runny nose combined with strong crosswinds provides for an interesting combination, which I won't elaborate on here.

My health began to improve as I entered

Arizona, where I passed several geographical areas where John and I had ridden on our "virgin" ride three years earlier. Pleasant memories brought a huge smile to my face on several occasions as I passed through Kayenta, Arizona, through Page, and near the North Rim of the Grand Canyon.

The frigid weather of the mountains assisted me in my decision of where to camp, and I decided to head down in elevation and camp near Pipe Springs Memorial, where it was much warmer. I found it virtually impossible to find a place to sleep because most of the land was fenced off. I finally found a side road and literally had to push my bike through soft dirt, sand, cactus, and creosote bushes to adequately hide myself from the road and bed down for the night. I again used my camouflage technique and covered my bike with creosol bush branches to blend her in with the scenery the best I could. I wasn't sure if the bike was badly stuck or not, but I really had no desire to know until morning. Because I was beginning to feel much better health-wise, it felt good to camp again. I was relieved and fairly confident that my trip would indeed end on a good note after all. For the first time in three nights, I slept soundly.

As I was packing up my gear the following morning, I felt my hand brush up against something "sticky" and bumpy beneath the tarp. After turning the tarp over, I found that the sticky lump turned out to be a black widow spider who had decided to make her home there for the night. I had grown up with these little beauties in the country, and I really had no desire to be bitten at this stage of the game. Had I grabbed the tarp about two inches to the right, it would have been a guaranteed poisonous bite. I had certainly experienced the gamut of spiders on this ride.

I rode through some gorgeous Arizona canyon country and on to Hurricane, Utah, where I grabbed some lunch, then took I-15 toward Las Vegas. My feelings began to run wildly as I approached my home state of California. The entire trip almost seemed as if I had dreamed it, and the many individual experiences and faces seemed to melt into one another. A few days earlier, I had felt that I wanted to get home as soon as possible, but now my feelings were beginning to change. Now, I didn't want it to end. I had been so far from home for so long that I felt like a foreigner heading toward my own state—feelings I had never felt before.

My plans had originally been to return to my Southern California abode, but as I thought more about it, I decided to complete the circle the way it should be completed, by returning to my real home, to my family in Lodi. I decided to continue northward through Nevada instead of staying to the south. It would be a good way to end this exploit. It would be good to see my family.

The weather turned very hot once I descended onto the desert floor near Las Vegas. Because it was a Friday, there would be no affordable motel deals in Vegas that night. I knew it would be too hot to camp, and I needed a shower very badly...very badly! I continued on to Pahrump, Nevada, and rented a cheap room there. I would ride through Death Valley the next day and then spend the night at the exact spot where I had camped that first night of my journey more than 100 days earlier. What a perfect and unexpected ending that would be!

While I was checking in, I met an ex-fireman from Pennsylvania who was on a ride of his own. He had more of the late-sixties look, with tie-dyed clothes and hippy-like mannerisms. All he owned was what he had on his back and whatever was packed on his Honda Gold Wing. He was planning to head to Central America with very little cash, and all he could really talk about was the quality of drugs down in that area. We had slightly different motivations.

He made me think of the many "free spirits" I had met on this trip. It seemed that different people were fueled by different motivations or reasons. I had seen those who were on the road for pleasure, and I had seen those who were on the road to escape. Some wanted a break from the realities of the world, and some never wanted to go back. It made me wonder what my true reason was for taking this trip. Had it been connected somehow to my unsuccessful marriage? Was I escaping from life and its pressures? Perhaps I was simply realizing a dream I had always held close to my heart. Maybe a little "all of the above."

When I began this pilgrimage, I certainly did not view it as a series of lessons that would be laid out before me like a college course curriculum. I had known I would grow in some areas and that I would have the time to explore those areas of my life that I had ignored in the past, but I certainly had had no preconceived ideas on what I would think about or what I would be taught. For the most part, I had just assumed that this type of a trip would be fun. In looking back, I was very relieved that this trip had been more than fun. We seldom grow during fun times. Had this trip been only for selfish pleasure, it would have been a trip of memories only applicable for that period of my life. If I had turned against my value system, it would have been intermingled with regret and hypocrisy. As it turned out, this trip provided me lessons I could use the rest of my life. Suddenly, my lost salary and commission revenue paled in comparison to the priceless wisdom I had gained.

I didn't know what the future held for me, but one thing I did know was that I would work hard to enjoy life no matter where my circumstances placed me. Whether I was single or married, owned a successful business or a failed business, I would try not to let myself dwell on that which cannot be changed. There would be plenty of work to be done on those things that could be changed. My goal would be to become a free spirit, no matter where I found myself.

When I awoke the next morning, I knew it would be a fairly long day of riding if I were to make it to my original campsite by dark. Although I couldn't help but feel a bit depressed at the realization that my trip was near its finale, I was also excited at the prospect of seeing my most favorite campsite again. I looked forward to sitting in the exact spot as that first night, closing my eyes, and reliving the feelings I felt that first special evening.

I rode out that morning and aimed my bike straight for Death Valley. I had visited there as a very small child, and although I had lived in Southern California all these years, I had never taken the time to investigate this low wilderness. Passing the "Welcome to California" sign hit me hard, as it confirmed the realization that my journey really was nearing its end. My thoughts reverted back to that night in Newfoundland, when I had felt so far from this sign. I stopped at the Death Valley Museum and took my time looking at the exhibits and savoring the last educational stop of my ride.

It was over 100 degrees outside, and I made sure the tank was full of gas and that I had plenty of water. Vehicles were scarce as I crossed this expanse of desert, and I spoke to my bike often, urging her to hang in there despite the intense heat. Because of the bike's leak, I was now adding about a quart of oil every 500 miles or so, and I made sure that I kept a very close eye on the oil level because this was her primary way of cooling herself.

Several hours later, I began to climb out of the hot valley of death and continued past the famous historical landmark called Scotty's Castle, returning to Nevada as I continued north. I rode hard and fast and made it to the Mono Lake area just as the sun was dipping behind the majestic Sierra Nevada mountain peaks. I had a little trouble locating the dirt road that led to my favorite spot, because I was entering from the opposite direction, but I finally managed to track it down.

I made a left turn onto the dirt road that served as an entrance to my sacred place and began plowing through the deep sand and dirt, struggling to keep my bike upright, much like I had done that first night. Feelings began washing over my soul that rivaled those same feelings experienced at L'Anse aux Meadows, Newfoundland. I was literally yelling at the top of my lungs, yells of victory and accomplishment! I could hear my voice echoing off the mountains around me, even over the pulsating sound of my loud Harley engine. I had officially completed the circle, and what a circle it had been!

I found my spot, parked my bike, and sat on the same log I had sat on that first night. Tears came to my eyes as I bowed down on one knee, looked up to the sky, and thanked the Lord for the safety he had shown me on this expedition. So often, it seems that reality does not match our expectations, but I could now look back and realize that my expectations could never have matched the reality of this tour.

After setting up camp, I ventured into the small town of Lee Vining that night, bought a margarita, and toasted myself in a private little celebration. I didn't feel like making small talk with anyone this time. This was my private moment. God had seen me through almost 18,000 miles without a single serious close call. He had totally blessed me on this voyage, and what I felt during that moment was nothing short of sheer accomplishment and thankfulness. I was in the same restaurant where I had spoken to the German couple on my second day of the trip, and I thought of how much I had changed since that time, 104 days ago. I sat back and basked in the warm glow of emotions enveloping me like a satin robe…feelings that will never leave me for as long as I live.

I left Lee Vining fairly late at night. About five miles out of town, my bike sputtered and quickly stalled. I checked my mileage on the odometer and, based on my calculations, figured I should have had at least thirty more miles to go before my reserve switch would need to be activated. Then I remembered how hard I had pushed my bike over the mountains to make camp before nightfall. It had taken a real toll on my mileage.

Camp was twelve miles away from town, and I now had a huge decision to make. I could turn back into town for gas, but I was unsure if the gas station was still open at this late hour. If it was closed, there was no way I could make it back to camp and then back to town in the morning. If I continued back to camp on reserve, I had a chance, but it would be tight. I decided to take the chance and go on.

The night was cloudless and crisp, and every star known to mankind seemed to have come to the party that night. I cruised the secluded road very slowly to conserve gas as best I could, and whenever gravity permitted, I shifted my bike into neutral and coasted for as long as possible. I made it back to camp and savored my last evening. I tried staying awake for as long as I could, desiring the night to never end.

About three in the morning, I was abruptly awakened by the sounds of wild coyotes. If you have ever heard coyotes scream and howl in the night, you know it is one of the most inauspicious sounds you will ever hear. I am not talking of the gentle howling that one hears on the TV westerns but about loud screaming as if they are in pain during a death-defying fight, in the highest, shrillest voice you can possibly imagine. It is an eerie sound that will easily push your heart rate up to a healthy aerobic level. Hearing this when alone and in the dark is intensely frightening.

The coyotes finally and slowly faded away, and I once again drifted back to sleep, only to be awakened, about an hour later, by a loud owl hooting his brains out directly above my tent. I would later remember this "sign" as a symbol of my increased wisdom that I had gained through this journey. Hey, it could happen.

When I awoke the next morning, the weather was absolutely perfect, just as it had been that first day. I started a fire to warm up a bit and sat back on my log, looking up at the lone tree I had claimed as my own that first night. I restated my vow that I would be the one to stand out in the crowd and not let conformity take hold of me once I returned to "civilization," to attempt the things others would not do and to become more of a leader.

I grabbed my journal and looked back at what I had written the night before:

> I am sitting at the same place I camped that first night, facing the lone tree on the ridge I have claimed as "John." My joy was giddy as I wrestled my bike down the gravel road to this spot. I just read my first day's notes. Little did I know there would be many nights like this. The craters no longer have snow and there is no full moon tonight, but I am experiencing feelings of joy and accomplishment that most people could never relate to. The unknown is no more, as far as this trip is concerned, but what lay ahead of me three and a half months ago has changed me and made me wiser. God has blessed me beyond what I deserve. This campsite will always be my special place. Whenever I look at my tree, I will be reminded that those who are great, both in deeds and faith, will separate themselves from the crowd. Conformists do not promote change, nor do they lead. Thank you, Jesus, for everything. This is why I came.

I copied these words on a piece of paper. I then took my Harley lighter, which I had bought on this trip and which had lit many a cigar, and put them both in a plastic container. I walked over to one of the huge dead trees and found a place that would be protected from the harsh weather, and I placed these important symbols of my journey inside. I plan to visit this location many times throughout my future and will read these words every time I visit. I know I will be touched by these words and by this adventure until my dying day.

The routine of packing up my gear and placing it on my bike had a new-ness about it that morning and certainly was not the drudgery I had experi-enced over the past few weeks. It is funny how we take things for granted until we are about to lose them. Then they seem to suddenly take on new meaning and importance in our lives.

I remembered my gasoline dilemma from the night before and would do my best to conserve the precious liquid so I could make it into town to fill her up. I took one more look at my ridge and rode out to Highway 120 toward Lee Vining. I turned north onto Highway 395 and felt fairly positive about my chances of making it to town.

I knew it would be close and also knew that the entrance into Lee Vining was a fairly steep incline so coasting her into town would not be an option. I was tucked in behind a large motor home, taking full advantage of the wind break he was providing me, when the first sputter hit. "No, not this close," I moaned. The sputtering hit again. I started shaking the bike from side to side, hoping to use every last drop of flammable liquid that was still in the tank.

That worked for a while, but not long enough. The dreaded sound of silence soon fell upon me, and I coasted in behind a Chevy Camaro that was pulled over on the gravel shoulder of the highway. I noticed the head of an older woman in the passenger side and thought that she perhaps could help me out. I was only a mile or so from town and was amazed that after 17,800 miles, I had not once run out of gas, until now.

As I dismounted my bike and slowly began walking to the car, I noticed the old woman's head was nervously glancing from over one shoulder to the other. Knowing she would probably be a little apprehensive by my looks and by the situation, I greeted her with a smile and said with a reassuring tone, "Hi, I just ran out of gas."

"So did we," she said. So much for help.

Her daughter had just left to walk back to their mobile home a ways down the road, so I figured I would forego walking into town and talk to the old woman for a while. She was a local Piute Indian woman who was probably in her late sixties or early seventies. She had raised nine girls and two boys prac-tically on her own and had lived with an alcoholic and abusive husband most of her life. I admired her strength as she told me story after story of her past.

To make matters worse, a few of her daughters were also battling alcoholism and she was put in the position of raising a number of grandchildren as well. Her genealogy was extensive in this region, and she had lived in the area her entire life. I thought how tough it must have been to raise all these kids in a mobile home during the harsh winters the Sierras inflicted on their inhabitants at 7,000 feet. My respect for her grew with each story, and I could tell that although her body was old, her mind was very sharp.

Once again, out of a negative situation, a positive experience was born. How many times had that happened? I don't know, I had lost count. As the woman's daughter drove up in another Camaro, we poured a little gas into my tank. I wrote down her address and promised to stay in touch. As I drove off, I was very glad I had run out of gas that morning.

The weather was fairly brisk, and after gassing up, I decided to take the only mountain pass road that I had never taken before. An hour after leaving Lee Vining, I turned west onto the Ebbets/Monitor Pass road. It was absolutely beautiful, and the road provided me with a wonderful array of tight and twisty turns. In fact, much of the road was void of center-line markings or road signs constantly warning me to slow down for tight curves. What a great way to end this ride!

As I neared my true home in the country, I chose to not stop this time, but drove by it more slowly than the 55 mph limit allowed, thinking of how much had happened since the last time I had gazed at this familiar place more than 105 days earlier. As I slowly passed, I glanced at my speedometer and could hardly believe what I was seeing. My trip's distance turned exactly 18,000 miles almost directly in front of the place I would always consider home. *Fitting*, I thought, as the circle really did seem complete now. Fifteen minutes later, I pulled into my mother's driveway, a different person than the one who had driven away more than three and a half months earlier. This time, her son did come back.

I returned a highly educated student from the road scholars. I learned to not judge people by their looks or first impressions. I realized there are many good-hearted people in this land. I understood the history of this county like I'd never experienced it before. Poor people are generous and nonjudgmental. People have achieved amazing things on their own. Family relationships are like gold. Everyone has amazing stories. And the list goes on.

I mentioned in the beginning that this was a great lesson plan...I had no

Crossing the Mississippi River

Max & Diane - Cottonport, LA

My old riding buddy John

New Mexico - Long and a little dull

Tarantula in New Mexico

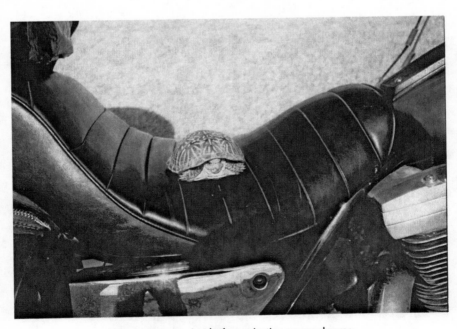

Tortoise on seat - Just before uninating on my chrome

Heavy rains in Oklahoma

Arizona has cool school buses

Stuck in Arizona Desert

Colorado River Grand Canyon w Rafters

Circle is complete - Back at Mono Craters & original campsite.

idea how great it truly was. Thank you, teachers...I salute you all.

Epilogue

Hindsight may be 20/20, but risk-taking is blind as a bat. To know the result before doing is an advantage that seems inviting at face value and seemingly guarantees success before the risk is taken. But the world does not allow such a reality, and it is not necessarily the optimal option. Would the prize be as cherished if we knew the outcome? Truth is, endings must be the result of discovered experiences, and those experiences need to be treasured because of the uncertainty in their successes, and yet the question often torments us, echoing in our minds: "Is it worth taking the chance if we don't know for certain?"

It is fitting that in a book recalling a once-in-a-lifetime adventure, I can answer that question without hesitation...hindsight shared from fifteen years later. Although it was my intention to write and publish my manuscript soon after I arrived home, let's just say that life got in the way of this particular goal. In that 20/20 hindsight, I'm glad it did.

Without that divine delay, I could not answer the questions Would I do it again? and Was it worth the financial sacrifice? and Did it really change my life?

Looking back after more than a decade has passed, I can truthfully say that this was one of the most important events in my life.

Now, before the Hallelujah chorus begins to play, let me quickly infuse some reality here. Life has thrown its share of curve balls at me over the past years, like it has at everyone else. I have found myself deep in some of the same ruts that I felt I was in before my ride. I got caught up in the frenetic lifestyle I so enjoyed being away from when on the road. Real responsibilities and financial successes and setbacks once again became part of my life.

It was slightly different this time, however. Securely filed away in my memory, this trip lived on, and I knew I had accomplished something I had always wanted to do. I was provided a gift on which I cannot place a price and which I can scarcely put into words...a gift of memory that allows me to close my eyes at any given moment and revisit any part of the adventure I wish to live again, transporting me from the rigors and stress of life not to an imagined scene but to one that existed, and of which I took a starring role. But as it turns out, this simple ride bore many gifts and shaped my future in ways I could never have imagined.

When I arrived back in Lodi, I spent several weeks there visiting with my family and spending time with my wonderful mother. The look on her face when I rode up the same driveway I had left more than three months earlier was one of relief and love. I'll never forget her smile.

After returning to my home in Southern California, I chose not to go back to work right away but decided to work on my manuscript full time. One day, I chose to visit the local chamber of commerce to discuss a little side business I was thinking of trying, and there I met Leo, the marketing manager. Leo was a large, portly man, his size more centered on his girth than his height. He sported a perfectly groomed gray beard and a full head of gray hair, and suffice it to say, he would have looked much better on my Harley than I. His deep baritone voice was immediately impressive, and we seemed to click right away. Leo was a definite people person. He became quite intrigued with my story, and he decided to invite me to a chamber mixer. Well, that sounded real tempting, except for one minor detail...it was a chamber mixer and I was unemployed. He said, "You're an author!"

I said, "No, I'm a manuscript writer."

"Close enough" he countered, and he gave me directions.

The mixer was located within a condominium complex, in the pool area, on this day, which turned out to be a real scorcher. When I arrived, there was no parking, it was hot, I was wearing a sport jacket, and I wanted to be just about anywhere else but there. But then, my eye caught that a sight that was most beautiful, especially when you are unemployed...free food, and lots of it. Suddenly, I had an overpowering urge to share my vast experience as an author with others and made my way through the gate.

About an hour later, I was sitting down, talking to a couple about my adventure, when Leo walked up with one of the most attractive women I had ever seen. It was there that I was introduced to Anna.

I remember sitting in the tavern in Corner Brook, Newfoundland, waiting for one of my newfound friends when up on the giant screen had come a video of Shania Twain singing her first country hit, "Whose Bed Have Your Boots

Been Under." I remember thinking that if I could meet a girl who looked like that, physical attraction would definitely not be a problem. Anna was about 5'4" and had a perfect figure, long brunette hair, and the prettiest face I had ever seen. Out of my league? Oh yeah.

Leo left us, and we spoke for about ten minutes while I rudely sat the whole time and she stood looking down at me. Thinking me the outdoor type, she gave me her card and said if I wanted to join a number of her friends for a mountain hike in a few weeks, I should let her know. I came to find out later that she had very little interest in me but thought I was "nice."

Coincidentally, I had just rewritten the first two chapters of my manuscript because of the interest of a publisher in New York. A few nights later, I called the number on Anna's card and nervously asked her for a favor. In talking with her at the mixer, it had been evident to me that she was not only beautiful but incredibly intelligent and well-spoken. Because she didn't really know me, I figured she would make for a most excellent and unbiased editor for those two new chapters. Although she really did all she could do to get out of the unwanted chore, I was uncharacteristically diligent. Begrudgingly, she said she would read them over the weekend.

Well, those first two chapters introduced John Hodel to her in a truthful and sincere way that was further manifested through self-paced and relaxed reading instead of awkward dating conversation. She was able to learn about me through the medium of the written word inspired by a trip I had wanted to take since I was a kid. Little did I know that those childlike dreams would introduce me to the love of my life, who is my wife today.

Exactly ten years later, in the summer of 2005, I found myself returning to the Midwest to attend the Hodel family reunion in Illinois. It was my second reunion since my ride (zero before). My sweet and dear eighty-six–year-old mother pondered whether she should go to this one. She recently had lost twenty-five pounds and had been noticeably weaker as of late. These trips were no longer easy for her, and she had come to the conclusion that her traveling days would be over after this.

To make matters worse, she was fighting a harsh cough she had been battling for about a year and was awaiting some tests. We knew this would probably be the last time she would see her sisters, Millie and Margaret, so with some trepidation, she agreed to go. It was a tiring trip for her, but she had a wonderful time, and I will never forget reminiscing with my family of the epic motorcycle journey one decade earlier. I laughed with Millie about the pizza and with Margaret about when she was too sick to cook. We still give Uncle Mark a hard time about when he had called my bike a Harvey Davidson and how I had thought he was going to total my motorcycle when he had ridden off out of earshot. It seemed like yesterday.

I will never forget the looks on the sisters' faces when they said their last good-byes, knowing this would be the last time they would see my mother—their sister. I beheld hugs that will never again take place and seeing the tears in eighty-year-old eyes, struggling with the finality of it all. It is an image that will forever be pressed deep into my soul and one I will always cherish. My connection with that family in the Midwest was created on the back of a Harley, and I will always be in its debt.

The following week, Mom was diagnosed with terminal cancer. The timing of the trip seemed surreal, and I was taken back to that day, ten years ear-

In Memory

Mabel (Mom) Hodel

lier,
when
I had

toured her house in Iowa and sauntered through the rooms where she had learned to walk, where she had played with her sisters, where she had laughed as a little girl. In a way, I was experiencing her circle of life, from that house where she was born to an ending of which I would be a part. This mother had let me back my motorcycle out from her garage with nary a sign of forbiddance or apprehension, even though she later admitted she had thought she may never see me again...like one other son in 1967.

Mom went to be with the Lord on Labor Day, September 5, 2006. On that day eleven years before, I had been riding in the Smokey Mountains and had gone to a Brave's game with my friend Jim. What a great day that had been...what a horrible day this was. But that's life.

CPSIA information can be obtained at www.ICGtesting.com
Printed in the USA
LVOW062340191012

303681LV00001B/6/P